MW00526702

I CANNOT
CONTROL
EVERYTHING
FOREVER

# I CANNOT CONTROL EVERYTHING FOREVER

A MEMOIR
of MOTHERHOOD,
SCIENCE, and ART

## EMILY C. BLOOM

ST. MARTIN'S PRESS
NEW YORK

First published in the United States by St. Martin's Press, an imprint of St. Martin's Publishing Group

www.stmartins.com

Gwendolyn Brooks's "The Mother" reprinted by consent of Brooks Permissions.

Library of Congress Cataloging-in-Publication Data

Names: Bloom, Emily C., author.
Title: I cannot control everything forever : a memoir of motherhood, science, and art / Emily C. Bloom.
Description: First edition. | New York : St. Martin's Press, 2024. | Includes bibliographical references.
Identifiers: LCCN 2023038135 | ISBN 9781250285683 (hardcover) | ISBN 9781250285690 (ebook)
Subjects: LCSH: Motherhood. | Exceptional children.
Classification: LCC HQ759 .B6166 2024 | DDC 306.874/3—dc23/eng/20231108
LC record available at https://lccn.loc.gov/2023038135

Our books may be purchased in bulk for promotional, educational, or business use. Please contact your local bookseller or the Macmillan Corporate and Premium Sales Department at 1-800-221-7945, extension 5442, or by email at MacmillanSpecialMarkets@macmillan.com.

First Edition: 2024

10  9  8  7  6  5  4  3  2  1

To my daughter

[T]he gods who govern our affairs
Arrange them unpredictably:
What we expect does not occur,
For some god always finds a way
To bring about the unforeseen.

—Euripides' *Medea*,
sung by the women of Corinth[1]

# CONTENTS

## AUTHOR'S NOTE

The names of many of the people who appear throughout this book have been changed. I refer to my daughter as Willie; this is the name that I gave to her when I was pregnant and she was still a part of me. This book tells the story of several pregnancies and my daughter's first four years. Her birth name and those of the family, friends, and healthcare providers that I met along the way are theirs alone to use to tell their own stories in their own way. Everything that I set out to tell is true with allowance for any mistakes, errors of omission, or lapses of memory that came about from recalling seven years of pregnancy and parenting.

I CANNOT
CONTROL
EVERYTHING
FOREVER

# Introduction

The warmth of spring creeps up on the late-morning playground and children shed layers like snakes shed their skins. Benches are littered with jackets and sweaters, announcing that summer will soon be here. The daisies planted along the perimeter are turning to face the sun in expectation of more to come. A mother sits on the bench amid the discarded clothes and her face looks up from her phone and turns toward me; she nods in recognition that we are both here in the park on a warming day. She has twin toddler boys that look to be the same age as my daughter, Willie, as well as an older girl who appears to be around five years old. Our children begin to play together. Willie wants nothing to do with the boys but craves the attention of the older girl, trying to stun her into submission with a series of loud squeals. It works, and the girl begins to notice the bald-headed person half her size. She hands her small rocks and they begin to assemble a primitive cairn. A landmark to steer an unknown visitor.

The girl looks intently at Willie before quietly standing up and going back to her mother, who has disappeared again behind the rectangular façade of her phone.

She tugs at her mother's T-shirt. What does the baby have in her ears?

The mother looks at Willie and then at me. Go ahead and ask.

What does the baby have in her ears? I hear the question at closer range.

I explain that she wears hearing aids. I tell the version that I tell children at the playground. Do you know anyone who wears glasses? Your dad? Yes? It's like that, but instead of helping you see better, they help you hear better.

So, she doesn't hear good?

No.

The mother looks on, encouragingly. She approves of the curiosity. Is grateful for the exchange of information.

She tells her daughter she did a good job asking nicely.

She brushes the wispy hair from her daughter's face and tells her how lucky she is to have good hearing.

More parents arrive. More children. Willie loses interest in the cairn and is now pleading for another child to share his toy cars. I continue to watch her with that strange combination of rapt attention and boredom that I've come to associate with these outings. Two months ago, Willie was diagnosed with Type 1 Diabetes. Willie was born with congenital deafness and, a year later, was diagnosed with diabetes. These are hard words to write because they reduce her vitality, her sense of humor, and her indomitable will to two labels that define her by a lack: she lacks normative hearing; she lacks a functioning pancreas. Willie is deaf and diabetic. She is not yet two years old. Shortly after her diabetes diagnosis, I stepped away from my job at the university: family emergency medical leave followed shortly thereafter by my resignation. It felt less like a step than a push. My husband, Evan, is still teaching English at the same university and I watch his career unfold like a vision of the future that I had planned for myself and, somehow, lost.

I am trying to get to know other parents and caregivers, to have more people with whom to make playdates and compare potty training strategies and share sympathetic glances over temper tantrums. Days with a toddler are long. The weekdays that were once filled with meetings with coworkers and students are suddenly emptied out, and a different type of time creeps in to fill its place. This time is measured in diaper changes and squeeze pouches and block towers built and demolished. It is the sped-up time of urgent cries—sudden hungers, unexpected fears, and unfathomable needs—and the slowed-down time of filling and refilling the same pail in the sandbox. For me, it has also become medicalized time: three hours between glucose checks, five days of a hearing aid battery's life span, and three months between medical checkups.

I'm learning to make small talk at the playground. Light topics, safe topics, about the weather or a preferred brand of crackers. I'm looking for that stray mom or nanny who I might get to know better and who might want to get to know me and Willie. I have just met one, although I don't know it yet. And she called my daughter unlucky. I think about what it means to call a child—my child—unlucky. She wears hearing aids. The mother and daughter noticed those, but they didn't notice me pull out a needle from my backpack and surreptitiously inject Willie with insulin as she ate that preferred brand of crackers. Willie did not protest. She rarely does anymore. The shots have become as routine as diaper changes; they are part of the rhythm of our days.

Here's what I carried to the playground that day: a small pink pouch covered in pictures of llamas and filled with an insulin pen and needles to regulate Willie's blood sugar when it is too high; *Sesame Street*–themed juice boxes to treat low blood sugar;

hearing aid batteries as a backup for when the current ones run low; an FM system (a small disk-shaped microphone) attached to the lapel of my shirt, which allows me to speak directly into the hearing aids at a noisy playground; and, of course, my phone, an all-purpose device that I use to take photos, to check social media, and, later, when we get a continuous glucose monitor, to track Willie's blood sugar.

When Evan is working, these hours are mine and Willie's. In these toddler hours, my circle of friends has winnowed away. Most of them—with or without children—are at work. And when we are able to reconnect, a gulf has started to form. I've lost the thread of connection. I try to talk about what my daily life with Willie is like, but I don't know where to start. When I meet other caregivers, I hesitate to share too much too soon. The details are so technical: low blood sugar or a dead hearing aid battery can overtake the basic patterns of feedings and naps and refusals and cuddles. There are parts of my day that are re-latable and others that are not. There are parts of my day that are easy and fun and there are parts that are not. I fear talking about the parts that are not; I fear the note of complaint that rises in my throat. I am afraid that I am becoming an automaton or an auto-mom—merely responding to a set of needs without a driving force of my own and, surrounded by all these devices, becoming a mere custodian for these beeping, blinking, surging machines. The very fabric of mothering, for me, has fundamen-tally changed. This change, more than anything, is what I wish I had the power to share with someone.

In my head, I craft a response to the mother at the play-ground. Willie is not unlucky, I want to say. I am not unlucky. We are both alive and well on this beautiful spring day. One day in the future, she and I will become friends; our kids will go to school together and we will serve on the parent board; one day a twin will accidentally kick her in the abdomen and it will hurt far more than expected; the twins will come over and play with Willie as their mother undergoes a cancer screening; she will be diagnosed with cancer and, after a tough battle and several rounds of chemotherapy, she will beat it. We all—Willie, the other mom, and I—are extraordinarily lucky. We live in a time and a place where these medical interventions are possible. We are both white women, I might add, who do not experience systemic racism in medical settings. We are among the lucky few who have access to good insurance and a reliable safety net. And yet, what is harder to articulate holds the echo of an ancient truth: we have each been so busy heading off catastrophe that we have driven headlong into our fates.

I PACK UP our things to leave the playground—a shovel and pail abandoned, half-buried, in the sandbox. Willie doesn't want to leave at first but as soon as she nestles into the swaying pocket of the stroller and can feel the ground vibrating beneath her, she falls asleep.

The word "unlucky" continues to worry my mind. If she is unlucky, what is the cause? In another time and another place, I might have said it was the will of the gods.

Willie's favorite book right now is an illustrated copy of the Greek myths. She has developed a grim fascination with its gory tales of heroes victorious and monsters vanquished. Again and again, we read the story of Pegasus: how the hero Bellerophon set out on an impossible task to kill the fire-breathing Chimera—a fierce beast with the head of a lion, the body of a goat, and the tail of a snake. Luckily for the hero, the goddess Athena comes to his aid, giving him a golden bridle to tame the winged horse Pegasus. Like all mortals, the hero requires supernatural intervention to kill a mythic beast—he needs a tool or a device of some sort to supplement his frail human body. The Greek myths are full of these assistive technologies—a mighty shield, a bag of wind, a ball of magic string. We humans need tools, the stories tell us, to survive the chaotic violence of the natural world.

Of all the books I am no longer teaching, it's the Greek epics and tragedies that I return to when my mind wanders. They mean something different to me now than they did in the classroom: I run lines through my head as if they might give me some insight into the place where I find myself. I shuttle back and forth between ancient texts and modern diagnoses. The more time I spend filling out daily logs of blood sugar levels, insulin dosages, and developmental charts, the more I hunger for words and images that can arrange this data into a meaningful pattern. As my tools threaten to overwhelm me, exerting their own chaos into my life, I'm reminded that stories are also tools, that art is also a divine gift handed down to help supplement the frailty of our minds and the insularity of our personal experiences. The golden bridle in the Pegasus myth is an object of art in its own right. The Greek word *techne* is the root for the English word "technology," but it once referred more broadly to any form of craft knowledge. The Greeks distinguished *techne* from *epistēmē*, which was considered a more rarefied form of theoretical or scientific knowledge. *Epistēmē* was cerebral, whereas *techne* was manual; one was a way of thinking with our heads and the other with our hands.[1] Athena places the golden bridle—a tool, a piece of art—in the hero's hands and he uses it to control his destiny. At least for a while.

After destroying the Chimera, the hero feels invulnerable. Crowds cheer him and hail his superhuman strength. He yearns to take his place on Mount Olympus, the celestial home of the gods. He mistakes a powerful, beautiful tool with godliness.

As he rides Pegasus into the sky on his quest to reach Mount Olympus, Zeus sees his intentions and strikes him down with a lightning bolt. The fallen hero spends the rest of his life lamed by the accident and shunned by his fellow man. He becomes untouchable. The golden bridle that tames Pegasus is a tool and a temptation—it helps the hero conquer the foe and it leads him down a path toward ruin. Once he has bridled Pegasus and defeated the Chimera, he sees beyond the limits of his human fate and believes himself to be a god. Our tools, the Greeks remind us, can also be our undoing.

Reading this story to Willie over and over again, in that recursive rhythm of children's stories, I think about the golden bridle. The best *techne* are both beautiful and useful: they allow us to live a better life without relinquishing the ordinariness of experience or the boundedness of our humanity. As my use of technology becomes more extensive, I seek that beauty and boundedness that I find in a different kind of craft knowledge— the kind that I have often found in great works of art. Poems, novels, paintings, sculptures, music. I have gratitude for all these tools that help me understand something about life. Perhaps it is an idiosyncracy of mine, but I have held on to the belief that old books and pictures in museums and live theater and music can help me better understand the *techne* of our twenty-first-century lives. I want to listen to a song that can teach me about the electronic sound of cochlear implants, or look at a painting that shows me a different way of visualizing pregnancy other than the tests and ultrasounds that have become my primary intermediaries. These realms of science and art might seem impossibly distant, but they both represent ways of knowing, craft knowledge, that help me get a handle on the vast sea of information that threatens to drown me or, more likely, might leave me numb in the face of unfathomable depths. The golden bridle is beautiful and useful, but it is also dangerous. It is a tool to maintain control in a violent, apathetic world and, also, a temptation to push myself and others too far.

The illustrations of the hero's defeat of the Chimera in Willie's book of Greek mythology are especially lively, with smoke and flames billowing from the Chimera's snarling fangs as her goat-hooves tread on the bones of her other victims.[2] Pegasus swoops from above, rearing away from a spray of the poisonous venom as the hero shoots arrows, one piercing the goat body and another going straight down the lion jaws. The chapter ends with a vermilion pool of blood and the word "Victory!"

Like many monsters of Greek mythology, the Chimera is female. Similar to those other hybrid beasts—the gorgons, sirens, and harpies—she is composite in nature, made up of more than a single being and, therefore, monstrous. But chimeras are not merely creatures of fantasy: they exist among us. Biologists use the term to describe genetic material from one entity that crosses over to another, as occurs in the grafting of one organ onto a host body. We do not often think of transplant recipients as chimeras, but they are—someone who has received a bone marrow transplant will, for instance, continue to produce a mix of their own and their donor's blood cells for the rest of their lives. At least at the cellular level, their bodies will contain two sets of DNA. This is true during pregnancy as well. Studies have found fetal cells throughout the maternal body, in kidneys, livers, spleens, lungs, hearts, and brains, even long after a child has been born.[3] The unwieldy term "fetal microchimerism" refers to this process through which cells pass back and forth through the placenta in a bidirectional flow that leaves a mark long after a pregnancy ends.

It is a cliché to say that pregnancy changes a person, but this phrase becomes more vivid and alarming to me when I consider how I have retained pieces from each fetus that I have carried in my body. A parent contains genetic material from the children they carry and, in the cases of miscarriage or termination, from those that weren't born. For some, this sharing of genes can become a superpower, aiding lactation, preventing certain forms of cancer and Alzheimer's, and possibly contributing to longevity. And yet, it may also trigger dangerous autoimmune responses and other forms of cancer. The fetus's cells can be found throughout our bodies, including in the brain—an organ so complicated that the possibilities of its impact there are endless. There's an evolutionary purpose to this sharing of cells—placentas are easily traversed so we can share resources more easily—but for all the benefits of cooperation, there is the risk of two human systems sharing a body and competing for limited resources.

I have been a mother once, but I have been pregnant four times. One chemical pregnancy. One late miscarriage. One termination. Willie is my only child. Thinking back on these pregnancies, I often consider the term "microchimerism." How much of an imprint did each of these pregnancies leave on my body? And, if these stray cells were in my body when Willie was gestating, how much of a mark did they leave on her too? We are all chimeras, hybrid beings, both miraculous and monstrous at once, bound up together in ways that we will never fully understand.

I STILL HAVE some time before I need to be home from our outing to the playground. It has been two months since Willie's diabetes diagnosis and I am still measuring my outings in three-hour increments. Three hours between lancet pricks on those delicate fingers. Three hours to determine whether Willie's tiny endocrine system requires more insulin. Home has become a tethering pole that expands outward in a precise three-hour arc.

Willie nods off in her stroller and I stop along my route at Riverside Church where I sit on the cigarette-littered steps below a bust of a saint praying with clasped hands. I'm not a religious person—my messy identity as a Jewish daughter of a Catholic mother has made religious identification tricky and, often, undesirable. Evan, on the other hand, grew up a Texas Baptist, and although he's moved far from the religion and place of his youth, he remains touched by a spiritual life that I can never quite reach. Even in our harried life in New York City, amid doctor's visits and career pressures, he retains a slow, reflective manner of seeking depths beneath the surfaces.

As the toddler sleeps on, I open the notes feature on my phone and begin to type, creating tentative patterns of meaning out of the jumble of facts. I write about Willie's diabetes diagnosis and the events that came before that. I write about her birth and the events that came before that. I stretch back in time to other pregnancies, other diagnoses. My body becomes a Russian doll enveloping other lives and other possibilities. What am I trying to discover in all this feverish typing on my phone? I suppose that I am trying to understand the gap between my expectations surrounding parenting and the reality that I have encountered.

This is the first time that I have written anything for myself since Willie's diagnosis. My only other writing this year has been in the form of data logs and medical histories: lists of foods consumed and insulin injected, examples of receptive language and expressive language, and symptoms and dates of diagnosis. I look back at what I have typed on my phone and realize that if I want to try to understand where I have found myself, then I'll need to keep writing, and if I keep writing about my personal experience as a mother, I will also need to address the specter of "motherhood." In his famous treatise on motherhood, the psychologist D. W. Winnicott describes the "good enough" mother as someone who attends to her newborn child completely, intuitively, and with no interference from others. He is not sentimental about this state, describing "a mother's love" as "a pretty crude affair. There's possessiveness in it . . . and power, as well as humility."[4] Arguing for an intuitive approach to mothering, Winnicott claims that the natural state of mothering is one where the mother and child are left alone together to get to know each other and to find pleasure in each other's company without the interference of medical professionals or well-meaning advice-givers.

But mothering does not come naturally for everyone. In Adrienne Rich's *Of Woman Born: Motherhood as Experience and Institution,* she writes, "My children cause me the most exquisite suffering of which I have any experience. It is the suffering of ambivalence: the murderous alternation between bitter resentment and raw-edged nerves, and blissful gratification and tenderness."[5] Rich distinguishes "mothering" from the institution of "motherhood." While she can appreciate the complexity of mothering as an experience, she condemns motherhood as an institution for requiring her to sacrifice her personal needs and wants to satisfy an impossible set of social expectations. In her preface to the 2021 edition of *Of Woman Born,* Dani Mc-Clain points out that the book's "understanding of motherhood is tied to [Rich's] specific experience of white womanhood."[6] The experience of motherhood that Rich describes comes out of a particular white, middle-class, American set of expectations and assumptions: a mid-century version of domesticity featuring a two-parent household with a breadwinning father and a mother at home. In contrast to this portrait of white motherhood, the poet Cynthia Dewi Oka describes how "[w]omen of color have been violently punished and stigmatized for mothering."[7] The history that Oka traces is more than bleak: the forced removal of children from Black women to slaveowners and from indigenous women to Christian boarding schools; genocide and sterilization under eugenics laws; a grim narrative of institutionalization, co-erced adoption, removal to foster homes. And it is a history still very much with Black mothers, who die in childbirth at higher rates, denied the same care or the same rights as white mothers, and with migrant workers who mother others in conditions of low pay and exploitation. Neither the cozy image of mother and child that Winnicott imagines nor the stultifying togetherness that Rich experienced are possible for everyone.

Winnicott and Rich were formulating their ideas about motherhood in the 1960s and 1970s, and since then our under-standing of motherhood has changed and broadened to include trans parents, queer parents, adoptive mothers, and parents who give birth through surrogacy; and yet, even with this expansion, the expectations that weighed so heavily on mothers of earlier generations have not disappeared. If anything, advances in the science and technology of bringing children into the world and caring for them have raised the stakes of what it means to be a good mother. Winnicott and Rich were writing before the ex-istence of many of the sources of worry that shape motherhood now: social media, surveillance technologies, genetic testing, and biotechnology. Now parents have unprecedented power in making decisions that will shape their children's future—decisions about genetics, assistive technologies, and medical interventions. While parenting may have changed, motherhood, as an institution, isn't going anywhere.

Social historians have described the rise of "scientific mother-hood" as a new set of expectations for mothering in the twen-tieth century and continuing into today. Scientific knowledge about nutrition, bacteria, infectious diseases, and genetics, as well as new standards of measurement to assess whether a child is reaching developmental milestones, have led to healthier children and lessened infant mortality, but they have also created an environment of constant medical assessment and surveillance. A "good mother" is now often defined not only in terms of traditional standards of nurture and care but, increasingly, by the degree to which a parent protects their child from environmental harms and works alongside a medical team to track development and intervene when their child goes off track. Historian Rima D. Apple describes how, for American middle-class mothers in the twentieth century, "the image of the 'good' mother, the 'proper' mother, was a woman who sought out experts for advice on childrearing and who followed the advice she was given."[8] Notions of "scientific motherhood" that emerged in the twentieth century were tightly wound with the rise of eugenics; the good mother of glossy women's periodicals and textbooks and "better baby" contests and formula advertisements was explicitly represented as a middle-class white woman.

In the twenty-first century, the procedures and interventions that are available exceed anything that the most scientifically minded mid-century mother could have imagined. For a cost, we are offered the possibility to surmount infertility, eliminate genetic disorders, and intervene with biotechnological tools. And the costs themselves—the impossible price tag for those without insurance and the accumulating costs of seemingly endless interventions for those with insurance—are creating a steeper socioeconomic divide between parents. For mothers who adhere to the standards of "scientific motherhood," as well as for those who fall outside the margins, the situation is defined by anxiety. Mothers worry about whether their child is "normal"; whether they've been exposed to harmful bacteria, diseases, allergens, or contaminants, especially in a society where environmental risks like air quality and water quality are not distributed equally; whether authorities—doctors or social workers—will deem them unfit; whether they are doing enough—and there is always more to do.

In this climate of constant assessment and scrutiny, writing about oneself as a parent, as a mother, feels like the ultimate act of selfishness. It is taking time away from one's child to navel-gaze. We often use that term, "navel-gazing," to describe the self-involvement of first-person writing. Melissa Febos observes that this description of memoir carries a whiff of the feminine and the maternal: "I don't think it's a stretch to wonder if the navel, as the locus of all this disdain, has something to do with its connection to birth, and body, and the female."[9] Looking down at my own navel, I'm not only looking at myself, but I'm reminded of what connects me to another—my child, my mother. I've become reflective lately, watching Willie so closely over the days, but in observing and watching and waiting, I have become more of a writer than I ever was before. Winnicott himself compared a mother to a writer: "Just as a writer is surprised by the wealth of ideas that turn up when he puts pen to paper, so the mother is constantly surprised by what she finds in the richness of her minute-to-minute contact with her own baby." But where Winnicott sees a binary—mother *or* writer—I see a common thread. By becoming a mother, I'm also becoming a writer. And yet, these two selves (mother, writer) remain hard to reconcile. Writing a memoir blurs the lines between private and public, taking something inherently intimate and broadcasting it outward. It is a dangerous thing to do, reckless even. You are not writing for yourself alone, but writing a story that implicates others. The story of my daughter's birth is not my story alone but, in writing it, I'm claiming for myself the narrative that is also rightfully hers. I'm grasping the golden bridle and trying to steer the course of our lives into a meaningful direction. At the same time, I know that our lives are intertwined with more divergent strands than I could ever shape into a single narrative.

Trying to write now, on the steps of the church with a sleeping baby beside me, I think about fetal microchimerism and how this dangerous blending of parts—the self and the other—defines the experience of pregnancy. You carry something inside you that is part of you but that may become someone who is not you. The boundaries between the body and the outside world start to blur and collapse. If I try to write about this experience and the years that follow, everything that I type out is compromised, composite. So, sitting on those steps, I make a decision to lean in to this difficulty and go ahead and write. I write because, foolish as it is to admit, I think that I have something to say and that there might be someone out there reading these words who nods and agrees and says, yes, that is what it is like. I keep typing, random thoughts, about fate and genetics; about art and science; about the cascade of devices that save me and bury me; and about the deep connection I feel with my child and the desperate loneliness of mothering.

After several minutes, several more sentences, I put my phone away, take a deep breath, and slowly leave the church steps to make my way home.

Willie is not awake yet and, entering our apartment, I still have some time before we need to test her blood sugar. I pick up the toddler, warm with sleep and willing to cuddle her fuzzy head into the crook of my neck. Evan is grading papers in bed and puts them aside so we can climb in with him. Willie allows us to transfer her from her stroller to the bed, stirring softly in a twilight state between sleeping and waking. We still have time. Willie nestles between Evan and me—her toes knead Evan's arm, while her fingers lace themselves in my hair. Her fingers and toes work in elaborate braiding patterns, weaving herself out of the fabric of our being.

If a camera were to record us with one long exposure, it would trace these moving creatures as two wobbly vertical lines with a restless horizontal pattern shifting between them. We would appear before the eye of the camera as an imperfect double helix, marking our way through the passage of time.

PART ONE

# PREGNANCY

1

# On Being and Not Being Pregnant

Pregnancy tests remain memorable only if you don't take too many. If you buy them in bulk packages and test and retest, each result loses its power to shock and awe. After more than a few pregnancies that don't come to term, you forget which test you took where. Were you at home? Alone? Was your partner watching the wand alongside you as its color changed and a line or two came into view? Was that second line clearly visible, or did it appear as a faint haze of pink that you scrutinized for hours? All I can say for certain about my first pregnancy test is that two pink lines slowly materialized before my eyes and that my sense of what those lines meant was not yet what it would become.

Evan and I had moved to New York City a month before I took that test. I did not yet have a doctor. Or a dentist, or a hairstylist, or a favorite bar in the city. I hadn't yet learned how to take a crosstown bus or switch from the local to the express train. I didn't know which museums offered free admission after 5 p.m. or where to get a cheap lunch. The city was a Minotaur's maze that seemed to block access at every point of entry. I found a gynecologist's office through my insurance provider and tried to book an appointment. They could only see me a month from now. Wouldn't that be late? No, they said, that's a normal time to wait to see if the pregnancy is viable.

Viable. The word, uttered by an impatient receptionist, was my first introduction to the precarious and sometimes hostile landscape of early pregnancy. When I took that first pregnancy test, it all seemed straightforward. You sat on the toilet seat and held the magic wand under a stream of urine. It was better, I would learn, if you had to pee just the right amount. The test itself was as straightforward as possible. Depending on the brand, you would simply wait for a plus or minus, one or two lines, pregnant or not pregnant. These binary options didn't allow for the possibility that one might be just a little bit pregnant—that a tiny clump of cells would do their best to generate a spark of life but, in the end, they didn't have all the right information. These cells might manage far enough along to create two pink lines, but then they would break up, falling away as bloody detritus: the same mess experienced every month, but this time with the poignancy of lost potential.

When bleeding appeared before the scheduled doctor's visit, I called the office and was told that it was most likely a "chemical pregnancy."

Should I be seen by someone?

No. As a first-time patient, there was no cutting the line. It wasn't an emergency.

The bluntness with which these words were delivered stung. For the receptionist on the phone, this was run-of-the-mill. Not all pregnancies are built to last, I would learn.

People move to New York City for many reasons. Ambition, adventure, fame. Sinatra sang a song about it. Evan had gotten a job here and if we wanted to have a child together, I'd need to move too. We were looking down the barrel of our thirties. Time was running out. So we moved, we tried, and it all proved rather complicated.


I KNOW A guy who works in advertising. I've known him since middle school when he asked me to a dance organized by a Jewish youth organization. The dance was in Bloomfield Hills, outside of Detroit, and I remember standing in a crowd of teenagers I didn't know, cold in my spaghetti strap semiformal dress and awkward in my semi-Jewishness. In the years since that dance, I'd kept up with him and watched over social media as he transformed himself from a husky thirteen-year-old in a yarmulke to a sleek advertiser in San Francisco. He worked for an agency that was known for cheeky, irreverent advertisements. My favorite thing that he posted on social media from that time, when we were both in our twenties, was a television ad for a Clearblue Easy home pregnancy test. The ad is shot like a scene from *Star Trek*, with a white pregnancy test slowly coasting through black space. The music recalls the slow crescendo of *2001: A Space Odyssey*. A deep male voice intones the ad's catchphrase: "The most advanced piece of technology that you will ever pee on."[1]

I watched the ad on my friend's social media feed, but I rarely saw it on the air after that. At the time, I was neck-deep in graduate work in English literature, and my focus shifted to the blue screen of my computer and the pile of books that I needed to read. But I never forgot the ad. It goes against the basic logic of home pregnancy test advertisements, with their emphasis on joyous couples celebrating positive results. These ads want you to focus on the happy consequences of a positive test that reveals a sought-after pregnancy. In the Clearblue Easy ad, we don't see any people at all and the results of the test are inconsequential. The focus is on the test itself as a technological marvel. Like a spacecraft from a science-fictional universe. I love that final punch line. It's advanced technology that we pee on. High tech meets lowbrow.

The first laboratory test for pregnancy, the Aschheim-Zondek (A-Z) test, was invented by Jewish-German scientists in 1927 to detect the hormone that is now known as human chorionic gonadotrophin (hCG).[2] The placenta produces hCG, which is secreted after the embryo implants itself into the lining of the uterus. This hormone stimulates a cyst on the ovary called the corpus luteum to produce progesterone, which is essential for maintaining the pregnancy. As the pregnancy advances, the placenta will begin to produce progesterone itself. But in the early days, a blast of hCG is needed to help the embryo along before the placenta can take over. This is why hCG is an important indicator of an early pregnancy, before an ultrasound would be able to visually capture an image of the embryo.

The A-Z test required five immature lab mice. Each mouse was injected with the patient's urine twice a day for three days, after which they were killed, dissected, and scanned for signs of ovulation, which would not have otherwise occurred in such young mice. If any of the mice had ovulated, the patient was diagnosed pregnant. It was not far off from a sacrificial offering.[3] Five mice for one pregnancy. Later versions of the test used rabbits. In the TV show *Mad Men,* the advertising executive Roger asks his former lover Joan whether she's had a "rabbit test" to know if she's pregnant. Because of the difficulty and expense of animal testing, A-Z tests were used only in extreme cases, often when a woman was ill and doctors needed to determine whether she might be experiencing a rough early pregnancy.

From the grisly origins of the rabbit test came a series of innovations that led to the home pregnancy test. In the U.S., the FDA approved the home pregnancy test in 1976 and aggressive marketing for the first devices began in 1978. The e.p.t Early Pregnancy Test tapped into the emancipatory rhetoric of the feminist movement to promise customers "a private little revolution any woman can easily buy at her drugstore."[4] It also introduced the idea of at-home diagnostics; as historian Sarah A. Leavitt observes, "home testing was an unusual occurrence for most Americans, who probably counted the thermometer as their only home diagnostic tool."[5] No longer relegated to the specialized domain of white lab coats, pregnancy tests brought advanced medical technology into the home. Early tests, unlike the sleek modern versions, did not hide their origins in the laboratory. They consisted of elaborate test tubes and droppers like a child's first lab kit. Users needed to follow nine intricate steps to get the results they sought.[6] With the shrinking and streamlining of the pregnancy test over the years, the devices have become more efficient to use. Now you can buy them in packs of ten or more to use as early as a week after ovulation. They are packaged like a set of disposable razors, meant to be used as often as possible and thrown away.

EVEN AFTER MOVING to New York City for my husband's job, I was occasionally staggered by the sheer conventionality of my decision. We had spent the previous three years accommodating my job. I was hired as an assistant professor of English literature at a public university in Atlanta that was excited about supporting my work as a young, energetic teacher and researcher. The job was a major coup coming three years after the financial collapse of 2008, when universities were slashing tenure-track positions left and right. The runner-up for the position was an Ivy League PhD who double majored in English and computer science and was fluent in a handful of languages. Getting the job fell somewhere between miracle and cosmic joke. The faculty were warm and inviting, but they were disappointed to learn that I was married to another energetic teacher and researcher. Even worse, his energetic teaching and researching was in precisely the field they were least interested in expanding. Their disappointment registered on their faces at cocktail parties and welcome dinners. Evan and I had started dating as graduate students in the same PhD program in English at the University of Texas. Although I was a year ahead of him in the program, we had met on equal footing—both students, both bright enough, both painfully aware of our points of weakness. But pursuing careers in the same field meant that we would always have to balance on a swinging teeter-totter of prestige and insecurity. One plus sign for another minus sign. My two lines for his one, or vice versa. There were so few jobs and our fields were so specialized that it was unlikely we would ever find positions in the same city.

With good grace, Evan spent those years as a trailing spouse, applying for the jobs he could find and hoping one would land him in the same region. We lived on my salary and the small income that he brought in from adjunct work. And then, unexpectedly, he landed *the* job. The shiny, big job in his field that everyone wondered who would get. The kind of job that got you talked about at conferences. The kind that stirred up professional animosity and made people rethink their previous dismissals of your intelligence, aptitude, and fitness. It was the kind of job you didn't turn down. The unwritten rules of scarcity and prestige governing our profession demanded acceptance.

I had wrenching discussions with friends and family about whether to live apart or resign from my job. My dissertation advisor—a wittily acerbic British expat living in Texas—described it as my "Elinor or Marianne" predicament. She was referring to the two main characters of Jane Austen's *Sense and Sensibility*. The elder sister, Elinor, is reasonable to a fault, while the younger sister, Marianne, is romantic and impetuous. One is all head and the other all heart. While both sisters face trials, Austen goes to astonishing lengths to punish Marianne, whose raptures push her just nearly over the brink of polite society and almost lead to her death. Did it have to be a choice between the two extremes? I wanted to argue that we're all a little bit Elinor and a little bit Marianne. Wasn't that, after all, what made the novel so appealing? But, like the binary options of the pregnancy test, I could be only one or the other. Choosing to move with Evan would make me a Marianne and, as such, I should be prepared to suffer.

I did the thing that everyone said was unthinkable, and I resigned from my university position. Suddenly, I was the trailing spouse. I was offered a one-year visiting position at the university-one-does-not-turn-down. I taught my classes, met with students, presented papers, signed a contract for my first book. The position would end at the end of the year and I wanted to see if there was any possibility of extending the time. There was not. Universities-one-cannot-turn-down, it seems, did not offer open-ended positions to trailing spouses, especially ones who were trailing from southern public universities. One senior faculty member in the department sat down with me to discuss my professional options. She was brimming with advice about going back on the job market. The challenge, she said, was how to spin this decision to leave a tenure-track job. This disastrous decision, she implied. How could I describe this choice without making it seem so "wifey"? It would be one thing if you were pregnant, she went on, but it will be hard to explain leaving such a job for a *husband*.

And so that little clump of cells, before they had a chance to be anything more than a chemical spark that lit up a pregnancy detector, was already a missed opportunity to justify my decisions.

I BLAME MY father, a urologist, for my fascination with the role of urine in the sacred rituals of twenty-first-century pregnancy. Prominently displayed in his office is a framed print of a medieval physician wielding a matula—a glass flask used to visually examine urine samples. Uroscopy, the study of urine, is one of the oldest branches of European medicine and involved a physician inspecting a patient's urine to determine the nature of an illness. Sometimes they would taste it to detect sweetness or acidity. The diagnostic skills of ancient "piss prophets," as they were known, included pregnancy detection. The use of urine to detect pregnancy was not limited to Europe. Much earlier, in ancient Egypt, papyrus manuscripts from 1350 B.C. describe urine tests to detect early pregnancy. Two bags were prepared—one with barley seeds and one with wheat—upon which a woman would urinate every day. If the barley grew, it would be a boy. If the grain grew, it would be a girl. If neither bag germinated, the woman was declared not pregnant. This test and later versions operated through an analogy between a woman's fecundity and the germination of seeds.[7] It would be easy to write off such a test as unsophisticated in comparison to modern technology, and yet, when later physicians replicated the test, they found it could predict early pregnancy 75 percent of the time.[8] It seems that estrogen can stimulate the growth of seeds; the grain and barley responded to the elevated level of estrogen in pregnant women's urine.[9] The Egyptian papyrus had a curious afterlife—the reference to "grain" was mistranslated by a German physician as "needle" and sixteenth-century women were instructed to place sewing needles in their urine; later, an English physician again mistranslated the "needles" as "nettles" and Englishwomen were soon peeing on the leaves of the nettle plant and looking for red spots to appear.[10] One thing these early tests tell us is that there is nothing new in the desire to confirm a pregnancy as early as possible with some form of outside verification. I wonder about how these tests would have provided a different way of imaging a pregnancy. A flowering shaft of grain; an oxidizing needle; red spots on a nettle plant. These tests are all different ways of making a pregnancy visible to the outside world. Without them, pregnancy was a private feeling—a somatic experience known only to the woman herself; she might guess she was pregnant from her morning sickness or tenderness in her breasts, or she could wait for the "quickening" of the pregnancy, the first signs of movement in the womb. Yet, these feelings did not count as diagnostic proof. Seeing is believing, after all.

While urine tests have long been a form of early verification for women who think they might be pregnant, they are far less accurate and informative than blood tests. This is an old family conflict for me. My father might have been a urologist, but his father—my grandfather—was a hematologist. They had a difficult relationship. My grandfather was a dominating personality whose sense of humor could easily slide into ridicule. A first-generation American, he was born to Yiddish-speaking parents from western Russia. He had witnessed the horrors of Auschwitz as a medical officer in World War II and had attended the Nuremberg trials. Deeply intellectual, he did not suffer fools or extend much grace to those who fell beneath his contempt. He worked in private practice, seeing patients in Buffalo, New York, long after his eyesight and health had given out on him. My father, on the other hand, has always been lighter and easier with a loving, if slightly feisty, nature and a willingness to change his mind. I tend to anthropomorphize blood and urine in this way: one dark and deep, the other light and insightful. The battle lines were firmly established in my family tree.

Although it feels like taking sides, blood wins out over urine when it comes to pregnancy detection. In 1972, Judith Vaitukaitis developed a test that did not require animals to determine the presence of hCG. She began her work studying the hormone in order to detect certain forms of cancer, but the implications for pregnancy testing soon became apparent.[11] The blood test that she developed, though it led directly to the manufacturing of commercial pregnancy tests, was much more sophisticated than the urine test we use at home. It could make more specific claims about a pregnancy beyond a simple yes or no. This test revealed the levels of hCG in the blood (not just its presence), to show whether there might be a complicating factor, such as ectopic pregnancy, in which the egg has implanted outside of the uterus.[12] In the case of an ectopic pregnancy, the urine test would tell you that you are pregnant, but a blood test would reveal that the pregnancy is most likely not viable. What you experienced as a plus sign should have really been a plus with an asterisk—a pregnancy with a difference.

When Vaitukaitis published her findings, she said that this new test "will permit earlier diagnosis of pregnancy, which, in turn, would permit earlier therapeutic intervention if desired."[13] The knowledge of a pregnancy, enabled by a pregnancy test, meant very little if there were not actionable consequences to this knowledge driven by therapeutic needs and individual desires. The adjective "therapeutic" is doing a lot of work here. By emphasizing the therapeutic nature of any possible intervention, Vaitukaitis and her coauthors tacitly acknowledged cultural anxieties about the motives for intervening in a pregnancy. Early debates about the home pregnancy test focused on what women would do with this newfound knowledge about early pregnancy.

Should women be trusted with this information? Would there be more abortions as a consequence? From a doctor's point of view, diagnosing a pregnancy early allowed for quicker responses to complicated cases in early pregnancy, again including the ectopic variety, where the life of the mother may be at risk. In many cases, therapeutic intervention meant abortion. A year after Vaitukaitis described the possibilities for therapeutic interventions generated by home pregnancy tests, the U.S. Supreme Court maintained the legal right to abortion in the case of *Roe v. Wade* (1973). Pregnancy tests and legalized abortion in the U.S. share a timeline—information about when a pregnancy started went hand in hand with the right to make decisions about what to do about it.

From these tangled roots, pregnancy testing and the U.S. abortion debates have influenced the experience of miscarriage in America. Historian Lara Freidenfelds argues that home pregnancy tests coupled with the heated rhetoric of the pro-abortion and anti-abortion movements in America have increased the poignancy of miscarriage for many women. Early testing alerts women to pregnancies long before previous generations of women would have known they were pregnant, at a precarious stage when miscarriage is very likely: about 30 percent of detectable pregnancies are lost, most often in the early weeks.[14] In a culture in which anti-abortion advocates push sentimental images of life in the womb, which women are meant to protect as a sacred principle, and pro-choice advocates emphasize the control that women should exert over their choice to be pregnant or not, miscarriage stands, in Freidenfelds's words, as "a silent repudiation to both sides" or "a denial of life and choice at the same time."[15] The at-home pregnancy test is a preliminary step that precedes the highly medicalized experience of twenty-first-century pregnancy, but it is an essential one that allows for therapeutic intervention and that shapes attitudes toward pregnancy.

It gives the illusion of certainty and the expectation of control with a graphic, highly visual image of a pregnancy confirmed.

STANDING ON A sandy beach in James Joyce's imagined Dublin, Stephen Dedalus thinks these words to no one but himself: "The ineluctable modality of the visible."[16] I've taught this passage of *Ulysses* many times and each time I have to look up two words in the dictionary—"ineluctable," "modality." What is he trying to say about vision, visibility, seeing? To be ineluctable is to be inescapable. The connotation is negative—you want to get away from something but cannot. And what about modality? That which relates to a mode or style or manner, but not the substance of the thing itself. So, the ineluctable modality of the visible, glossed in inelegant descriptive prose, means: we cannot escape the style of what we see. Or, that which is visible is known to us only through its style, not its essential nature.

Seeing a pregnancy through an at-home test, for instance. We buy it over the counter at the drugstore (it is a commercially available medical supply); it is often white and comes individually packaged (surgically clean); and it is shaped like a wand (magic!). Once we've peed on it, we wait a few minutes and something is revealed to us. A plus or minus, one line or two. Once we see those symbols, we cannot escape them. They are the manner through which we first see and know ourselves as pregnant. And yet, what did we really see? We saw a binary response to the presence of hCG in our urine. In the case of a positive response, we did not really see confirmation of a baby—the essence that those two lines claim to represent—though it feels like we did. There is something mirage-like about an early pregnancy. It is there and not there, existing only incompletely in the mind and in the body.

I held on to the common superstition against telling people

I was pregnant before fifteen weeks. And yet, people had a way of knowing. During one pregnancy, I spilled the secret myself—telling Miranda that I was pregnant as we sat outside on a beautiful sunny fall day at the Met Cloisters, surrounded by medieval art. Miranda had been my closest colleague in Atlanta and leaving her was one of the hardest parts of my decision to go. She was a quick-witted know-it-all who was fierce in her loyalties and convictions. Hers was an alpha personality that hid a deeper vulnerability. She reminded me of my mother. We'd come to the Cloisters, nestled at the top of a rocky cliff overlooking the Hudson River, to find a particular sculpture of the Virgin Mary. Miranda specialized in literature of the American South and wanted to find this sculpture because it was especially beloved by Flannery O'Connor, who sought it out repeatedly when she lived in New York City, far from her home in Georgia and hungry for a familiar companion.

After an hour of searching, we were still not sure which sculpture O'Connor would have visited. Was it the one with the soft smile whose child playfully tugged at her mantle, or the rosy-cheeked one who was missing her arms? There were so many Virgin Mothers. My current, distinctively less immaculate conception had been confirmed by a doctor just the week before, and I was not planning to tell Miranda during our outing, but a morning spent submerged in the iconography of pregnancy loosened my tongue. I couldn't take my eyes off the paintings of the Annunciation. In these works, the artists were depicting a divine form of early pregnancy detection. The archangel Gabriel visits the Virgin Mary to announce that she is pregnant just as the Holy Ghost arrives to make it so. I stood in front of one of the most famous iterations of the Annunciation, Robert Campin's *Mérode Altarpiece,* a fifteenth-century Dutch triptych. In this version of the Annunciation, Mary sits in a domestic space, leaning against a bench and absorbed in the book that she is reading. She doesn't notice Gabriel kneeling on the other side of the table about to deliver the news. Meanwhile, above Gabriel's head a minuscule white figure—the Holy Ghost, who appears like a tiny homunculus—dives through the window on a sunbeam, carrying a cross and cruising with high velocity straight toward Mary. To know she is pregnant is to be told by Gabriel and, perhaps at the same moment, to experience a collision with the Holy Ghost. On the left side of the triptych, a wealthy Dutch couple, the artist's patrons, kneel and observe, while on the right side, the carpenter Joseph plies his trade, not knowing what Mary will soon know. This altarpiece catches its figures in a strange moment between knowing and not knowing, between not being pregnant and being pregnant.

Miranda had guessed I was pregnant before I told her.

But how?

She couldn't say. There was something about the way I was behaving. An air of mystery she hadn't seen before.

There are people who seem to have a preternatural sense of detection. The more often you are pregnant, the more times you will encounter these folks. Your colleague who notices you pass

on the sushi hors d'oeuvres at a reception. Your friend who takes you out for dinner and looks at you askance when you order sparkling water. The subway passenger who magisterially gives up her seat even though you are not showing yet.

When Keira came to town from LA, I was ten weeks pregnant and, despite some morning sickness, was not yet showing any signs of pregnancy. Keira was a college friend who now worked in museum curation and so her trip to New York would be filled with museum visits, which was just fine with me. I suggested we go to the Harlem Studio Museum to see an exhibition of Alma Thomas. We passed enormous canvases composed of wide brush-strokes of primary colors—blues, reds, yellows, greens—arranged in long lines, like colorful scripts of an unknown code. On some canvases, the strokes were arranged in neat vertical rows, and on others they were arranged horizontally with peaks like mountains. Thomas was a Black DC-based artist who did not begin paint-ing professionally until the 1960s when she had retired from a thirty-year career as an art teacher. We stopped in front of a can-vas where the lines of colorful pats of paint were arranged in cir-cles surrounding a central black dot. It could have been a planet or an embryo. As I stood immersed in this technicolor canvas, a security guard approached me. At first I thought I had done something wrong. Brushed too closely to a canvas, perhaps.

He wanted to congratulate me. He was sure it would be a boy. Something about the way that I was walking.

I looked at the guard and looked at Keira. I didn't know how to hide my confusion. How could he have known I was preg-nant? What made him think that it was a boy? Was I uncon-sciously mimicking the movements of pregnant women I had known? A slight bend of the pelvis. A hand resting against the small of my back. Or maybe I was giving off the mythical glow that people talk about? Was there a dreamy abstraction on my face as I stared into the center point of Thomas's canvas and wondered whether a life lay within? Keira and I did not discuss it later and the pregnancy did not come to term. There was a blankness, after all, at the center of the canvas.

WHEN YOU ARE a woman of a certain age on social media, it is likely that your feed will be flooded with ultrasound images. Posting an ultrasound photo online is one of the strange rituals of twenty-first-century parenthood. It is the first image of the future child and, as such, the imperatives of social media demand that it be shared. But what kind of image is an ultrasound? It is a grainy representation of a protohuman that, with the help of medical experts, we have learned to interpret as possessing human characteristics. That is an arm. That is its heart. The technician gestures to a certain area and we nod our heads.

Unlike other photographs, it is not produced by light, but rather, by sound. Ultra-sound.

The story of ultrasound technology does not begin with the human fetus: it begins, instead, with bats. In 1793, the Italian physicist Lazzaro Spallanzani first described how bats are able to navigate in the dark through the use of echolocation. They experience physical spaces not through sight, but by casting sounds into the darkness and measuring the presence of obstacles and obstructions through the reflection of those sounds off surfaces. The same principle would be invoked after the sinking of the *Titanic* in 1912 when scientists and public officials registered the importance of detecting obstructions—an iceberg, for instance—underwater. Through the first half of the twentieth century, ultrasound technology would develop as a military and industrial tool. The first ultrasound technicians were not medical providers, but naval officers charting the presence of enemy submarines and engineers looking for dangerous flaws in metal structures. The same principle was at work in both cases—sound was passed through a medium (water, metal) and any disturbance in that medium (submarine, flaw) would register as a blip in the otherwise seamless transmission of the sound.

The technology would need to evolve dramatically to create fetal ultrasounds, a sonic map translated into a visual picture. The British physician Ian Donald is credited with developing the technology for fetal ultrasounds. His training as a medical officer in the Royal Air Force during World War II brought him in close contact with the radar and sonar technologies that he would later import into the world of obstetrics and gynecology. In the 1950s, he borrowed an industrial ultrasonic metal flaw detector from a company of boilermakers and began experimenting on whether he could use them for imaging samples of fibroids and ovarian cysts.[17] In 1959, he first used echoes to measure a fetal head and used this measurement to determine its size and growth. With time, these rudimentary diagnostics eventually matured into complex images derived through sound. In contrast to X-ray imaging, another technology for representing our insides, ultrasounds pose no threat to the fetus and can be used at any stage of a pregnancy, from intravaginal ultrasounds, in which an uncomfortably large wand is roughly inserted inside a woman to document the early stages of pregnancy, to 3D ultrasounds that are now popular for late-term pregnancies and that produce rather creepily animate images of a fetus that is nearly ready to emerge into the world.

From an early stage, Donald worried about the ethical implications of ultrasound. That by giving parents early information about the physical characteristics of the fetus, ultrasounds might encourage selective termination on the basis of sex or physical abnormalities. In reality, ultrasounds have become a more powerful tool on the other side of the abortion debate, capturing images of a fetus that connect us to its developing human features and allow for emotional appeals regarding personhood at early stages of a pregnancy. These images would be mobilized in the ongoing battle between the pro-abortion and anti-abortion movements. Ultrasound technology was born on the battlefront and has returned to its place of origin, providing ammunition in the culture wars that have emerged in lockstep alongside advances in pregnancy detection. On a road trip through the U.S., you'll see ultrasounds blown up to enormous proportions. Billboards dot interstate highways proclaiming: "Choose Life"; "Abortion Tears Her Life Apart"; "Ask to Hear My Heartbeat, Mom."

What is more intimate than a snapshot? Here, in the technician's office, the ultrasound seems to offer us the first visual document of family life. We leave with a photo that we can slip in between the leaves of a baby album or post on our social media account, below which an aunt responds with a heart-eyed emoji. It doesn't matter that it is a grainy snapshot made with sound, not light, developed to detect obstacles, threats, and flaws. Not a flattering angle at all. I have a box of ultrasound photos that never made it into an album, that no one ever responded to with heart eyes. There they lie, abandoned and unclaimed, the uncanny relics of a failed ritual. For many, these photos continue to live online, haunting the present. Intrusive reminders pop up as "memories" on our phone, never letting us forget that we shared a photo of an ultrasound on such and such a date however many years ago.

Even for those of us who do not share photographs, our online searches in the days after a positive pregnancy test begin to tell the data-collecting bots that we are expecting a baby. The internet, with the subtlety of a sledgehammer, translates interest in pregnancy-related topics to the certainty of the expected outcome—a healthy, living baby. Omar Seyal, a department head at the image-sharing social media site Pinterest, calls this "the miscarriage problem."[18] At the first sight of a positive pregnancy test or the first glimpse of an ultrasound photograph, you might start searching online for ideas for redecorating your office into a nursery. You start a Pinterest account to look at images of nurseries, and so, according to the predictive skills of the machine, it is most likely that you will eventually end up decorating a nursery. Seyal calls this the "bias of the majority problem."[19] Most people end up with nurseries. A minority do not. The algorithms lay out a certain future that unfolds before your eyes and that belies the uncertainty of pregnancy itself. Long after the pregnancy passes, your Pinterest account continues to be overrun with nursery photos and you still receive ads for cribs, strollers, and baby clothes. There is no baby.

A line of flash fiction attributed to Ernest Hemingway reads, "For sale: baby shoes, never worn." It is often cited as a reminder of how much pathos a writer can pack into a single sentence. Because what is sadder than the dimming of the happy expectation that went into buying a pair of baby shoes? Now the algorithms do us one better. We are haunted by innumerable pictures of baby shoes, never bought.

I WAS THIRTEEN weeks pregnant when the bleeding started again. I called the doctor's office and was told that this was not uncommon but that they would check in at my next appointment, which was scheduled for that week. They would do an ultrasound and we would get more information.

The technician was upbeat and friendly. She lathered my stomach with jelly and began to knead it with a bulbous wand as Evan and I stared, with eyes transfixed, at the monitor that was set up to give us a glimpse of the movements within.

There is the head, she said, and the back, and the legs . . .

Her voice trailed off.

And what else, we wanted to know. But she couldn't say. We would have to wait for the doctor.

After hastily wiping my stomach clean and rearranging my robe, she left.

Our doctor came back more quickly than expected with a grave look of someone about to deliver bad news. I'm afraid the pregnancy has miscarried, she told us. It had not happened recently but had probably terminated a few weeks back. It must have happened as I was going about my business, teaching my classes, buying groceries, reading a book. While I was eating or opening a window or just walking along.

What had caused the miscarriage? I wanted to know.

It was impossible to say. Most likely it was a chromosomal abnormality. The genetic code may have gotten scrambled, in which case it would have been only a matter of time. Many pregnancies are lost in the first trimester. Even though we thought that we had made it safely into the second trimester, we had, in fact, not.

The doctor said that we needed to wait a week to see if the miscarriage would pass naturally, or whether I would need to come in for a surgical procedure. During that week, I was scheduled for a second-round job interview. It was for a local community college. The first interview had gone well. I had sat around a table with six members of the search committee and answered questions about research, teaching, and whether I was a good fit for their college. The latter round of questions was the most stringent; the student population was working class, predominately Latinx and Black students, and I was a white woman coming from a prestigious university, even if my connection to this university was loose. My former university in Atlanta set national records for supporting low-income students. I loved the students I had taught there and was eager to work at a public university with comparable demographics. I was still grieving leaving that job and was hopeful that I'd find myself at a similar institution. Though I could readily admit that there were better-qualified candidates for the job, I was looking forward to the opportunity to meet the students and talk more with the faculty. The committee members were confident enough in my fit to bring me back for a second interview, which would involve taking over a first-year writing course for the day and teaching a subject of my choosing.

In the days after learning about the miscarriage, I never once considered rescheduling the interview. There were very few jobs opening in my field that year and this was the only interview I was likely to have. Under the best of circumstances, a teaching demonstration would be nerve-racking, and these were not the best of circumstances. I would be going into a class without having had the opportunity to build a rapport with the students and teaching a lesson that may or may not fulfill their expectations for the course. I would be watched by a panel of interviewers who were scrutinizing my every move.

On the day of the teaching demonstration, I put more care than usual into what I was wearing, as if I were dressing in a coat of armor—not one to prevent external injury, but one that could trap something inside from getting out. I wore the kind of bulky maxi pads that one has to wear after a miscarriage, and obsessively checked the line of the seat of my pants to make sure it was unobservable. Above all, I tried not to think that there was something dead inside of me that my body was struggling to release. The images from the ultrasound lingered in my mind's eye.

I met with the chair of the department before going into the class. He seemed piqued. I had reached out to them too late to see if there would be a projector in the room. There wouldn't be. He was irritated that I hadn't contacted him earlier. When I got to the classroom, I felt more at ease. The students were already assembled and the teacher gave me a friendly greeting. Then the interviewers came in. Though each had been hospitable with me during the initial interview, not a single person greeted me or made eye contact as they came through the door. Even so, I taught my heart out. The students were magnificent, responding to every question and offering rich interpretations of the material. Like many other inherently shy people, I feel more comfortable in front of a group than in one-on-one interactions. I'd been teaching for twelve years, enough to know the difference between a good class and a bad one. This was a good one.

As the class ended and the interviewers filed out of the room, not a single one of them gave me a nod of assent or recognition. They remained stony-faced and unimpressed. As I packed up my papers with as much composure as I could muster, I thought, this is the limit of grit: steeling myself before this impassive audience at the back of the room, which has already decided I am the wrong candidate for the job. No amount of armor could protect me from the feeling of having failed in the face of success.

Only one faculty member stayed to have a word with me after the class. As the rest of the committee filed past, he asked if anyone had arranged to take me to lunch after the demonstration. They had not. He suggested a diner across the street.

During lunch, he told me about the negative consequences of a female-dominated department. Women, evidently, needed to do everything by committee. There was too much gossip, too many feelings. I quickly realized that he was the department pariah—someone who had developed an adversarial relationship with the rest of the department and wanted to feel out a potential new colleague to see if she would be on his side. When the waiter asked me what I wanted, I ordered grilled cheese. Something about the sandwich, in its childlike gooey simplicity, felt necessary. The conversation, warmed by the melting cheese and greasy fries, at least seemed human, flawed and strange as it was. I listened and found myself nodding along, anxious to please the only committee member left.

I went home to an apartment that felt suddenly smaller. There was no room to mourn. If I tried to creep into one corner, I was confronted with a laptop, open books, to-do lists. In another corner was the kitchen with its call to practicality, its lulling drumbeat of rhythmic tasks, its homey odors and pungent necessities. Only staring out the window, watching the tugboats slowly chugging along the Hudson, was I able to stop and feel something.

Months later, when my waking mind had made peace with what had happened, I had a vivid dream that wrenched me back. I dreamed that I was living in a half-empty hotel trying to care for a new baby that I did not know how to handle. I was by myself but visited by lonely guests who wandered in and out of the rooms. Everything about the dream suggested a Gothic novel—the kind that I especially like to teach. The rooms were decrepit, the guests were aged and spectral. Not knowing how to breastfeed, I tried to feed the baby using my cell phone. A woman gently tapped me on the shoulder and told me to try my breast instead. Then a clear fluid flowed out—not quite breast milk but not water either. Just as I began to settle into something like a ghostly version of motherhood, the baby looked up at me. It looked at me with a face of recognition that was not a baby's, but something more knowing, more fully adult. The baby saw me and let out a heart-piercing scream.

LINDSEY IS IN town for a conference and we decide to meet up at the Museum of Modern Art. It's January and bitter cold. I'm pregnant again and, once I enter the warm atrium, I am immediately running hot. She is not pregnant and is running cold. I check my coat and she hangs on to hers. Since we first got to know each other in Atlanta when she was a graduate student, we've been meeting up over the years. She is now working on a book on women's craftwork. She's interested in the homegrown arts that have long been considered part of a woman's sphere— knitting, crocheting, quilting—but that are rarely considered high art.

A special exhibition is running on the paintings and print work of Louise Bourgeois. She's an artist who interests us both. Lindsey is drawn to Bourgeois's use of fabric cuttings and embroidery, while I—at eight months pregnant—have a visceral reaction to her representations of motherhood. Throughout her career, Bourgeois created a highly personal iconography of motherhood. Some of the imagery hearkens back to her own mother, a French tapestry maker. Her most famous works are enormous sculptures of spiders whose webs recall the tapestries her mother wove. On a smaller scale, she created prints and paintings embedded with textiles that also recall her mother's handiwork. Other work by Bourgeois meditates on the experience of pregnancy and her role as the mother of three boys. The color palette of these works is unvaryingly red, as if the bloody experience of childbirth has left a mark on the page.

I can't look away from one image above all others. It is the sixth image in a series called *I Go to Pieces: My Inner Life*. The work is comprised of three parts arranged like a triptych. On the leftmost panel, Bourgeois has sewn a collage out of strips of red, pink, and white fabric. Tangled together, the fabric slopes into a V shape like the hairy triangle of a pubis or, given its red color, the sunken lump of a placenta after it has left the body. The discarded fabrics recall the leftover scraps in Bourgeois's mother's tapestry studio. In the center of the triptych is a painting on paper of a pregnant woman. The woman is shown in profile with her distended belly pushing toward the right edge of the frame. From her belly button runs an umbilical cord that projects out of her stomach, around her body, and enters and exits through her head. The umbilical cord wraps around her in a tangled mass, mirroring the fabric on her left. It is as if her pregnancy is both inside her body, piercing her womb and her mind alike, and reaching outside into the world. Her pregnancy is private and public, internal and external, bodily and cerebral at once. It is an entanglement with the world, with one's own mother, and with one's self.

On the right-hand panel of the triptych, Bourgeois includes another fabric panel, but this time, instead of strips of fabric, she has embroidered words arranged in a column like a poem. The words read:

I go to pieces
I lose

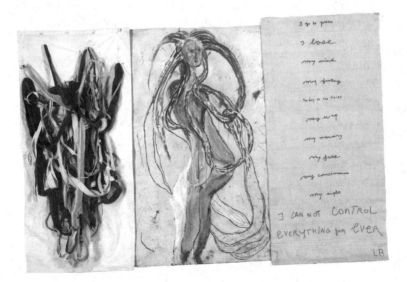

my mind
my footing
the key to the fields
my way
my memory
my faith
my consciousness
my sight[.]

And then, at the bottom, in slightly larger letters: "I can not control everything for ever."

Pregnancy tests and ultrasounds are not entirely dissimilar to works of art, in that all are crafted by people to reveal something about reality. They all make claims to truth (though only one promises 99 percent accuracy), but they also alter the reality that they represent. Looking at Bourgeois's painting, I feel my pregnancy differently. I imagine the fetus not only in my womb, but in my mind, intruding into or sharing my thoughts. I also imagine it extending its being out into the world, connecting me to my environment, but also making me vulnerable to its influences and incursions. It is no longer a plus or minus sign—a marker of success or failure. Bourgeois's painting is a darker representation of pregnancy. It is not composed of the cheery pinks and antiseptic whites of the pregnancy test nor the dreary gray scale of the ultrasound. And it does not promise happiness. Pregnancy, as Bourgeois depicts it, expands our understanding of our bodies and our relationship to the world, and this expansion is nothing short of terrifying.

After the exhibition, Lindsey and I buy overpriced coffee and pastries in the canteen. We sit and talk about motherhood, fabric, and careers. I met Lindsey when she was a graduate student and I was a newly minted assistant professor. Even after five years and as her career has eclipsed mine, I've had a hard time shaking off my role as elder statesman, try as I might. Like a figure skater hugging the sides of the rink, I circle the topics that press on me most intimately. As she tells me about the difficulties that she's faced in her first year in a new job and a new city, I respond with advice when I should be sharing my similar trials. I'm about five years older and yet feel a thousand years older. She has large doe-like eyes and loose curls that fall over her shoulders. It's reassuring, in some ways, to be with someone who thinks my advice is valuable even if I leave the conversation feeling like I've been playing a part. She is open and unguarded, talking easily about her marriage and the costs of professional success, while I remain more reticent about my life outside of work. Up to a point, she and I have similar stories. She and her partner attended the same graduate program and she got the first job—the big job. Since then, he had struggled to find his footing. There were no academic opportunities for him near her and he wasn't sure he wanted to stay in academia. Our stories were similar with a significant gender reversal. She's the one who had made it. Another version of binary logic: man and woman; success and failure. I listened to her talk and it was hard not to project my big what-ifs onto their relationship. What if we had stayed in Atlanta. What if I had gotten the job. What if one of the earlier pregnancies had come to term. A voice spoke in my head. I cannot control everything forever.

Things were tough for them since they left graduate school. It had been a rocky move.

I wondered if they wanted children but didn't dare ask.

There are some topics that can't be broached over museum pastries.

I felt the baby kick. Unmistakable. The quickening. A strange lurching in what I might have called my stomach, but now must think of as my womb.

As we each nodded and listened in turn, Bourgeois's painting throbbed as an afterimage behind my eyes. I cannot control everything forever.

The words were embroidered in looping red cursive thread. I imagined how Bourgeois would have sewn them into the fabric. A quick stab of the needle followed by the luxurious pull of the thread. Her finger and thumb pressed lightly together, holding the needle steady, while the other three fingers curved upward in a gentle signal of calm. I wanted to stay in this moment of creation forever. To embrace the uncertainty of Bourgeois's unknowing. I touched my stomach and repeated: I cannot control everything forever.

# 2

# Genetic Testing and Me

The Dadaists made chance a central principle of their artistic production. Man Ray cut strings of different lengths and tossed them onto a canvas to see where they landed. This act of casting the strings might reveal a beautiful pattern. It might not. Ray's concept took the artist down a peg. The artist was no longer the god of creation, sculpting life out of the raw materials of nature. The artist was now a mere instrument for the vicissitudes of chance.

I'm back at MoMA again, this time with my dad, who is in town visiting. We look at the pictures in the Dadaist room. Cold and unaffecting, they confront us with their mechanistic view of the universe. Pictures are hung according to a throw of the dice. A screen projects images where film was randomly cut and rearranged or marked with nails and other household objects. *Flash* and we see what looks like twinkling lights in the darkness. *Flash* and rows of thick lines appear like Morse code or redacted text. Another *flash* and a woman's naked torso shimmers on-screen, covered in the striped pattern of the blinds. She looks part woman and part zebra. *Flash* and all is darkness again. Over the sound system, a haunting chant is projected. A placard tells us that the music comes from four voices—Man Ray and his three sisters singing random notes that were pulled out of a hat.

My dad walks up to the security guard standing impassive at the room's exit. He asks the guard whether he is getting hazard pay for listening to this all day.

A dry chuckle. The real hazard is his pay.

They both laugh at that and the singing voices drone on, dissonant and discomfiting.

I look up at the film again. It is called *Le Retour à la Raison (Return to Reason)*. Played on a loop, it cycles back to the beginning and repeats its three-minute cycle yet again. The images start to look familiar to me. For an instant, the screen is covered with white circles dotted in the center with a black hole. Like toilet paper rolls seen from above. Or like a zygote with a black center. They bounce and jostle each other in a mesmerizing dance. Another *flash* and X-ray-like images appear in white against a black background.

The images start to blur and I see, projected on the screen in my mind, early images of DNA—the kind that Rosalind Franklin painstakingly captured. I see Franklin's "Photograph 51": a round cell with a white center and four squiggly strands radiating outward in the shape of the letter X. Rosalind took this photograph by bombarding DNA with X-rays.[1] This process, known as X-ray diffraction, requires that the scientist first crystallize the molecule so that it sits still, and then use X-rays, the only light source powerful enough to allow something so small to cast a shadow, in order to picture the presence of the molecule through the negative space created by its shadow. Siddhartha Mukherjee describes the technique as follows:

> To understand the basic outline of this technique, imagine trying to deduce the shape of a minute three-dimensional

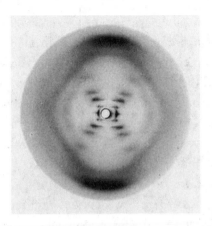

object—a cube, say. You cannot "see" this cube nor feel its edges—but it shares the one property that all physical objects must possess: it generates shadows. Imagine that you can shine light at the cube from various angles and record the shadows that are formed. Placed directly in front of the light, a cube casts a square shadow. Illuminated obliquely, it forms a diamond. Move the light source again, and the shadow is a trapezoid. The process is almost absurdly laborious—like sculpting a face out of a million silhouettes—but it works: piece by piece, a set of two-dimensional images can be transmuted into a three-dimensional form.[2]

As Rosalind Franklin's photographs became clearer and clearer, an unmistakable X-shaped pattern began to appear. In 1951, she gave a talk at King's College in London to share some of her findings with the scientific community and she noted seeing a helix structure with chains.[3] A young James Watson was in the audience and was energized by the structure she was just beginning to tease out. Before Franklin had a chance to publish her findings, and without her consent, the chief of her lab, Maurice Wilkins, shared her photographs with Watson, a Cambridge researcher who, along with Francis Crick, was attempting to model the structure of DNA. They saw in the photograph the double helix structure that they were looking for. Crick and Watson published their findings in *Nature* and went on to win the Nobel Prize along with Wilkins for their discovery.[4] Franklin had died four years before of metastatic ovarian cancer, a genetic disorder. The woman who first photographed the double helix would not live to see her own illness spelled out in the code she helped uncrack.

When I look at Man Ray's curious film and see Rosalind Franklin's photograph, am I projecting meaning onto meaninglessness? Most definitely. And yet, here they are in my mind, the zygotes, the strands of DNA, Franklin toiling late into the night on a discovery for which others will be acclaimed. I see shadows emerge out of the substance that is invisible to my eyes. Ray's film, named for reason, created by chance, landed on something familiar. In art as in genetics, strings are thrown against the canvas and we wait to see where they land.

WHEN I TOLD my ob-gyn, Dr. Patel, that I would prefer not to do genetic testing, her nose scrunched up just slightly. She put more urgency into her words. She was concerned that I was a likely carrier for a number of genetic disorders. First of all, there was my age to consider. Though she rarely brought up my age, she needed to remind me to make the point. I was over thirty-five years old and there was a greater chance that I would carry a child with the extra chromosomes that cause Down syndrome. This was not the best tack for her to take. It confirmed my fears that genetic testing was mainly designed to screen for developmental disabilities. The implication for this testing was, I reasoned, that I would automatically choose to abort a pregnancy if Down syndrome was detected. I was sensitive on this point; my brother Alex is developmentally disabled and I had grown up in the company of children and adults with Down syndrome. I saw my brother's peers go on to live full, meaningful lives and, for me, there was little to fear in such a diagnosis. Then Dr. Patel reminded me that I was descended from Ashkenazi Jews and therefore could carry genes for genetic disorders such as Tay-Sachs, which had long been associated with Jewish ancestry. This was something I knew less about. These were not disorders that I had experienced personally or that I had read much about. My resolve was slipping.

When my sister Jenny was pregnant with each of her three children—my nephews and niece—between 2003 and 2007, all of her friends opted for genetic testing, but she did not. The testing, as she understood it, was mostly for Down syndrome, and, with her experience as Alex's sister, she did not want to terminate a pregnancy for that reason. It was not a big deal to opt out of testing with the first pregnancy, but she noticed a shift between the first and the last, a stronger urging from her doctor. She was thirty-two by the time of the last pregnancy, so hers was still not a "geriatric pregnancy" like mine. Instead, it felt like something had changed in the culture of pregnancy in those intervening years, and now, even more so, between Jenny's first pregnancy and mine. By the time that I was pregnant, at least in the New York City hospitals that I was visiting, genetic screening had increasingly become a standard part of the picture of prenatal health. With this expectation came changes to underlying assumptions about what it means to conceive a healthy child. Genetic screening tests are now common pregnancy gateposts, allowing prospective parents to decide if they want to continue on their current path to parenthood. Writing in 1999, the anthropologist Rayna Rapp described genetic testing through amniocentesis as "the most routinized of the new reproductive technologies," and what was true then is even more true of the newer noninvasive tests that are flooding the market and bringing genetic screening into the home.[5] In medicine, the word "screening" is used to describe a test for an asymptomatic patient. I was not sick and the fetus I was carrying showed no signs of distress. From all outward appearances we were a healthy mother and future child. But a screening test could determine whether something was likely to go awry. In this sense, a genetic screening was not unlike a film screening—it was a projection onto a blank space. The blank space was the future. The film was the genetic code. Or rather, several possible reels were projected onto the screen at once, any of which might show the future.

Like the pregnancy test, genetic testing is a medical test that people are increasingly opting to conduct themselves. Commercial noninvasive prenatal testing kits (NIPTs) are now aggressively targeting consumers, playing up the rosier side of the tests, that parents could now learn the sex of the fetus before they are big enough for ultrasounds. A 2013 *Today* show segment first introduced a mainstream audience to NIPTs and popularized the procedure as a fun way to discover the sex of your future child with an on-camera gender reveal. The poet and bioethicist George Estreich described the segment as effectively humanizing the technology by focusing on the "good news" about gender rather than the potential "bad news" of a Down syndrome diagnosis.[6] A 2019 study predicted that revenues for the NIPT industry would exceed 2.5 billion dollars by 2025.[7] One of the questions that no one seemed to want to directly address was what to do with the information. It is one thing to discover a child's gender and pick out paint swatches. It is another thing to discover a disability or an incurable illness. The language that Dr. Patel used was vague—more information was better, she said. You can make an informed decision, she repeated. But information is not neutral. It is a loaded gun cocked in the first act of a play.

It is easy to see why genetic screening has become so common in early pregnancy—a pregnancy that is preceded with an ovulation tracker and then inaugurated by an at-home pregnancy test finds the logical next at-home test to be the genetic screen, which reassures parents that the child is genetically "normal" and that the pregnancy should proceed. But a genetic screening test, unlike a pregnancy test, is not a simple yes or no. In fact, you are not testing the fetus at all. Some tests involve blood samples from the parents that are used to sequence the parents' genes and, from these, estimate the probability of an inherited trait. For these, you do not even need to be pregnant to screen likely inheritances of a future pregnancy. Other NIPTs test the blood of the gestating parent in order to detect cell-free DNA. This kind of test is often used to test for non-inherited chromosomal abnormalities like Down syndrome. Both methods are screening tests rather than diagnostic tests, meaning that they determine the probability that a fetus might be a carrier for a genetic disorder. By taking genetic information from the bloodstream, they predict the possibility that the fetus will have inherited or possess a certain trait. If a prenatal screen determines that the fetus is a probable carrier for a genetic trait, parents still need a diagnostic test such as amniocentesis or chorionic villus sampling (CVS) to take a sample of the fetal cell and confirm diagnosis. Because these tests carry a slight risk of miscarriage, they are usually performed after a screening reveals a high likelihood that the fetus carries a genetic disorder. What the screening tests reveal is the probability that your pregnancy may be impacted by the genetic traits that show up in the blood sample. They offer betting odds wrapped up in the illusion of certainty. And they are not possible for everyone. In the U.S., the tests cost around $400 and are not always fully covered by insurance.[8] Even in countries with universal healthcare, NIPTs may require a co-pay, which is deliberately imposed to inhibit their use.[9] The divide between those who can afford a highly regulated pregnancy, complete with genetic screening, and those who cannot continues to grow. And with this divide is the feeling of judgment that mothers, in particular, feel about their decisions not to screen. Mothers of children with Down syndrome, for instance, describe feeling judged for the simple fact of having a child with Down syndrome; strangers immediately ask—out loud or to themselves—why the mother didn't undergo genetic screening or, if they did, why they chose to bring the child to term.[10] Genetic screening, like swearing off wine and soft cheeses, has become one of the many prerequisites for being a scientifically minded "good mother" in the twenty-first century. And, as such, it obscures many of the socioeconomic factors (the expense and time investment, most notably) that make this definition of motherhood inaccessible to so many.

DURING THE PREGNANCY that I miscarried at thirteen weeks, I had refused Dr. Patel's suggestion to undergo genetic testing. During those first three months, when a few people had intuited that I was pregnant at the Cloisters and the Harlem Studio Museum and riding on the subway, I was carrying a fetus that I knew very little about other than the information I had gleaned from a pregnancy test and a few ultrasounds. I felt secure in that knowledge. But the experience of miscarriage changed my relationship to the next pregnancy. When I saw two pink lines on a pregnancy test again, I knew it would be different. I felt a compulsion to have more information this time around.

This was our first full summer in the city, the first time I'd experienced the unexpected languor of the usually frenetic New

Yorkers as they slowed down under patches of blue sky. Tinny
tunes of ice cream trucks played all day, the sound traveling near
and far along their cryptic routes. And as the heat rose, a miasma
of trash smells would waft up from the sidewalks where bags
were dumped every week. The memory of the miscarriage ached
as a dull reminder of past pain, but I was ready to try again.
The human body has a way of patching itself up. Even that most
sensitive instrument, the brain, begins to heal itself with time.
After my failed attempt to find a permanent job, I'd picked up an
adjunct teaching position at a local public university. I was going
to be underpaid to teach one class on world literature as part of
the general education curriculum in the fall. My students would
be mostly business majors knocking a requirement out of the
way. And yet, it would be a pleasure to be in the classroom again.
Writing up my syllabus for the fall, I would touch the spines of
the *Odyssey*, *One Thousand and One Nights*, *The Tale of the Heike*,
*King Lear*. My soul felt parched for the slow wisdom of old texts.

Dr. Patel asked again. Would I do genetic testing this time?

Yes, I would.

Anything they could tell me about this next pregnancy, I
thought, would be helpful information. I was not willing to simply
roll the dice again. What I didn't realize was that genetic testing was
no crystal ball, but rather, a series of possibilities and chances that
would require further testing, more risk, and many difficult
choices. The first pregnancy taught me that the way ahead was
less secure than I had imagined and that I could easily lose my
footing again; and so, as in the story of Pegasus, I set off to battle
my Chimera, grasping for any aid that the gods had to offer.
If genetic testing could show me something about my next
pregnancy, why wouldn't I want to see it? It was easy to imagine that there was a technological solution to the problem of my
last pregnancy. Wasn't this the message that I had received time

and time again, through advertisements and newspaper articles and medical consultations? But genetic screening, it turned out, would give me harder decisions to make, decisions that would challenge my values and force me to confront what the Dadaists saw as the irrefutable force of chance.

The company that handled the genetic material was called Counsyl. On their informational brochure, they described the test as follows: "The Counsyl Family Prep Screen (version 2.0) utilizes sequencing, maximizing coverage across all DNA regions tested, to help you learn about your chance to have a child with a genetic disease." The language was a mix of advertising jargon (maximizing coverage), web-speak (version 2.0), and predictive forecasting. We would learn about the *chance* that our child would have a genetic disorder. On their website, they assured us that the screening would "identify couples at risk to pass down serious, prevalent, clinically actionable genetic conditions." I paused at the phrase "clinically actionable." Above these words, the website showed a photograph of a man and a woman with a young girl, perhaps five years old. The girl sat between the couple, playing a small ukulele that she cradled in her lap. She was smiling away from the camera, at her mother, who beamed down at her from beneath a fringe of trendy bangs. The girl wore a turquoise headband that held in place her cochlear implant. Was this meant to be a family that had undergone genetic screening or one that had not? How had this couple acted, clinically, on the information they had received? They all looked very happy.

They needed only my blood sample, not Evan's, to start. This would let them know if there was anything to be worried about. A week after sending in my blood sample, my results arrived in my email inbox as a PDF. Of the 103 conditions that I was tested for, it appeared that I was a carrier for one. It was a disease I had never heard of before: something called Pompe Disease. Being a carrier meant that I did not myself have the disease and, as an autosomal recessive disorder, it was only a risk if my partner was also a carrier. It seemed very unlikely. They would need a sample from Evan now, which we sent along to Counsyl for processing.

The pregnancy continued. I went to visit my parents in Michigan and help my friend Siobhan who was in town to exhibit her paintings in a local art fair. It was early enough that I didn't tell them that I was pregnant. I didn't want to get anyone's hopes up this time. I helped Siobhan set up a tent at the fair to display her pieces. The heat was blazing and I tried to conceal my increasing panic that I was harming the fetus inside me by working in the direct sun, inhaling the white spray paint that she was applying to pieces of wood. Her work was gold and silver and the glare from the metallic brushstrokes seemed to magnify the sun's rays. I drank copious amounts of water. I found excuses to stand in the shade.

I thought back on that day years later when Siobhan told me about 23andMe. She had ordered a kit in the mail and it came with a swab and a little hygienic container to mail back to the company. The results came back within a week.

And what did she discover?

In a surprise to no one, she was mostly Irish. We both had great-grandparents who came from the south of Ireland—this much we both knew. Then, they broke it down into percentages. She was a whopping 80 percent Irish, followed by a mix of German, English, and Swiss. Each was assigned a percentage.

The real kicker was that she was part Spanish on her mother's side. That really surprised her. No one had ever followed her family tree that far back. Where did it come from?

I put on my professor voice and spoke about the myth of the

"Black Irish," who were thought to be descendants from survivors of the Spanish Armada who had washed up on the shores of Ireland in the sixteenth century.

Siobhan never much cared for my professor voice. She had known me for too long to put up with that.

I saw this new information clicking into her conception of herself and her family tree. There was a new percentage of her family tree that she now understood to be Spanish. What did that mean? Here are some facts about Siobhan: she is an artist and had attended college on an athletic scholarship, but she doesn't think of herself as 80 percent artistic and 20 percent athletic. There is no bloodline or gene attached to these traits, and yet they define her sense of who she is. Genes certainly played a part in her athleticism and creativity, but what part, and was it quantifiable? I thought about my own blood sample sitting in a lab, waiting to reveal something about the identity of the fetus I was carrying. These two tests could not be more dissimilar. Both were genetic tests, but one was marketed as genealogical—a fun way to know your roots—and the other as medical—a way to determine risk. In either case, one came away from reading the results with a numerical sense of self. A body mapped out by percentages and fractions.

To use the language of medical and marketing acronyms, a NIPT (noninvasive prenatal test) and a DTC (direct-to-consumer genetic testing kit) are both tools for discovering genetic information. They contribute to what scholars Dorothy Nelkin and M. Susan Lindee describe as "the DNA mystique," or the way in which genes have become "a cultural icon, a symbol, almost a magical force."[11] Sociologist Alondra Nelson refers to "the special status afforded to DNA as the final arbiter of truth of identity."[12] NIPTs and DTCs also exist in a feedback loop with each other. The information that we send to these companies contributes to the sample pool from which the data derives. Many samples from individuals of Western European background, for instance, contribute to the accuracy of future samples showing Western European heritage. The information is also sent to third parties such as pharmaceutical companies and academic researchers.[13] The genes of those who participate in genetic testing become big data that fuels further research.

Had Siobhan, in sending her nasal swab to 23andMe, contributed to the knowledge that would allow for more and more comprehensive genetic tests? What disorders, disabilities, and traits would we be testing for in another generation? In addition to the 103 conditions that were currently being assessed in a lab far away, would a later pregnancy be screened for traits like blond hair, blue eyes, athleticism, or artistic ability? When Siobhan and I tried discussing 23andMe years later, the conversation was awkward and halting. Our thoughts on genetic testing were pushing in opposite directions.

But on this day, I set a last plexiglass display case onto the stand that Siobhan and I had erected. Once we had finished meticulously arranging the tent, we went home. That night the weather turned on us. The branches on the trees began to undulate as the wind picked up its force. The sky was suddenly streaked by fast-moving clouds. A gale blew through the fair, ripping the tops off the tents and sending displays flying through the street. It was hard to believe it had been so still just hours before. The meteorologists had reported only a 30 percent chance of rain.

*   *   *

A WEEK AFTER sending Evan's blood to Counsyl, we got his results. Another PDF. The words were printed in a bold font on the first page.

**POSITIVE: HIGH REPRODUCTIVE RISK.**

Evan was also a carrier for Pompe Disease. The PDF was open on his computer. We both looked at it blankly for a few moments. It took time to rearrange the furniture of our minds and make sense of this new fact. It didn't belong among what we knew about ourselves or our family trees. For one, it had nothing to do with my Jewishness—it was unrelated to the kind of risk that Dr. Patel had invoked. It was a rare genetic disorder that no one in my family had ever mentioned. And Evan's? No known history. It didn't illuminate any of the puzzles of our earlier pregnancies. It had nothing to do with the miscarriage. It was a new, immensely complicating revelation and we did not immediately understand the implications. Evan and I were both carriers. What did that mean, exactly? Nearing the second trimester mark, the one we had almost cleared once before, we discovered this disease had been there all along, lying in wait in our bloodlines. Having the gene was, in itself, harmless. It was only dangerous when it found a partner in another set of genes, when the right two people got together.

High reproductive risk was a numerical prediction. It meant that it was now 25 percent possible that any child we carried would have Pompe Disease. It was crushing news, but a one out of four chance meant that the odds were still on our side.

The PDF that Counsyl sent us included a description of Pompe Disease. I opened that file innumerable times, trying to read between the lines in order to interpret what kind of life expectancy was possible and, even more dangerously, how much pain and suffering would be in that short life if our child was diagnosed with the disease. I tried to parse the medical terminology to understand what this disease would really mean for us. I learned that Pompe Disease is a rare genetic disorder that results in the breaking down of the body's muscles, including those that operate critical organs like the lungs and heart. It is the result of a deficiency in an enzyme called acid alpha-glucosidase that is responsible for processing complex sugars in the body. Without this enzyme, the sugars build up in the muscles, which causes them to break down. The document ended with a note of sympathy, and finality: "Unfortunately, this disease will greatly curtail the life span of those affected. Most people with Pompe Disease will die from lung failure."

Only 1 in 40,000 people is a carrier for Pompe Disease. The bad luck that we were both carriers was astounding.

Evan and I had always felt that we had met each other against all odds. How I had ever started talking to and, stranger still, fallen in love with a divorced Baptist from a military town in central Texas defied all logic. How he had found himself entangled with a secular Jew from a college town in the Midwest was equally astounding. What were the odds of that? One in 40,000?

With a 25 percent chance that the fetus had Pompe Disease, I was still determined to feel hopeful. Evan was less optimistic but tried to hide it. I'd come to know a pessimistic streak in him that was easy to miss beneath his warm and affable exterior. This facet of his personality had been gathering into a steady conviction over the course of the last few years. Most people wouldn't have noticed it, but I heard the slight delay when he would respond to my more cheerful assessments of our situation. It was a quiet restraint, just the shortest hesitation that let me know that he was readying himself for bad news. To test the fetus, we would have to perform a CVS exam, which meant collecting chorionic villi cells from the placenta and testing them for the genetic disorder. Evan was scheduled to teach during the earliest time

the doctor was available. With the first trimester already pass-
ing, performing the test quickly was the most important thing.
I called my sister Jenny who lived an hour away in Westchester
County. Could she come? She would be there.

Before the procedure, I was scheduled to meet with a genetic counselor to discuss the implications of any results that
they would find. The counselor's office was high up in NewYork-
Presbyterian Hospital, overlooking the Hudson River. The waiting room was filled with pregnant women awaiting their own
genetic consultations. Many of these women were Orthodox
Jews in heavy wigs wearing long, loose black dresses that barely
gave away the impression of their growing bellies.

Jewish communities had been some of the earliest adopters
of genetic testing. Tay-Sachs disease was discovered in the late
nineteenth century and was soon found to have a higher inci-
dence among Jews, but it was not until the availability of genetic
testing and the legalization of abortion, beginning in the 1970s,
that there was any means to manage this incurable disease.[14] Like
Pompe Disease, Tay-Sachs is an autosomal recessive disorder,
meaning that it requires both parents to be carriers for there to
be a 25 percent chance that the child would inherit it. Sociologist
Shelley Reuter describes how genetic screening came to be perceived as a marker of Jewish immigrants' belonging in the U.S.—
their willingness to screen for genetic disorders amounted to a
self-policing of genetic risk at a time when immigrant groups
were associated with contagion and when immigrants felt the
need to combat eugenicist claims about the weakening of the
American genetic stock and the inferiority of "Jewish blood."[15]
Taking responsibility for one's own genes became a way of proving model citizenship. The legacy of that history was apparent in
the waiting room, with Orthodox women patiently waiting their
turn to see the genetic counselors and learn about their risk.

Screening cannot itself prevent a disease. Once a reproductive risk has been determined, choices need to be made. The nature of those choices will depend on when you undergo screening. If screening occurs during a pregnancy, you will need to decide whether you want to have an abortion. Take a step earlier and screen yourself and your partner before pregnancy, and you'll have to make a wrenching choice about whether you should have children together at all. Screen earlier than that, when you're dating, and, assuming you both want children, you might call things off before you decide to take that next step. None of these seem like happy solutions. Screening gives us more information about what the future might entail, but it does not tell us how to act. More knowledge does not translate to less risk.

Sitting in the waiting room, I wondered what the genetic consultation meant for these women, many with lives and values quite different from my own. Would the counselor describe the same options, with the same tone? Was each woman in the waiting room going to hear the same words, the same advice, and the same notes of sympathy? The implications of a genetic test would have to be powerfully influenced by religion and culture. While many branches of Christianity have absolute edicts against abortion, other religions like Judaism and Islam do not rely on a unifying organizational authority, and include a range of views.[16] In Judaism, rabbis will often prioritize the life of the mother over the unborn child and, in the case of known disease and illness, emphasize the mitigation of harm rather than life at all costs. Where did the role of the genetic counselor weigh into a decision that, for many, would raise questions of faith and morality approached from a dizzying range of backgrounds and traditions?

Genetic counseling is still a relatively recent part of the landscape of pregnancy. It emerged as a professional field only in the

1970s with the increased use of amniocentesis to detect genetic chromosomal abnormalities and other disorders that were detectable during pregnancy. It is a newcomer in the history of medicine, just now entering middle age. In her history of genetic counseling, historian Alexandra Minna Stern describes the field's challenges excavating itself from its origins in the eugenics movement and improving diversity among its mostly white and female providers; despite these ongoing obstacles, genetic counselors are in a unique position to "translate test results and technical language" for their patients and to aid them "with equal doses of scientific acumen and human empathy to make decisions about their options."[17] The genetic counselor was introduced to help parents assess risk and make decisions. They are the risk managers of the medical field, considering the relative dangers and costs of a particular disorder and helping parents decide what to do next. The main question that most parents ask when faced with a rare, incurable, and high-risk genetic disorder is whether to terminate the pregnancy. It is a moral, ethical, and biological question all wrapped up in one. It is also a decision that falls heavily on mothers who have become, in the words of Rayna Rapp, "moral pioneers" charting a new bioethical landscape with few precedents and not enough emotional support.[18] And what of the role of the genetic counselor? What type of person has the skills to assess this kind of risk? It would ideally be someone with a strong medical background, an ethical sensitivity, and a deeply humane ability to talk to people faced with the challenge of what it means to determine the quality of a life. A lot to ask of one professional.

The counselor that we met that day had a slight build and quick, intelligent eyes. She asked me to map out a family tree beginning with a circle representing myself, round and generically feminine, connected by a thin line to my husband, who was an architecturally solid square. From there, the lines radiated up-ward and outward, connecting squares and circles back through time. As each line folded in another family member by marriage or birth, the branches became a tree. This was the stuff of ele-mentary school projects and yet, here, presided over by a genetic counselor, each branch bore new weight. This was no longer the stuff of family lore—who married who way back when—but it was a hazy blueprint for a life that was yet to be. Somewhere in these tangled links lay a fatal gene that was lying in wait. It had not yet made itself known; it was biding its time.

And yet the consultation was not entirely unpleasant. The counselor had an intellectual enthusiasm for the subject that al-lowed me to forget, if briefly, that it was my genetic material laid out before her. I was transported back to biology class, studying the Mendelian peas with their smooth and wrinkly seeds.

The genetic consultation may have been a cerebral exercise, but the CVS examination that followed was brutally physical. Lying on a hospital bed in a spare room for outpatient proce-dures, I held my sister's hand. They tried to extract the cells with a catheter that was inserted through my cervix. It felt no worse than the various ultrasounds that I had been getting on and off over the last two years. But my placenta was twisted away from the doctor as if hiding from the suction. They would have to use a needle and insert it through my abdomen. I gripped my sister's hand and made sure to keep looking at her face. Not at the needle; I would certainly not be looking at the needle. I saw my sister's steady, encouraging smile with a veil of fear behind it. I watched her watch as the needle was inserted into my stom-ach. I felt my uterine muscles contract painfully like a menstrual cramp as the needle went further in, probing toward the fetus inside. There was a risk that the procedure would itself harm the fetus and I was acutely aware of the possibility of losing the pregnancy because we'd opted for this procedure. This was week thirteen, the same time that the last pregnancy suddenly ended. Like eating a forbidden soft cheese, this was one of the preventable dangers that was easier to focus on—here I could assign blame to myself as the cause of the misfortune. There was a moment of calm before the needle came out again and I felt more of the familiar cramping.

My phone rang after I finished teaching my last class of the day and I saw that it was Dr. Patel. I was walking along Amsterdam Avenue as delivery trucks rumbled past and ambulances blared, their sirens coming and going from Mount Sinai. This was not the street I wanted to be on to hear this call. But home was still fifteen minutes away and I could not wait. I tapped the button and pressed the phone tightly against my cheek.

Is this an okay time? I'm afraid it's not good news.

The ambulance noises suddenly muted and a ringing now echoed between my ears. I listened as Dr. Patel explained. The fetus had tested positive for Pompe Disease. There was no ambiguity in the results. I could take a little time to process the news, but we would need to make a decision as soon as possible about how to proceed.

The conversation was quick. I wasn't able to formulate follow-up questions, so I focused all of my energy on controlling the tremor in my voice and responding politely to the doctor. I kept thinking how awful it must have been for Dr. Patel to make this call. She told me how sorry she was. We were both very sorry for each other by the time the phone call had ended and I was halfway home.

Once we hung up, I considered how I would tell Evan. He

would be in the apartment, probably starting to prepare dinner. The peppers he'd be cutting would be stacked along the cutting board like dancers all raising their arms in perfect unison. He would know right away that something was wrong. Would I ask him to sit down? No, too theatrical. I slowed down my pace on the sidewalk, as if I could buy myself a few more minutes in which Evan did not know. Two minutes, maybe three, before we had to discuss what to do.

Neither of us remembers the conversation. I couldn't tell you if he was, in fact, cooking dinner when I arrived. And I don't know who was the first to ask the question: What's next?

This would be the only question in our lives for the next two weeks. Every waking minute—and there were many minutes through sleepless nights—we discussed what we would do. In one painful phone call after another, we told family members and close friends what little we knew. No one had heard of Pompe Disease or recognized the symptoms in any member of our vast family trees. After further conversations with Dr. Patel and the genetic counselor, as well as late-night online searches, we began to have a fuller picture of what Pompe Disease would mean for a child and a family. There was no known cure, but enzyme therapy had been successful in giving people some extra time. It would be a life dominated by hospital visits and painful treatments. As the muscles gave way, the child would lose their bodily autonomy piece by piece, shifting to a wheelchair and, eventually, feeding tubes and ventilators. Giving birth to this child would be welcoming it into a world that it would quickly and painfully begin to leave as soon as it arrived.

Imagine a first birthday party. If we were lucky, we might imagine a decade of birthday parties. And on each one, I would conceal from that child what I knew with absolute certainty. That this might be the last. I could imagine the balloons, the cake, the presents. They felt like a mirage, an elaborate ruse to hide the truth from a child who would be too young to understand. Were any of us old enough to understand such a truth?

Friends and family who were part of the discussions felt that I should spare a child this life. More important, I believe that they wanted me to spare myself. And yet I continued to weigh my options. What if there was a cure on the horizon? I looked into research and the only treatment I could find was the difficult process of enzyme replacement therapy, which would only delay the inevitable. Furthermore, the rarity of the disease meant that there were not huge research funds being funneled into finding treatments or cures. It was treated by professionals in rare disorders that handled a vast coalition of tricky diseases like this. I tortured myself with hypotheticals. Would I make the same decision if I knew that my child would have MS or ALS, two diseases with later-onset muscular degeneration but for which I knew many people who lived complete, fulfilling lives? Would I make the decision if I was facing a different chronic illness? Most torturously, I asked whether my mother would have made the same choice if she had known of my brother Alex's disability in advance. I did not think of myself as the kind of person who aborted a fetus based on genetic information. Or rather, I was not the kind of person who had ever been faced with this situation before. It went against everything I believed about myself and yet, for me, there was a difference between the certain knowledge of terminal illness in early life and the uncertainties of life with disability. I could imagine facing one reality, but not the other.

Hours before my call with Dr. Patel, I was sitting around a table with my students, a faded copy of *Antigone* between my hands. To a class of distracted twenty-year-olds, faces illuminated blue by their laptops, I read these words out loud:

Blest, they are the truly blest who all their lives
Have never tasted devastation. For others, once
The gods have rocked a house to its foundations
The ruin will never cease, cresting on and on
From one generation on throughout the race—
Like a great mounting tide . . . [19]

The words came back to me now and tolled in my head like a great bell. For Sophocles, it is the gods who visit ruin upon a house and it is a ruin that spreads, gathering force through each generation and touching every hopeful new birth with a tragic end. It is not chance that leads to ruin, but a wrong turn, an evil deed, or a poor choice that leaves its mark in the bloodlines. What Sophocles attributed to actions and deeds we attribute to genes. But Sophocles understood something of the nature of genetics—that a trait, be it a cleft chin or a terminal illness, could show up again and again in a family throughout time.

But, surely, genetic testing was not the Oracle of Delphi. Dr. Patel, calling from her Manhattan office, was not sending me vague hints about the future or cryptic riddles to solve. Without knowing it, Evan and I had gone about our lives silently carrying a sleeping gene in our DNA. We had found each other, traveling hundreds of miles from our birthplaces for each identical gene to meet its dangerous partner. Only now did we realize that in coming together, we had created something deadly.

"ABORTIONS WILL NOT let you forget," Gwendolyn Brooks sang out from a 1940s South Side apartment in Chicago.

You remember the children you got that you did not get,
The damp small pulps with a little or with no hair,

The singers and workers that never handled the air.
You will never neglect or beat
Them, or silence or buy with a sweet.
You will never wind up the sucking-thumb
Or scuttle off ghosts that come.
You will never leave them, controlling your luscious sigh,
Return for a snack of them, with gobbling mother-eye.[20]

I came across this poem, "The Mother," by chance when I
saw that it was the centennial of Brooks's birth. Sitting at my
laptop, I could think of only one other Brooks poem—"We Real
Cool"—so I entered "Gwendolyn Brooks poems" into the search
bar and "The Mother" popped up. From the first line, the poem
resonated deeply—no, I thought, they did not let you forget. It
is not that you do not forget the procedure: the deed itself is
inconsequential in the poem—the poem features no hospital,
no waiting room, no doctors, no bleeding—but what you don't
forget is the conditional future that is not to be. Brooks is not
sentimental about this unrealized future: she imagines potential
love or abuse, hunger or satiation, silence or song. She presents
the possible child in terms of probability and chance—a simple flip of the coin and you might get one or the other: a child
with little or no hair, one who grows up to become a singer or a
worker, and a relationship defined by love or neglect. You might
speculate about the future, but it is, in the end, unforgettable
because it is a future that has been foreclosed. In the poem, the
speaker wrestles with the terrifying power of motherhood, which
she aptly describes as something from a Gothic fairy tale: the
"gobbling mother-eye." Later, she tries to ask questions about the
morality of abortion but decides that these questions are inadequate. What matters, in the end, is love. The love of a mother that
underlies birth and death.

Believe me, I loved you all.
Believe me, I knew you, though faintly, and I loved, I loved you
All.

When I try to put words to my decision, I realize that the very language, even in my own head, is overdetermined by political and religious cant. It was the most difficult decision of my life. This was true. It was heart-wrenching. Indeed, it was. But how to put words to something without reducing the experience to phrases that might come from a political pamphlet? Gwendolyn Brooks had been able to express these complexities. But wasn't that setting the bar awfully high?

Once the decision was made to terminate the pregnancy, it felt correct. I had looked at the issue from all sides, spoken with family members and friends, and everyone agreed that this was the thing to do. But it never lessened the sense of sadness that this pregnancy, which was so badly wanted, would end and that the future that we had imagined was not to be.

On the last visit before the surgery was scheduled, the doctor's office required me to consult with the surgeon on my own, without Evan or anyone else present. Theoretically, I was fine with this. It was clearly a protection against abusive partners pressuring a woman into some kind of decision. Evan went with me as far as the waiting room and then I was shown into a small, clinical room and asked to disrobe and put on the paper-thin hospital gown. There I sat for five minutes, and then another five. By the tenth minute the thoughts in my head started drumming a hypnotic beat of accusation. My heartbeat was accelerating, and I started gasping for breath. I padded out into the hallway in my bare feet and didn't see anyone—no nurses, no doctors. I was abandoned to my thoughts. Back in the room, I tried to breathe slowly. As I focused on slowing down my breathing, I started gasping harder and harder as if my body was out to spite my best efforts at self-control. Total lung failure, I thought. I poked my head out of the clinical room again and saw no one. This time I raced down the empty corridor back to the waiting room. When Evan saw me, eyes red and streaming, clutching my gown, I must have looked like a hysterical woman in an eighteenth-century Bedlam print. Together we marched to the front desk and demanded to be able to wait together for the doctor. Five minutes later, as we sat side by side on the hospital bed, the doctor finally came.

I needed Evan with me for this. It was my choice, yes, but why did it have to be faced alone? To be separated now felt like an act of cruelty that finally had a human face. This would not be the last such terrible moment. Others would come and, every time, once I proved myself strong and capable in standing up against big "F" Fate, I would then fall apart with the actions of small people doing their jobs.

Evan sat with me until my breathing became steadier. The walls were no longer closing in. I could answer the doctor's questions.

Yes, we were sure.

The statement felt like both an overstatement and an understatement at once. Yes, we had thought this through (and through and through). No, we would never be sure.

They could schedule the procedure right away.


WE MADE PLANS to get out of the city and spend our four-year wedding anniversary weekend in a small town in the Catskill Mountains near the Pennsylvania border. As we drove outside of the city, the sky became bluer and the air felt crisper. It was already late into the fall, but the trees had retained their autumnal colors, though they'd begun fading from bright reds and yellows to duller oranges before they would turn to brittle brown paper and fall away. It was 2016 and a presidential election was coming up. The polls were declaring that the Democratic candidate had a significant lead. Everyone we knew had become armchair pollsters that autumn, parsing the odds and creating elaborate projections of the electoral college to show which states would secure a victory for either party.

It was a good time to get away. On the drive, the highway was studded with signs. On the outskirts of the city we saw an equal sprinkling of "I'm with Her" and "Make America Great Again," but as we drove farther upstate, the ratio of the signs began to change. Suddenly we realized we were thundering into the countryside with a steady beat of "MAGA" flashing against the side windows. It was like shaking a Magic 8 Ball and seeing the future spelled clearly against the glass.

A few days after my procedure, the two candidates had appeared on national television in a final debate. Playing to his pro-life base, the right-wing candidate described how a doctor performing a late-term abortion would "rip the baby from the womb." Although mine was not a late-term abortion, the callousness of the description and its distance from my experience made my stomach churn in indignation. The doctors handling the procedure spoke to me sympathetically and explained what they would do in detail before putting me under sedation. It was a teaching hospital and I was surrounded by gynecologists and anesthesiologists in training who held my hand and asked me questions as I nodded off. The day of the procedure was the closest I had come to clarity about this decision. There were no more nerves or second thoughts, only the calm following through of a complicated intention.

The sun was falling as we drove, and the political signs

became more sinister in the gathering darkness. I thought about polls, probability, and chance. Everywhere, we were placing our sense of the future on predictive models. Meanwhile, the whole countryside seemed to be gathering its forces. It was twilight before we reached the small inn tucked against a bend in the river. Evan and I held hands for a moment before leaving the rental car and moving forward toward whatever was coming next.

# 3

# Designing Futures

We watch the tape again. Alex has pushed this banged-up VHS into the tape player more times than I can count. Every Sunday night when my brother comes over for dinner, he sneaks down to the basement to watch old home movies. This is one of his favorites. The recording shows a sunny day when our family went to visit Alex at the Benedictine School, a residential school for developmentally disabled boys and girls. I am three years old in the video and Alex has been at the school since shortly after I was born. The school lies on a sprawling campus outside of Annapolis, Maryland, and is run by nuns in the Benedictine order. In the video, I clasp my small hand to my brother's skinny legs and circle around and around him like a lone child wrapping herself around a maypole or a small planet orbiting its sun. The little girl in the video is unaware that this is the last time she would see him before our family moved from Maryland to Michigan and visits like this would become rare. Ambling in the background is my mother, eight months pregnant with my younger brother Sam, and wearing a tentlike black dress that makes her look like an incongruous nun among the habit-wearing women who run the school. Alex would come to our new home in Michigan each summer, but during the school year I would see him only on holidays. I couldn't have known at the time that my birth was an exchange for this loss. On the grainy video, I twirl around and around in a blue dress that billows out against the velocity of my movement, as my brother stands, patiently, looking out into the distance.

As the tape comes to an end, crackling with white static, he presses rewind and starts again.

When Dr. Patel asked me to name Alex's developmental disability, I could not give her an answer.

Did I know whether it was genetic?

I did not.

She was surprised by my answer and I could understand why. As an intellectually curious woman in my late thirties, I had never inquired into the nature of my brother's disability.

I couldn't explain to her the climate of our household growing up—not one of secrecy but, rather, of a reluctance to define or label. There was a tacit understanding in my family that certain things should be understood in their particularity and that labels could be harmful. I'm not entirely sure where that came from. We didn't talk about it, but we had two family taboos growing up—one was that we never used the word "half-sibling" to describe our relationship to each other, and the second was that we never questioned what made Alex who he was. They were both, in effect, taboos about determinism—about letting other people's ideas about blood or genes supplant our knowledge of each other as individuals or the choices we made about our relations to each other as a family.

While I was still in college, I visited my sister Jenny in her basement apartment in Chicago, which she shared with two other young women and someone's pet flying squirrel. It felt very grown-up at the time. She got me a fake ID that said I was seven years older than my actual nineteen years. I would have to answer to the name Heather. We came back to the apartment that night, tipsy and exhausted, but not too tired to stay up talking.

She looked at me sheepishly. Did I ever ask Mom about Alex? What happened?

No, never.

Jenny paused for a moment. She had heard that his umbilical cord had gotten wrapped around his neck. He had lost too much oxygen when he was still in the womb.

That had never occurred to me, but it seemed plausible.

There was a hush in the room and then a creak from across the hall. A door had been opened.


LOST TAPES COULD always be found in Alex's room. In the summers when he was home with us and after he moved back to Michigan permanently at age eighteen, he was constantly listening to music on his tape player, but he especially coveted Jenny's music. As the next oldest sibling, she had tapes with an aura of cool that no one else's could surpass. She resorted to increasingly elaborate methods for hiding her tapes, but Alex would find them. Once she put them in the bottom of her laundry basket—under the dirty laundry. He dug them out, leaving a pile of crumbled jeans, T-shirts, and underwear on her floor, and carried the tapes off to his room in triumph. He especially loved to steal her mixtapes with their handwritten scrolls on the liner and their odd assemblage of Billy Joel, Aerosmith, and Janet Jackson. Jenny would record some tracks directly off the radio, which led to abrupt starts and ends and the occasional voice of an advertisement or disc jockey bleeding into the mix. These do-it-yourself

tapes surpassed the polish and finesse of the professionally produced ones, and Alex had a way of seeking them out. He would
steal the mixtapes and, in an effort to pass them off as his own,
would write his name all over the liner. He wrote in all capitals—
A-L-E-X—over and over again, blotting out the band names and
track titles written in Jenny's neat hand. The tapes were recoded.
They were Alex's now.

I thought of these coveted mixtapes when I was introduced
to genetics in Mr. Friedenthal's high school biology class. It
was my group's turn to give a presentation and we had created
a color-coded diorama to explain meiosis, the process through
which eggs and sperm come to carry half of a parent's genetic
material. We showed the class two chromosomes—one from the
mother and one from the father—and modeled how these chromosomes are copied once and then divided twice to create four
daughter nuclei, each with different arrangements of the original
chromosome. Throughout the process, the chromosomes trade
parts, crossing some genes across to the new chromosomes in
different arrangements. During fertilization, the resulting zygote will contain a mixture of one of four possible arrangements
from the parents' original chromosomes. Our model zygote was
a colorful assemblage that contained a rearrangement of the parents' genes. Or you could say it was like a mixtape—a bit of Lauryn Hill's *The Miseducation of Lauryn Hill* combined with Joni
Mitchell's *Blue* to express the individuality of the fifteen-year-old
mastermind whose name graced the spine of the new tape.

We rely on models and metaphors to explain and understand
DNA—a complex weave that defies immediate comprehension.
One of the first scientists to explore the structure of DNA, Arthur
Kornberg, compared it to a tape recording. In his Nobel Lecture
in 1959, he told his audience that "DNA, like a tape recording,
carries a message in which there are specific instructions for a

job to be done. Also like a tape recording, exact copies can be made from it so that this information can be used again and elsewhere in time and space."[1] Kornberg, like many scientists speaking to public audiences, used the most up-to-date technology of his time to explain complex biological processes. The analogy worked to illustrate how information is encoded in our genes and, also, how it functions as a mechanism for reproduction—copying the same code over and over again in new arrangements. It also helped explain a tension between understanding genes in terms of their expression of the code (playing the tape) and their role in replicating the code (copying the tape). As technology advanced, scientists would look for more contemporary analogies to describe this process, but I keep coming back to the tape recording in part because my understanding of genetics has been shaped so completely by Alex that I cannot think about DNA without thinking about those tapes covered with his name.

In my childhood nightmares, I was forever losing Alex. There would be a terrible flood. The waters would rise up from the Huron River that ran a half mile below our house in Michigan. We would watch them creep toward us and prepare to evacuate. The waters of the whole world would rise. We lived uphill and upriver and had lasted longer than most. But now all we had was a canoe in the garage. There were six of us and only five would fit in the canoe. I would wake up before the waters reached our door, but always with the same horrible awareness that Alex would be the one who did not get a seat in the boat. It was social Darwinism filtered through a child's imagination. Nature, dark and inexorable, was pressing in on us and our only resource—the small canoe—was not built for us all. Someone would have to decide who would survive the flood and who wouldn't.

Waking up from the dream the next day, feeling mournful and guilty about the bleak vision that my unconscious mind had produced, I would find ways to be particularly kind to Alex, making him a mixtape (never as good as Jenny's) or sitting with him to look through old photo albums. As if my kindness could dam the floods of my imagination.

These terrible scenarios of scarcity and choice, which I didn't allow myself during the day, came to me under the cover of night when my mental resistance went down. They raised a spectral vision of the world that scientists and social thinkers had been imagining since the nineteenth century and that climate change made all the more menacing.

AFTER MY PREGNANCY years, my mother sheepishly passed a book along to me. She admitted that it was pretty dated. But someone had given it to her when Alex was young. Another mother of a child like Alex. There was still a note from this woman, whom I'd never met. "This book hit home on many levels," the note said. My mother wasn't sure it hit home for her, but she had kept the book—and the note—and thought about it on and off through the years.

*The Child Who Never Grew* by Pearl S. Buck.

The cover was worn and green. It may have passed through other hands before her friend's. A chain of mothers that branched backward to some lost origin near its publication date in 1950.

In the book, Buck describes the experience of giving birth to a baby girl with blue eyes that seem to hold an otherworldly wisdom in their clear reflection. By the time the girl is a toddler, Buck starts to notice that she isn't keeping up with the other children as they develop. She hasn't spoken yet. She does not hold her mother's gaze. A toy would drop from her hands and she would sit listlessly without picking it up. As readers of

Buck's other work, including her Pulitzer Prize–winning novel, *The Good Earth,* will know, she was a white American expat in China, both at home and foreign in her place of birth. In telling the story of her daughter, she describes her time as a young mother in Nanjing where she encountered conflicting understandings of disability. According to Buck, her Chinese friends understood disability to be part of the plurality of human existence and spoke frankly about it without judgment. It was only in the company of other Americans that she confronted the experience of maternal shame. Walking down the streets of Shanghai, two American women witnessed her daughter dancing and said, "The kid is nuts."[2] As an expatriate, Buck didn't know the colloquialism "nuts." She had to ask a friend what it meant. It was a foreign word to her and it made her see her daughter as a foreigner. In the end, Buck turned away from the advice of her Chinese friends to keep her daughter at home and returned to America to find an institution for her daughter.

One of the tragedies of reading *The Child Who Never Grew* from the perspective of today is the fact that Buck felt the need to accommodate herself to the standards of American strangers over the acceptance of her Chinese friends. She decides to place her daughter in a home for the disabled in America and her Chinese friends try to talk her out of it. Buck writes:

> They feel that the helpless, young and old, should be cared for by the family, reasoning, and quite truly, that no stranger, however kind, can be trusted to be as kind as the family. There are no homes for the old in China, no orphanages except those started through western influence, no places for the insane or for the mentally defective. Such persons are cared for entirely at home, as long as they live.[3]

Buck had no such stable family. Her marriage was breaking up and her relatives in the United States were strangers to her. She thought often of what would happen to her daughter if she died and there was no one left to care for her. She tries to explain this difference in cultures: "Ours is an individualistic society, indeed, and the state must do for the individual what family does in older civilizations. It was hard to explain this to my Chinese friends, and hard not to be moved by their appeals to me to keep the child with me."[4] Without family support, Buck turned to institutions for help, but not just any institution would do.

Buck ended up finding a permanent home for her daughter at the Vineland Training School in New Jersey. Vineland was a modern, progressive institution for its time. This meant, first of all, that it saw itself as a humane alternative to the cruel and neglectful state and religious institutions of the previous centuries. Residents lived in quaint cottages with modern amenities. There were donkey-cart rides and social visits. When Buck toured the facilities, she was struck by a sign that read "Happiness Comes First." But Vineland was a modern institution in another sense too; it was committed to scientific research that aimed to eliminate "feeble-mindedness" from society. In the early twentieth century, Vineland had embraced eugenics research under the leadership of its first director of research, Henry Goddard. In a 1911 article titled "The Elimination of Feeble-Mindedness," Goddard coined the term "moron," which he used to describe the third category of the feeble-minded, which he classified as having higher intelligence than the other two classes—idiots and imbeciles—but who were still far below "normal" intelligence and therefore susceptible to vice, immorality, and unproductivity. Goddard argued that the "vast majority of feeble-minded persons are so because a parent or grandparent was feeble-minded" and that, therefore, the elimination of such disorders relied on preventing such people from breeding.[5] Conveniently, he believed that people who did not look or talk like him—those who were immigrants, poor, or Black—were more susceptible to carrying such genes. Goddard went on to play a pivotal role in developing methods of intelligence testing, consulting with the U.S. government on immigration and army recruitment and, in the process, establishing an indispensable database for scientific racism in the United States. The Vineland Social Maturity Scale, based on the work of Goddard's successor Edgar Doll, is still used to assess developmental and intellectual disabilities.

By the 1930s, Goddard was no longer on the staff at Vineland and the institution was dissociating itself from his more extreme eugenicist ideas. Meanwhile, his arguments for the forced sterilization of disabled people were taking off overseas in Germany, where they would reach their apotheosis in the containment and murder of millions of people deemed to carry inferior genes. Adolf Hitler encountered Goddard's studies of the Kallikak family, a dubious account of hereditary feeble-mindedness based on a resident of Vineland, which was published in Germany in 1914.[6] Although Goddard stops short of advocating euthanasia—noting that the murder of the intellectually disabled goes against our instinctive humanity—the forced sterilization policies that he promotes were legally adopted in several states, and American eugenics had a profound influence on subsequent Nazi programs.

Distancing itself from Goddard as Nazism was on the rise in Europe, Vineland continued to present itself as a humane institution committed to the eradication of intellectual disability. Buck was drawn to both aspects of Vineland—she wanted her daughter, Carol, to be treated with dignity and also wanted to prevent the circumstances that she believed had marred Carol's life and her own. Throughout the book, she returns again and again to the idea of proving the usefulness of her daughter's life and, by extension, her usefulness as a mother. Buck did not believe that her daughter's disability was genetic. In her book, she goes to great pains to explain her own good stock and that of the girl's father. Her search for answers led her to Vineland, which she hoped would not only provide a good home for her daughter but, also, help other families avoid what she had experienced as a profoundly sorrowful maternal experience. The book is a deep cry of shame from a mother who believes that her primary responsibility is to the well-being of a society that has repeatedly rejected her daughter's joy and her own maternal delight.

My dad met my siblings, his future kids, at a child's birthday party in LA in the late seventies. My soon-to-be-divorced mother was sick that day and had sent the two children, Alex and Jenny, with her sister while my bachelor father attended the party as the birthday boy's godfather. We have a photo of the three of them from that party. The two kids smile widely, exhilarated by the party atmosphere, the noise of the other children, and the sugar from the cake pumping through their veins. Jenny stands confidently in a white dress, arms folded across the embroidered chest. She looks like a child from an OshKosh B'gosh commercial; her raven-colored hair is shorn closely in an androgynous bowl cut and she wields a big gap-toothed smile. Alex does not look like a child in an advertisement. He has a matching bowl cut, though his hair is lighter brown than his sister's, and he wears thick glasses that wrap around his small crumpled ears and constantly slip down the bridge of his nose. He sits on a bicycle and looks away from the camera, distracted by the party and the noise of other children. Beneath his glasses are two of the palest blue eyes you've ever seen, deeply recessed behind the thick lenses. From a distance, he looks like the other denim-clad children roaming around the party while their parents sit around a pool smoking cigarettes and drinking Miller High Life. In the sepia-hued photo, Alex and my father somehow look alike—the same shade of hair (though in life, my dad's hair was vibrant red and the hair on top was nearly gone by the time the photo was taken) and the same thick glasses. But there is something different about Alex that people notice when they get closer. I don't know what it was that my dad first saw, but this first photo of the three of them has hung on his office wall as long as I can remember. At the time he met my future siblings, he couldn't have known how his life would become entangled with theirs.

My mother's first husband did not attend the party either. He was attending fewer and fewer family events like this. He was in the Air Force, an officer and graduate of the Academy, but he worked on the white-collar side of operations, far from the front lines of Vietnam. And now he was quietly slipping out of their lives. Not long after the birthday party, my mother would find herself a single mom raising two kids. Her husband bought a motorcycle one day. He rode off on it the next.

When I was twelve years old, I read Katharine Hepburn's autobiography. I'm not sure why. I had never seen any Hepburn films and there was no particular reason to read it, but someone had left it lying around and I decided to pick it up. In a vivid scene depicting the aftershock of the death of her lover of thirty years, Spencer Tracy, Hepburn speaks to the dead Tracy, trying to trace the seeds of his unhappiness. One seed, it seemed, was his son Johnny's deafness and the corrosion of his marriage that followed from the disparate paths of a husband and wife, in 1950s Hollywood, with a disabled child. Hepburn writes:

You—that lovely wild spirit full of laughter—yet so sad—were you sad? What was it—what? Was it John being deaf and you feeling responsible? Was it that you felt that you should have remained married? Well, you were still married to Louise. I think that this is what she wanted. She just could not settle for the fact that her marriage had been a failure. I don't believe that she realized that it is almost never another way when a child is born who is handicapped. The wife devotes her real center of energy to the child. And the husband somehow wanders off. Driven by an inability to face the reality that a child of his could be anything but perfect.[7]

In Hepburn's account, Johnny's existence troubled Tracy, as did his wife's reverential devotion to his care. Even decades after reading the book, I remembered this description of the son unsettling his father and Hepburn's easy dismissal of the situation as inevitable. The story is self-interested, providing justification for Tracy's unhappiness at home and his subsequent relationship with Hepburn. I wondered how different the version would be if it were told by Tracy's wife or, better yet, his son. As I read, I found myself projecting the little I knew about my mother's first marriage onto Hepburn's story. Perhaps it was because they shared a basic resemblance—my mother is tall and thin with dark hair. I thought she was more beautiful than Hepburn with less of the chiseled intensity about her but that, like Hepburn, she was arresting and other women found her intimidatingly so. But the part of the book that really stuck with me was the idea that fathers might have a distinctive ambivalence toward disability in their children and that this might be especially true of fathers of sons. Was it the same for my mother's first husband? Did he look at his son and feel guilt and shame that he was not willing to try to understand? Did he want a son who was a mirror that he could hold up and see a younger version of himself? Had he expected such a mirror, he may not have liked what it revealed.

After he left, my grandmother—my mother's mother—was sure that Mom would never remarry. She told me as much, sitting in her kitchen in Iowa where my mother was raised, speaking in the hushed voice of taboo confidences. She was Catholic and divorce was a sin. While she didn't blame my mother for what happened, she expected that being divorced would mark her for life. Being divorced with a disabled child put her in another category entirely. It could never be a normal life.

I like to imagine my parents as they were at the time of the party: my mother rising phoenixlike above difficult circumstances and my father emerging from a period of single-minded focus on his medical career, blinking into a strange light, and finding himself drawn to a reality unlike anything he might have expected. It was LA, it was the '70s, they had friends in common, cheap booze, and flared pants. *Annie Hall* had just come out and my parents fit that model: the nerdy, bespectacled Jew and the tall, sporty gentile. Nothing seemed impossible. But there was one obstacle—she wasn't sure if she wanted more kids. Once they began dating seriously, the question would pop up like a mosquito; it buzzed faintly and then, after it had stopped, you knew it was still hovering nearby. Was she willing to have more kids? Alex was nine years old and Jenny was six. The effort of raising Alex had left a mark. When he was born, he was not able to suck from a breast or a bottle and had to be fed with a stopper like an abandoned baby bird. He did not know his days from his nights and screamed with unstoppable fury when he was upset. At age nine he could communicate with family and a close inner circle, but he couldn't make himself understood to others. It would be a long road ahead, and expanding to a family of three or four kids seemed unwise. My father was acquiescent in most ways, but he was clear on this point—he wanted more kids. It may have been out of biological determinism—wanting to pass along his name and genes—but my dad was also genuinely good with kids and wanted to be there from the baby stage this time around.

They had adopted the LA ritual of watching the Academy Awards live on television every February. On Oscar night of 1980, my father bought a bottle of champagne and proposed. As Sally Field won for her role as Norma Rae, they cut to Jane Fonda sitting in the audience with her son on her lap. The previous year they had watched together as Jane Fonda won the Best Actress award for her performance in *Coming Home*. Wearing a gauzy pink dress grazed by a halo of loose blond curls, she'd delivered the opening of her speech in American Sign Language, recognizing what she described as her growing awareness of the "problems of the handicapped." In the ever-changing terminology of disability, "handicapped" and "special needs" were having their moment, taking over from pejorative words like Goddard's "moron," which has now been displaced today by the acronym IDD for "intellectual or developmental disabilities." Fonda signed the word "handicapped" by first pointing two fingers together and toward the camera for the letter "h" and then cupping her hand in the shape of the letter "c."

My mother said yes. They did not wait long. Within the year, they were married, had left LA for DC, and had their first or third child together, depending on how you do the math.

ONCE A COUPLE has been designated a "high reproductive risk," as Counsyl had labeled Evan and me, there are a few options. The first option is to not have children. To decide that the risks outweigh the rewards. Another option is to try again and hope for better results. This involves carrying the pregnancy to the thirteen-week stage when we could have amniocentesis or a CVS examination and determine whether the fetus tests positive for the disorder again. Then, a decision would need to be made again. Either the same decision or a different one. The other option, which Dr. Patel urged us to consider, is pre-implantation genetic diagnosis (PGD). This would involve undergoing in vitro fertilization (IVF) so that the doctors could screen the embryos before implanting them. Rather than waiting thirteen weeks for a genetic test of the fetus, we'd be testing the embryos for Pompe Disease and implanting only the ones that were free and clear.

Dr. Patel explained that we'd need more genetic information if we were considering PGD. They would need genetic information from all four of our parents so they could know the origin of Pompe Disease in our family and any other genetic disorders that they would need to look out for.

They would also need genetic information about Alex.

She didn't need to explain why.

I went home and read up on PGD. It was first introduced to clinical care in the 1990s to determine the sex of the embryos for known genetic disorders that were sex-linked. For instance, couples with a family history of Duchenne muscular dystrophy, which affects mostly men, could use in vitro fertilization to screen male embryos and implant only female embryos. The procedure immediately raised ethical questions about what constitutes an undesirable gene and whether it would be used for more superficial or biased reasons. Couples with no known sex-linked genetic disorders might simply prefer a girl or, more likely, a boy. If some people were comfortable with screening for Duchenne muscular dystrophy, others were concerned that the process would be used to screen for nonfatal disabilities or personal traits. What would stop families from using this procedure to choose embryos with favorable height or eye color?

But these slippery slope questions are, perhaps, not as important as the very real and immediate question of which parents have the opportunity to make decisions regarding gene selection and disability. PGD is an expensive treatment that is covered by insurance only in cases of a known risk for a gene-linked profound disability. Science may be leading us toward a world where certain gene-linked disabilities are eradicated, but, more likely, it is also leading us down a path where working-class and poor people continue to carry a disproportionate burden of care.

In the United States, PGD is regulated by medical associations rather than the government, but in some countries, regulatory bodies decide what constitutes an appropriate use of the procedure. A British couple received widespread attention when UK regulatory bodies approved them to screen embryos for BRCA, the mutations associated with breast cancer. Scrolling through these articles, I asked myself where my own ethical lines fell. What would I be willing to screen for, and what did I consider unacceptable? I had already made the decision that Pompe Disease would have prevented a child from having the quality of life that I felt was necessary to bring someone into the world. But quality of life was an unstable benchmark. How could I quantify Alex's quality of life? Or the quality that his life gave to mine? While I thought that I was capable of raising a child with an intellectual or developmental disability, many parents would not feel like they could handle it. Defensive as I am of Alex and the value of his life, the principle of choice rests on the right to make decisions that might differ from my own. Who am I to judge? I could not know whether my mother would have made a different decision if she had the same choices that I had now. If she had different options, she may have made different decisions that would most likely have meant that I was never born in the first place. She may very well have stayed married to her first husband. Meeting my father at a party, she might have found him funny and interesting to talk to, but that would have been the end of it. No Oscar night proposal, no move to DC, no Benedictine School, no me.

But my parents were not the kind of people who were interested in dwelling on hypotheticals. And they were not eager to take Alex back in for genetic testing. When his differences first presented themselves in the 1970s, doctors told my mom it was just a fluke of nature—nothing more to diagnose or examine. Over the years, as different tests were developed, doctors had urged them to test Alex and always the tests came back inconclusive. When Jenny was pregnant, her doctor encouraged her and my parents to determine whether there was a genetic basis to Alex's disability, but the tests that were on the market at the time revealed nothing. And yet, Dr. Patel reminded me, there were new tests available now that could test for genetic syndromes that weren't available for testing fifteen years ago. In asking them to test Alex again, I was breaking one of our family's unwritten codes. Dr. Patel insisted that it was necessary for a full picture of the genetic profile they were looking for when they began PGD. Alex was now forty-eight years old. He had gone bald rather prematurely; male-pattern baldness was another genetic trait in our family. As he aged, he began to look more and more like our maternal grandfather. They both even had the same tendency to pace, staring down at the ground, when they were nervous about something. I remember the end of a visit to our grandparents in Iowa and watching the two men, clearly related, crisscrossing the driveway as we said our prolonged goodbyes. We didn't need a blood test to see where Alex got his baldness or his nervous pacing. And yet, a blood test would tell us something that somehow seemed far more determinative: what his genes could reveal about a fundamental difference, something that he did not share with the rest of his family.

My parents took him in for the bloodwork and a few weeks later I received a message in the clinical style that my dad reserved for email: "Alex's test indicates he has a recently recognized genetic condition due to loss of some chromosomal material at the 1p36 location. That's the small arm of the first chromosome. Most likely a spontaneous abnormality and unrelated to Pompe. Let's talk this weekend."

1p36 deletion syndrome. It was utterly unfamiliar and impossible for me to remember. The string of numbers and letters couldn't quite stick in my mind. Dad included a link to Gene-Reviews with more information. What I learned was that the syndrome was most likely not an inherited trait, but rather a random occurrence. It was a genetic accident—a gene missed the bus when Alex came into the world.

I thought about the late-night revelation from Jenny, her mistaken impression that Alex's disability was linked to oxygen deprivation. In that case, one could attribute the disability to medical neglect. A doctor should have intervened earlier. If a doctor wasn't to blame, then the next place people would look was to the mother. Was it possible that she had done something to cause the child harm? Perhaps a disability could be attributed to a few too many drinks before she knew she was pregnant or a drug habit that was hard to kick. Unlike these possible causes that people are quick to attribute to maternal neglect, genetic mistakes are impossible to pin on a human actor.

I kept reading. The next section moved away from outlining causes and began defining characteristics of the disorder. Suddenly, the person who I had always known as a collection of quirks and idiosyncrasies was reduced to a cluster of traits and disorders. Among other things, the report said that individuals with 1p36 deletion syndrome were characterized by typical craniofacial features consisting of straight eyebrows, deeply set eyes, midface retrusion, a wide and depressed nasal bridge, a long philtrum, a pointed chin, and posteriorly rotated, low-set, abnormal ears. The description seemed like it could have been written by a nineteenth-century phrenologist. I was stuck on the description of the ears. Alex had adorably crumpled ears that provided just the smallest ledge for his thick glasses. I loved those ears and had never heard them described in clinical detail before or even perceived them as abnormalities. The report described the severity of his cognitive impairment, the probability he might have scoliosis (he did), the likelihood he could never speak expressively (he could), and then went on to describe specific behavior, at which point I had to stop reading. Here were intimate details of his personality explained as results of a missing gene. The most striking one was a description of affected individuals displaying the tendency to bite their hands. When Alex was very upset, he would bite his own hand. How was it possible that this specific behavior was connected to the deletion of a gene called 1p36? What information, exactly, was the missing gene communicating that led Alex to bite his hands at the height of his temper? Hearing these behaviors and traits defined did not make me feel like I knew Alex any better than I once did, but rather that his particularity, his Alex-ness, was now reduced to a type.

The diagnosis laid out physical abnormalities and aberrant behavior without any reference to the things that are wonderful about Alex: the way that his small hand hooks perfectly around the crook of my arm on a walk, or his affinity for animals, especially independent-minded creatures like cats and rabbits who allow him to pet them for a while before shaking their fur and bounding off, or his ability to recount the various repairs that his vacuum cleaner required over the years. What I once took to be Alex's complex and layered personality was now written up as if he were a defective player piano who was discordantly banging out a flawed, predetermined code. Had I been in a more positive mindset, I might have thought about the ways in which the diagnosis connected Alex's experiences to those of other individuals with that impossible label—1p36—all living their lives according to similarly switched-up genes. But I had never met any of these individuals and they remained abstractions to me. It felt as if the words of the new diagnosis were papering over the image of Alex that stood in my mind; it was harder for me to see him now than it had once been.

I closed the tab on my computer and did not open it again. I had seen enough.

PEARL S. BUCK never names her daughter in *The Child Who Never Grew*. It is as if she wants to keep some private connection even as she, metaphorically at least, gives the girl up for the sake of usefulness.

But she had a name. It was Carol. She loved listening to music on her phonograph player. Buck describes in loving detail her likes (Beethoven's Fifth Symphony) and dislikes (church music, crooning, jazz). Buck writes, "She finds her calm and resource in listening, hour after hour, to her records. The gift that is hidden in her shows itself in the still ecstasy with which she listens to the great symphonies, her lips smiling, her eyes gazing off into what distance I do not know."[8] Buck remarks with approval on Carol's exquisite taste in music, her ability to listen with deliberation and patience to a symphony in its entirety. Her musical aptitude included a technical fluency with the phonograph itself and the records that she knew backward and forward. "Her taste is unerring. By some instinct, too, she knows each one of her own large collection of records. I do not know how, since she cannot read, but she can distinguish each record from the others and will search until she finds the one that suits her mood." [9] Buck describes how Carol taught her to appreciate different ways of understanding and knowing, that the kind of intellectualism that was valued in her family was not the only way of understanding the world. But, in the end, it was not enough. Buck packed up Carol's records and sent them to Vineland. Carol would live there for the rest of her life with regular visits from her mother. As Buck's literary fame grew along with her financial resources, she was able to build a fine cottage at Vineland for Carol and fill it with more records. She came to see her often, sometimes weekly. On each visit, Carol would hold her mother tightly and ask to go home.[10]

At the end of *The Child Who Never Grew,* Buck describes the importance of places like Vineland as modern institutions that respect the humanity of people with intellectual disabilities, that provide care beyond what parents can provide. She also writes approvingly of Vineland as a site for scientific observation—where modern researchers could observe the behaviors and assess the capabilities of intellectually disabled children and adults in order to help eradicate such disabilities in future generations. Buck donated the proceeds of her book to Vineland to continue their work.

Throughout the book, Buck reserves her hopes for those nongenetic disabilities, which she understood as possible for science to cure. Genetically inherited disabilities were of another type that fell outside of her imagination. What she did not realize was that Carol's disability was very much a genetic one. In his book on the history of genetics, Carl Zimmer explains that Carol Buck had phenylketonuria (PKU), a rare recessive genetic disorder that Pearl Buck and her husband both carried in their genes and that had never manifested before in their known relatives. The disorder causes a defect in the gene that creates an enzyme that is necessary to break down an amino acid called phenylalanine. Without this enzyme, phenylalanine builds up in the body whenever a person eats foods with protein. The buildup causes side effects, including intellectual disability. PKU is now part of infant screening tests and can be treated with a severely restricted diet.[11]

While Buck was wrong in believing that Carol's disability was not genetic, she was right to imagine a future where Carol's or her own life might have been different. With a diet limiting phenylalanine, they might have avoided the side effects that resulted in intellectual disability. It would have been a relentless, day-to-day struggle to keep within the strictures of the diet, and it would have changed the course of their lives, in one way or another. In another alternative timeline, a twenty-first-century Pearl Buck might have undergone genetic screening and may not have had Carol in the first place. And yet, it is impossible to engage in these counterfactuals. A year after Carol was born, Pearl Buck had a tumor removed that rendered her infertile. She adopted a second daughter but would not carry another with her genes. Would not having had Carol look different to Pearl then—or now—depending on the timeline that we might imagine? And would it have helped her to know then that Carol had PKU and that, years later, her intellectual disability would be considered preventable?

Carol had her records. Alex has his tapes. I was struck by the similarity, both their common love of music and their fluency with the technologies of their day. One of the significant differences between records and tapes is the ability to manipulate tape; to rerecord it, splice it, and recombine it. In the seventy-odd years since Buck published her book, genetic disabilities have moved very much on the table for scientific cure. The mapping of the human genome has allowed for the possibility of genetic selection and modification on a scale that Buck could not have foreseen. If genetic information were stored on a tape, as Kornberg describes it, then we are entering the era where splicing has become possible.

The first gene-edited babies were born in 2018 using the CRISPR-Cas9 genome editing tool. This tool allows scientists to introduce a virus into the DNA that attacks certain undesirable genes and inserts a new sequence of genes into the genome. CRISPR was already in use for biomedical and agricultural purposes, but this was the first time it had been used on a human embryo. Gene-editing human embryos introduces much higher stakes than gene-editing a somatic cell in an adult organism. Somatic cells refer to cells other than the sperm and egg cells (also known as germline cells); editing somatic cells can change an individual, but those changes are not passed along to the next generation as they are in the case of germline editing.[12] When changes are made to an embryo's genome, these changes are passed along through the generations and can profoundly impact the human species. Even when there is a clear consensus that a child would benefit from a gene's alteration, scientific regulatory bodies remain resolutely against the use of CRISPR on embryos because of the possibility of introducing other complications that would then be inheritable.

Despite this near-consensus, the Chinese scientist He Jiankui brazenly pushed forward with using CRISPR to gene-edit the first human embryos. Journalistic coverage of the announcement represented the first gene-edited babies as either a consumer product (complete with a barcode tattooed on the body) or an eerily artificial "test tube baby." Looking at this early coverage, disability studies scholar Rachel Adams writes, "strikingly absent in the news has been any discussion of where the embryos developed, how the babies came into the world and who will care for them. That is to say, their mother."[13] We have a pseudonym for the babies, called Lulu and Nana, but the figure of the mother is shrouded in obscurity. The babies are described as "Chinese Frankenstein[s]" descending from the rogue ingenuity of their scientist-creator-father.[14] In fact, these babies were carried by a human mother and would be raised by one.

What do we know about this mother? We know that her partner was HIV-positive and that she agreed to participate in this experimental procedure that offered her free fertility treatments and the promise that her children would be HIV-negative. CRISPR would be used to remove a gene called CCR5, which produces a protein that unlocks cells for HIV to enter. It was believed that the removal of this gene would give the children genetic resistance to HIV. The mother undoubtedly wanted to protect her children from illness. It is also quite likely that she first came to He Jiankui because of his expertise in treating HIV-related fertility problems. Did shame play a role in her openness to experimental procedures? Perhaps the doubled and infinitely recursive shame of infertility and sexually transmitted disease? She is never named in reporting on the procedure, and we are told that this anonymity is a way of protecting her from scrutiny. A modesty screen pulled across the scene of birth.

We do not know the difficult decisions that led her to this procedure and that would surely follow. He Jiankui was later sentenced to three years in prison by the Chinese government for forging documents purporting to be from the ethics review board in his effort to recruit participants.[15] The consent agreement signed by the anonymous mother included provision for the twins' medical care until they reached the legal age of eighteen, but it is unclear if those promises have been kept. Rachel Adams situates gene-editing within a larger tradition of new reproductive technologies, such as ultrasounds, amniocentesis, and IVF, and notes that "CRISPR is likely to present pregnant women with more responsibilities and decisions, not remove them from the process."[16] Technological advances in reproductive science do not reduce the role of decision-making and day-to-day care that falls heavily on women. If anything, they've made the expectations for proving oneself a good mother to be a lot more work and a lot more expensive.

One of the prominent concerns regarding germline gene editing to human embryos is that, even if it begins with treatments for chronic illnesses such as HIV, there will be an easy slide down a slippery slope toward gene editing for "designer babies." If gene editing can be used for therapeutic purposes, then why not use it for the purposes of enhancing desirable traits like physical appearance, athleticism, height, or intelligence? Here we are entering the well-trod territory of science fiction, in which individual parental decisions have far-reaching consequences for the human species. In an article about the prospect of gene editing for enhancement, philosopher Robert Sparrow introduces the frightening prospect of genetic obsolescence—that a child born to any given generation will soon become "yesterday's child" as new technologies push the human species into further and further advancements.[17] Parents opting for gene-editing procedures would be creating a generation of children who would soon find themselves in competition with a younger generation that were designed to be smarter, faster, and stronger than them. Entire generations would be made redundant. Sparrow's argument is purely speculative; CRISPR technology does not yet allow for the possibility of human enhancement. There is no such thing, for instance, as an intelligence gene. Complex traits like intelligence are controlled by an exhaustive range of different genes, not to mention the inescapable entwining of environmental factors.

Unlike editing for intelligence, the possibility of gene-editing to alter genes associated with disease or disability is much closer at hand. In the race for perfect children, however we define perfection, gene editing could become a powerful tool in shaping the standards that define a good, happy, or useful human life. Here again, the emphasis is placed on the fate of children and the future of the species as a whole; with such high stakes, it is easy to lose sight of how this vision of the future would change our understanding of parenthood. What kind of procedures would parents be willing to endure, and who would be able to pay for them, in order to give a child the kind of life that they have come to believe is the only acceptable future? In this climate of infinite perfectibility, who bears the responsibility for imperfection?

My mother claimed to abhor the concept of guilt. If I ever asked her if she felt bad about being responsible for something or other, she would look at me aghast. Why should I? She had little patience for hand-wringing or self-doubt. She made a choice and marched forward. It sometimes seemed like a deliberate turning away from a Catholic background—thumbing her nose at the nuns who ran her parochial school in Iowa. She was a resolute believer in nature over nurture. Mothers really didn't do much, according to my mother. Her four children were all the people that they were going to be without much doing on her part. Including Alex.

During one of my pregnancies, my dad gave me a small green notebook. It looked almost exactly like the copy of *The Child Who Never Grew* that my mother passed on to me—it was the same soft faded green and nearly the same size and dimensions.

But this book was different. It was a diary that my dad had kept from the year that I was born. My dad was an army doctor at the time. He may have been the very last person drafted during Vietnam. After two deferments to complete two separate medical residencies, he was serving his time after the war had officially ended. The notebook came from the Office of General Supplies and Services and was stamped "Federal Supply Service." In the early passages, he wrote daily, adding a precise date at the top of each page. He also inserted photographs along the way, documenting my first days with words and images. In one photograph, Alex is holding me in his lap. I am maybe two months old. We are both facing away from the photographer, as if someone off camera is trying to make us both smile. I look confused, but Alex smiles widely, happy to be holding me in his lap, happy to

be in the center of the frame. My father's documentary impulses were another difference between my parents—and among the three of us. It would never have occurred to my mother to write down her experiences or to keep more than the barest baby book. She was baffled by the fact that my dad and I had this compulsion to record our thoughts and capture things on film. Hers was, instead, an impulse forward—she was an enemy of clutter, emotional or physical. My dad and I collected books, journals, and scrapbooks, all agents of dust and disorder. She didn't need them. She had a life to live and things that needed to get done.

Reading my dad's journal opened up another portal into my mother's life, one with all the insecurities and uncertainties of young motherhood, when the path forward was unclear. She was newly remarried, starting a blended family, and raising a son whose future she could not imagine. In one of our few conversations about her early maternal years, she had told me that when she was still in LA before I was born, soon after the doctors had confirmed what she already knew—that Alex was different from other children—she went to a group for mothers of handicapped kids, as they were called at the time. She had looked around at the other mothers and seen a group of distraught women, all bloodshot eyes and unwashed hair, who felt chained to an inexorable fate. It was not a club she wanted to be a part of.

Before she remarried—when she was still a single mother— she had earned extra money during the day making stained glass windows. She would assemble the dull-seeming glass, soldering it together with hot metal. Only when held up to the sun would it reveal itself as bright color distilled into light. A miraculous transformation of raw material into art. She did not keep any of the work she had made. I asked where it went, assuming it graced the high arches of churches. Mostly Denny's restaurants, she said. Their workshop had a big commission to create stained

glass windows for the restaurant chain. Perhaps they were looking for something more classic to distinguish themselves from
the high modernist aesthetics of a Howard Johnson's. I wonder if
any are still intact, adding a bit of glamour to a fading enterprise.

My dad's journal chronicled their first year after marrying
and moving from LA to the suburbs of DC when my mother was
pregnant with me. There were glimpses here and there of their
anxiety over the impact of my birth on the two older siblings and
how they would feel about this new, nontraditional family. My dad
came up with new routines and rituals to involve Jenny and Alex
as they all prepared for the new baby. He built a doll's house with
Jenny—a $30 project that became a $200 splurge on all the finest
trimmings and accessories. With Alex, Dad developed a bedtime
routine—a call-and-response song based around the story of a
lion and a kitty. I remember one iteration of the routine, which
they came up with to prepare Alex for his first time away at a summer camp for children with disabilities. Dad would begin, The
lion and the kitty went to camp, and Alex would respond, Meow.

The family changed shape again. Three months after they
came home from the hospital with me, they took Alex for his
first day at a boarding school an hour and a half away. My dad
recorded it all.


September 7, 1981

Yesterday M. and I drove Alex to the Benedictine School. We had
a late start as the Volvo needed a new thermostat. We packed up
the gear and got to the school in about 1¾ hours . . .

We unpacked Alex in his room. His prized tractor got locked up
safely where the bicycles are kept.

I saw him in the dining room—we went to say goodbye as he
was sitting with his group waiting for dinner. As we left, I turned

around and looked back at him. He called out across the room "Ba wrar"—his way of starting our "lion and kitty" routine. Somewhat muted I answered him back with a quiet "meow."

There's no doubt the school will be terrific for him. But somehow it's kind of quiet here tonight and M. is quietly kind of sad. We'll all miss him and look forward to the first visit in 5 weeks.

November 18, 1981

We all miss Alex at school, but the absence is the hardest on M. He depended so totally on her for so long I think the temporary lack of dependence has left a void. We called last night and he and I did our lion and kitty routine.

The Benedictine School had been recommended by an aunt who was a special education teacher in the DC area. She knew the school well and felt that the nuns who ran it would be able to teach Alex skills that he had not yet learned: verbal speech, basic hygiene like toothbrushing and applying deodorant, and zipping and buttoning clothes. He would never master the complicated requirements of shoelaces or learn which shoe goes on which foot. While there, he also learned some of the tasks that he would come to love—tasks that made him feel useful, like vacuuming a carpet and putting a fresh bag in a trash can. He would discover other favorite things too, like record players and dancing. In moving him into Benedictine, my parents believed, he would gain a more extensive social world that he could learn to navigate. He would become more independent of his family. This was at a moment when the tides were turning against residential institutions. There was increasing awareness about abuse, poor living conditions, reduced life expectancy. Benedictine had, and continues to have, a solid reputation, but the 1980s were the early days of mainstreaming and my parents' decision would have been seen by some as, at best, old-fashioned and, at worst, neglectful.

After the rest of the family left Maryland for Michigan, Alex went back and forth from the Baltimore airport to the Detroit airport for Thanksgiving, Christmas, and summer break. He loved the important feeling of taking a plane by himself with the stewardesses fussing over him and giving him a pair of wings to wear on the outside of his jacket. He memorized the flight number and, years and years later, would recite the numbers like a comforting litany. In the summers when Alex would rejoin the family, my parents would often bring in an older cousin or god-child or au pair to help watch the youngest kids and ferry everyone around to their activities. When the live-in sitter moved in, Alex and I would share a room. Like a tiny mother hen fussing over a chick twice her size, I would go to great lengths to make him feel settled. One night when I was seven, I tried to dim the small table light beside my bed so that I could continue reading without disturbing Alex after his bedtime. I set a photo album on top of the lamp not realizing how hot the bulb was. The lamp burned a small hole in the album's leather exterior. I still have the album and can see the little scorch mark on the back cover. Looking at it now, I wonder whether I felt some of the guilt that my mother had refused. Even as a small person, I felt responsible for my brother's displacement. Was this decorousness an attempt to compensate for having pushed him out of the nest in the first place? I could never shake the feeling that I was something like a cowbird, making its home in another's place.

When I was nine years old, Alex graduated from the Benedictine School and moved back in with our family in Michigan. I played teacher with Alex in the basement, pulling out a child-sized chalkboard and going over the ABCs and 123s. I was tyrannical in showing off my newly acquired knowledge to my older brother. Alex would humor me for ten minutes at most before drifting back to playing his favorite tape cassettes on a much-loved boom box—Huey Lewis and the News, Kool & the Gang, Neil Diamond, John Denver. There were fights over the television, most viciously between Alex and my younger brother Sam who, at seven years old, did not understand why he would need to give ground to his grown-up sibling. The one point of concord was the watching of *Top Gun,* which they could both agree on. As a result, *Top Gun* became the soundtrack of our lives, playing in the background at all times of the day. Throughout my childhood, Maverick was continuously flipping down his shades, spiking a volleyball, grieving Goose.

Four years into Alex's time back in Michigan, my parents decided they needed to make a plan for him to live more independently. He was twenty-four and they wanted him to have his own place in the world and a situation that would sustain him through his adult years. My mother researched independent living for adults with disabilities. In the early 1990s, living situations for adults with intellectual disabilities were often limited to the ingenuity, resourcefulness, and financial resources of family members, as they still are today. In the wake of institutions, terrible as they could be, there was no safety net once people aged out of the school system. My mom proved adept at navigating the byzantine system of resources. So, in 1994, my parents bought a house that they registered as Section 8 housing for Alex to share with a roommate. Community Mental Health provided aid workers during the day to help Alex with tasks like feeding himself and basic hygiene, as well as taking him to his activities. He volunteered at a food bank, was in weekly bowling groups and horseback riding groups for people with disabilities, and worked a few hours a week cleaning an Ace Hardware. The first roommate was a blind man who could be responsible for the house and their general safety over the night. It seemed like the perfect solution—Alex was nearby, he was busy, happy, and safe, and he relished the independence of adulthood. Whenever anyone made him feel like a child, suggesting he watch a cartoon or play with a children's toy, he would emphatically declare: "I am a man now." The house was, for him, a powerful symbol of this identity.

The hitch was the neighbors. Alex moved into the house on Brooklyn Street when I was twelve years old, just shy of my bat mitzvah. The neighbors circulated a petition trying to prevent a "group home" from coming to the neighborhood. They were afraid that having a house designated as Section 8 housing would drive down property values. The house was in a classic college town neighborhood with placards in the yards advocating world peace, nuclear de-escalation, racial harmony, and gay rights. These same residents, I realized, were the ones who could, without compunction, try to ban two disabled people from moving onto their street. They voted for progressive candidates, they had all the right opinions, but they did not want to compromise the property value of their homes if they had to share their street with two disabled people.

Where, I wanted to ask them, would you suggest they go? Where was far enough away for you to support their right to exist?


IN THE COPY of *The Child Who Never Grew* that my mother gave to me that a friend gave to her, Buck breaks periodically from articulating the suffering and anguish that defines her experience of mothering an intellectually disabled child and gestures toward a brighter understanding. She speaks of the ways in which

Carol transformed her understanding of humanity. Buck writes, "While I tried to find out its [*sic*] slight abilities I was compelled both by love and justice to learn tender and careful patience . . . So by this most sorrowful way I was compelled to tread I learned respect and reverence for every human mind. It was my child who taught me to understand so clearly that all people are equal in their humanity and that all have the same rights."[18] In the end, she places her faith, and her daughter's fate, in the hands of the scientists who will one day eliminate the forces that compelled her into a version of motherhood that she had not anticipated. And yet, reading over the book now, I am struck by whether Pearl S. Buck, without Carol, would also lose her sense of reverence for humanity and sense of equality. Would this version of Pearl S. Buck have become a novelist? Would she have won the Nobel Prize in Literature? If she could have edited out the genes that made Carol, what other futures would have been foreclosed?

Across this page of the book, where Buck muses on the value of human difference, someone has scrawled in green crayon. I do not know if the mark was made by a member of my family or one of the other families that owned this book before me. If I squint hard enough it looks like the broad signature that my brother practiced endlessly on the mixtapes hoarded in his bedroom.

A-L-E-X, in green, covering the page.

# 4

# The Night Watch

New York is a city of reunions—friends come and go, sometimes visiting, sometimes stopping for a while, and occasionally staying for years and years. After work, over dinners, drinks, walks, we catch up. Everyone I know is trying to get pregnant or trying not to get pregnant. We are entering the last of our baby years. It is now or never and the sense of urgency tinges our conversations. Some of us want a child and struggle; some of us do not want a child and likewise find ourselves in a constant battle against the visions of maternity that barrage us on our smartphones: gender reveal parties, baby room decorating tips, and mommy influencer videos scroll endlessly on our screens. We come from different backgrounds, but we all have the kinds of jobs that become identities in their own right— knowledge work that mired us in graduate education and precarious employment at the age when our mothers had us; and competitive, white-collar jobs that don't allow for an easy on- and off-ramp. The friends that I find myself talking to in my late thirties face difficult emotional, financial, and professional choices about whether to become a parent and how to go about it. We discuss the vast medical possibilities that are available to us only because we have good jobs with health benefits and maternity leave but, also, the limitations of what science can do and the risk that, in having a much-wanted child, we might compromise those good jobs with health benefits and maternity leave that made the pregnancy possible. I hear the stories at night, when the workday is over and our guards have come down, over the soft glow of city lights. These familiar voices sometimes echo and sometimes shout down the voices that reach me from social media accounts pushing narratives about the ease and inevitability of motherhood or those that lament infertility and child loss, sounding like lonely wails of pain in the dark. Over time, these voices of friends and strangers start to blur into a vast stream of hopes, ambitions, frustrations, and sorrows. I cannot tell the story of my pregnancies without hearing these other voices in my head.

A time traveler listening in on the conversations of previous generations would certainly have heard similar discussions among women of bygone days about whether they wanted to get pregnant and how many (if any) babies they hoped to have, but apart from advice about medicinal herbs, religious rituals, or sexual positions, these women from the past were less likely to discuss *how* they planned to get pregnant. The birth of the first "test tube" baby, Louise Brown, in 1978 shifted the conversation, allowing for the possibility that infertile couples, women waiting to have children later in life, carriers of genetic disorders, single people, and queer couples could become biological parents if (and this is a big if) they could afford access to assisted reproductive technologies. Choices for assisted reproduction now might include IVF, egg freezing, surrogacy, or the genetic screening of embryos, which Evan and I were now considering. In the future, parents may also be considering artificial wombs that allow a fetus to gestate outside of a body. Newspaper opinion columns and

science fiction novels argue endlessly about the societal ramifi-
cations of these changes, and while the future that such technologies lay out before us may be exciting to some and dystopic to
others, the toll of these decisions is also deeply personal.

In the U.S., the decision of whether to pursue assisted reproductive technology has serious financial consequences. It is a well-
known fact that the United States is an outlier among wealthy
nations for its lack of publicly subsidized healthcare. This means
that a single treatment of IVF will cost an average of 50 percent
of a person's annual disposable income in the U.S. Compare this
to 20 percent in the UK, Scandinavian countries, and Australia.[1]
Oftentimes, private insurance providers in the U.S. will not cover
assisted reproductive technologies, and many IVF centers in the
U.S. require payment up front. There are consequences to this
expense: where the costs of IVF and other assisted reproductive
technologies are higher, the treatment is more likely to be used
primarily by white, affluent, older, and more highly educated
people seeking pregnancy.[2] Because of economic disparities in
the U.S., Black and Hispanic women are less likely to have access to IVF treatment even though they experience infertility at
similar or higher rates than white women.[3] These disparities also
mean that individuals pursuing IVF at great personal cost are
more likely to take risks with the treatment, such as maximizing
their chances of implantation by using multiple embryos in a
single cycle. There are long-term financial and medical consequences to this as well; with the use of more embryos in a single
cycle, there is a greater likelihood of multiple births, which can
be medically complex and require further financial investment
and care. Although there are more choices around *how* to get
pregnant than ever before, these choices can be prohibitively expensive and come with hidden risks and further costs. And so, we
would-be parents continue to talk amongst ourselves and talk

online, trying to figure out the possibilities available to us and, with more difficulty, weighing what we ought to do.

Four people navigate the dark, wet-slick pavement of the West Village. We have known each other since graduate school in Austin and have lived itinerant lives since then. After five years apart, we happened to land jobs that took us all to NYC. Even in the gathering darkness, it would have been clear, to a distant observer, who went with whom. The other couple, Lynne and James, are both tall and blond; they manage to come across as both bohemian and patrician at once. They had been living abroad for several years, finishing graduate school and working in nonprofits. They still have a whiff of Europe about them, something about the angle at which they drape their scarves across their shoulders against the evening chill. How would Evan and I appear to an outside observer? We present less of a unified front, but we are the sort of adults who had been blond children and then darkened to muddy brunettes. We both have soft features that people usually perceive as kind, mingled with a slight aloofness. I inherited my mother's tendency toward distraction and my father's tendency to take on the role of observer in the company of others. Evan inherited his father's hearing loss, which people sometimes mistake for standoffishness. Both of us enjoy the company of extroverts, because it allows us each to hold something back—to keep a part of ourselves private. But now, with old friends who know us well, many of those inhibitions and misunderstandings have disappeared.

Making our way through the busy after-work crowds, we catch up on various things, the conversation threading the needle of oncoming traffic. We talk about searching for a new apartment, adopting a rescue dog, looking for a job.

We walk for several more blocks before stopping at the Strand to browse for books before it closes for the night. As Lynne and I look over a towering pile of new releases, I finally blurt out what I had been wanting to tell her all night. I terminated my last pregnancy. Lynne had been one of the few people who knew about that pregnancy; we had celebrated afterwards over sparkling water, expecting the news to be official within the month. It was now three months later, and I was clearly not five months pregnant. She had been polite enough not to mention this obvious fact, but I wanted to tell her what had happened.

She nodded and listened. She asked what we were planning to do next. Dr. Patel was encouraging us to try IVF with PGD. A string of acronyms that I had to add to the growing list. This procedure, or rather, combination of procedures, would allow the doctors to screen any embryos that might have Pompe Disease and choose only those that were not impacted by the disease. This preselected embryo would be implanted in me and I would, hopefully, carry it to term. We could be certain that the child did not have Pompe Disease before the pregnancy even began. I told Lynne that I was hesitant to go this route, that it involved a level of medical intervention beyond what I felt comfortable accepting. I didn't like the idea of tampering with genes. And after all, we were not infertile; why would we need to go through the ordeal of artificial reproduction?

Then Lynne told me that they had been trying to get pregnant these last three years. They were about to begin IVF. I felt the callousness of my last remark hang in the air, but she was kind enough not to make me feel worse about it. They had been meeting with a doctor who had outlined the whole process.

Lynne would need to start giving herself hormone injections every day. These injections would help her body produce a superabundance of eggs. Then, the doctor would harvest the eggs; the description made me picture a man in overalls with a straw basket. James would then "deposit" his semen into a sample jar at the doctor's office. I decided not to picture this. With the specimens collected, the doctor would fertilize the egg with the semen to create an embryo, which would then be implanted back into Lynne's uterus. Each step was precarious—they would cross their fingers and hope that there would be enough eggs in working order, that their doctor would be able to fertilize the eggs in the lab, that the implantation would be successful, and that Lynne's body would accept the embryo and allow it to grow to full term. They were hoping it would not result in multiple births, which are common in IVF procedures and can lead to difficult pregnancies and, sometimes, birth complications.

There were other worries involved—financial worries among them—but she was not daunted or sentimental about giving up on a "natural" pregnancy. They had waited long enough and it was time.

Having shared those confidences, the night went on, and over decaf espressos we turned back to the usual channels of talk—work, mutual friends, politics—but a new link had formed in the chains that bound us together.

ELEANOR AND I had known each other since college. She had moved to the city almost directly from school and started working for the same corporation that she worked for now, which allowed her to afford a nice one-bedroom apartment on the Upper East Side. She was making a steady income and saving for retirement when I was living with two roommates in Austin on a paltry graduate stipend. When she found out that I was moving to the city she told me that it was a good thing that I was not single. This is a terrible place to be single in your late thirties.

We had kept in touch sporadically over the years. Eleanor had become a serious athlete in the time we had been apart, running competitive marathons and triathlons and Ironman races.

We met for dinner soon after Eleanor returned from running a marathon in Tokyo.

I'm planning to freeze my eggs, she said. Her younger sister was married with kids. She loved being an aunt and would drive down to Philadelphia every month to see her nieces and nephews. She thought she might want kids one day, but she wasn't meeting anyone.

Even if she met someone tomorrow, the time it would take to enjoy a normal dating period would drastically reduce her fertility. She was shedding eggs as we sat there, enjoying our glasses of wine.

I want to be able to have kids when I'm ready, she said. Right now that means waiting to find someone that I want to spend my life with. That might change. I may decide to do it alone or not to have kids, but having the eggs gives me some assurance either way. I'm thinking about leaving the city. I've aged out of the dating scene here.

It was getting late and the wine was making me bleary-eyed and tired. I gestured that it was time for me to go.

You're lucky you're not single, she repeated.


EVAN AND I met up for dinner with Yvette after her third miscarriage. This one had been an ectopic pregnancy. The fertilized egg had attached itself to the outside of the uterus and the embryo never stood a chance of developing into a viable pregnancy. It was medically necessary for the doctor to perform an abortion to remove the embryo so that it didn't kill her. When we joined her for dinner at her apartment, she looked smaller than usual, as if the weight of each lost pregnancy were chiseled away from her body. We ate a meal that she had meticulously prepared. Every ingredient was carefully chosen according to advice from her acupuncturist. No meat, no dairy. She passed around a bottle of wine but didn't drink any herself.

The hardest thing lately has been the condolences, she said. She tried not to let them get to her, but they did. Her godmother sent a book called *Two Is Enough: A Couple's Guide to Living Childless by Choice*. It would be one thing if she had said she had stopped trying . . .

Her voice trailed off before picking back up again. She went on to describe the jealousy that bowled her over in unexpected moments. She couldn't log on to social media without seeing baby photos. They're everywhere and they make it look so easy.

I nodded. The worst, for me, was the pictures of sonograms. Whenever I saw a black-and-white, grainy image of a fetus curled up safe and sound in the womb, I wanted to warn the mother-to-be not to tempt fate that way. It wasn't here yet. It most likely would be, but it wasn't ready to be shown off. It felt like a wanton betrayal of privacy to expose its tiny bones to the world.


LANA WAS VISITING for only forty-eight hours and half of that time would be spent at a work-related conference. We had known each other long enough that our conversations held the candor of childhood friendships. Within minutes in each other's company we would disclose our secrets and fears. Adult friendships rarely worked this way and it was refreshing to be in Lana's company, even for a short visit.

The year after we graduated from college, Lana had an abortion. She was in a committed relationship, but they were not ready to be parents. Twenty years ago, I had listened on the other side of the telephone as Lana told me that she had made an appointment at the clinic. And now, many years later, Lana knew with more clarity that she did not want to have children now, and probably not ever.

We met up at a new Italian restaurant that was too trendy to take reservations. It was packed. Perched on stools at the bar, we ate oven-charred pizza while tucking in our elbows to avoid strangers. It was easy to talk about intimate things in a boisterous and loud public space. A hush would kill the conversation.

I told Lana that Dr. Patel had recommended PGD. Lana worked in the medical field and knew a lot about the procedure. She talked me through the details: preparing the body to produce eggs, extracting the eggs, fertilizing them, screening the embryos, and selecting the embryos that did not have Pompe Disease. In this way Evan and I could avoid having to wait until after the pregnancy to determine if the fetus was affected. It was a very painful and expensive way to avoid another traumatic decision later down the road.

And I would need to inject myself with needles.

Lana knew me well. You can handle it, she said.


BETWEEN PREGNANCIES, I had found a new job, an administrative position at the university-one-does-not-turn-down. I had fallen into it after meeting Jeanne earlier that year. Forty years earlier, Jeanne had been a graduate student in the department where I was then working. After finishing her degree, she had wanted to stay in New York City, where she had married and given birth to two children while still a graduate student and adopted another soon after. She had made the leap to administrative work after her PhD and took to it naturally. It had been a great career for her. She was able to balance work and motherhood in ways that she could not have done as a tenure-track faculty.

Someone in Jeanne's administrative unit had quit at an inopportune moment and, over brunch, she suggested that I apply for their job. I'd had no idea when the brunch was proposed that there would be a job on the table. I ordered a sprawling frittata with a heap of home fries. Jeanne ordered a side order of brussels sprouts that she speared with dainty pokes of her fork. If you're thinking of having a family, she added, this is a much better career than a faculty position. You have more stable hours and none of the pressures of tenure.

It was too late to find any teaching positions other than part-time adjunct work for the coming year, so I decided to try it out. See what else I could do. I pronged a greasy potato and said, yes, I would take the job.

Jeanne pushed aside her half-eaten plate of brussels sprouts. Excellent, she said. Now she had to run; she was late to her next meeting.

I started the job. It was both better and worse than I expected. The hours were not as advertised. I answered an endless stream of email from 9 a.m. to 5 p.m. and then attended evening talks, sometimes as many as three a week. The talks would end at 8 p.m. and were followed by increasingly tedious dinners with visiting speakers. These were people doing exciting, intellectually ambitious work; it should have been a fascinating job, but the same salmon dinner and glass of white wine at the same university-adjacent restaurant over and over again made me miss the solitary nature of research and writing. I enjoyed hearing about other people's work but I also felt that I had work of my own that was being buried under the mountains of email. I was managing two other staff members who, like me, were new to their jobs and looked to me for answers that I did not have. I had no idea how to navigate through the university's byzantine reimbursement system; honoraria went unpaid for months, and I could only send futile emails asking people to maybe try filling out the online form one more time.

The silver lining was that the pay was good and, unlike teaching as an adjunct, this job would allow me to take maternity leave. But I'd need to get pregnant and stay pregnant first. The question was, how would we do it?


IN VITRO IS Latin for "within the glass." It distinguishes a pregnancy that is conceived *in vivo*—"within the body"—from one in which the sperm fertilizes the egg within a sterilized glass in a laboratory. It is different from artificial insemination where sperm is inserted into a living organism. During *in vitro* fertilization, doctors fertilize the egg with sperm outside of the body and with any combination of parent or donor eggs and sperm. It is a procedure that allows a variety of childless people to conceive— whether they are infertile couples, queer couples, or single people wanting a child. The first generation of IVF pregnancies were dubbed "test tube babies" in the press, a moniker that not only emphasized the artificiality of the process, but diminished the humanity of the children themselves. Artificial reproduction was set against natural conception even as all aspects of pregnancy and childbirth were involving more medical and technological interventions. In the 1970s, when the first test tube babies were conceived, artificial reproduction was still the stuff of science fiction. Journalists repeatedly evoked Aldous Huxley's *Brave New World,* suggesting that with this procedure we were coming closer to the futuristic age that Huxley imagined, in which sex and family were eliminated in favor of vast medical nurseries for the creation and nurturing of future generations.

In reality, the first IVF babies were born to married couples who wanted to participate in the traditional rites of pregnancy and family: Louise Brown in the UK (1978), Kanupriya Agarwal in India (1978), Candace Reed in Australia (1980), and Elizabeth Jordan Carr in the U.S. (1981).[4]

I am exactly contemporary with Elizabeth Jordan Carr, whose baby picture would appear on the cover of *LIFE* magazine alongside the medical equipment that brought her into the world; we were both born, under different circumstances, in 1981. There was nothing futuristic about these children, nothing novel about their parents' desires. Their lives would play out on the same timeline as my own, in different places with different trajectories, but made of the same ordinary human stuff.

Artificial reproduction developed as something of an afterthought in the medical community. Infertility had previously been treated as an inevitable part of human life. Inasmuch as it was a problem to be solved, the solutions were often seen as individual—women should have children younger and men should restrain from smoking or frequent masturbation that might waste their sperm. Venereal disease was a common cause for male infertility and yet most of the stigma of infertility fell on the "barren woman" whose childlessness pushed her outside the community of mothers. Like the spinster, her unmarried counterpart, she was beyond the pale of womanliness. If a husband's venereal disease rendered a couple childless, this was often either unknown to the woman herself or private information within the household. Her barrenness, on the other hand, was a public fact.

The first use of artificial insemination in the U.S. was performed by William Pancoast in 1884 to impregnate a woman whose husband was infertile due to gonorrhea. When Pancoast performed the procedure, he used the sperm of a medical student who looked similar enough to the husband for the offspring to pass. He did not tell the parents that the sperm was not from the husband. Later, he would confess to the husband who, not shocked or angry, only asked that Pancoast not reveal the truth to his wife.[5] She would die believing her husband's healthy sperm had impregnated her with a little help from their friendly gynecologist. She was no longer barren. It was a miracle.

While artificial insemination began to take hold as a solution to male infertility, there were still no solutions for female infertility. And yet, patients continued to consult their doctors looking for answers. They were often met with a shrug. Women would turn to each other for homeopathic cures, sex advice, or tricks for promoting ovulation. If they turned to religious authorities, they would have been offered biblical examples of women granted children through prayer after long periods of infertility. Couples would be counseled to adopt a child from the orphanages that were teeming with children born to women who did not have the ability to prevent a pregnancy before the rise of modern contraception or legalized abortion, nor the means or desire to raise a child.

In the mid-twentieth century, fertility research started to gain traction, driven by the postwar population boom. Research money in the 1950s poured into work that was deemed much more important—solving the problem of overpopulation. There were too many children, too few homes for them to go to. The first scientist to successfully perform in vitro fertilization in rabbits in 1959, Min Chueh Chang, was also one of the researchers responsible for developing the oral contraceptive pill. A Chinese immigrant working at the Worcester Foundation for Experimental Biology in Massachusetts, Chang did not even consider applying in vitro fertilization to humans—he believed there were already too many people in the world.[6] Chang was not alone in this belief. In an increasingly interconnected world, the scientific community and their financial backers feared a swelling global population that often did not look like them. Medical researchers found vast pools of grant money from the Rockefeller Foundation, the Ford Foundation, and others to tackle population control. This research, stemming from a combination of good and bad intentions—ecological concerns about a burdened planet, feminist calls for reproductive choice, and a heavy dose of racism—led to the development of the contraceptive pill.

In the process of developing contraceptive technologies, the medical community learned a lot about conception. What they learned about conception in the attempt to prevent it led some researchers to consider infertility as a problem that might, in fact, be worth solving.

FIVE OTHER PEOPLE were at the clinic for our IVF training session. Evan and I were still unsure about whether we were going to go through with it, but wanted to get as much information as possible before making a decision. The others in our training session included a man and a woman with sleek dark hair and matching, stylish suits who had clearly ducked out of work for the session and were constantly checking their phones to see what they had missed. The other couple were two women who were a portrait of contrasts—one short, soft, and fair and the other long, sharp, and raven-haired. They asked many questions and sought out each other's eyes for reassurance during the thornier descriptions about dosages and injections. And then there was a single woman in her late forties whose wide brown eyes seemed to open up into a well of sadness. She looked down at her hands frequently, in a gesture of exhaustion and fear. I wondered why she was there alone. Did she have a partner who was too busy? Someone with a shift job and no unpaid leave, or a Very Important Person with a Very Important Job. Or was she single and turning to IVF as a last resort to have a child? Had she tried adoption and, like many other single women, been turned down? Or was she among the increasing number of gestational surrogates who would carry another couple's fetus for nine months before delivering the baby into their hands? The nurse droned on, her intonations betraying too much repetition of the same content. She rattled off a list of medications that we would need to acquire. She was not able to tell us whether they would be covered by our insurance or how much they would cost.

No one came to a session like this without a history. How many miscarriages did they share among them? How many discussions with themselves and their loved ones about whether it was worth it to have kids? Were they not happy already? What about the expenses, which averaged around $12,000, if they weren't covered by insurance? And they often weren't. A 2018 Pew Research study found that white women with postgraduate degrees were the group most likely to have used fertility treatments or known someone who has, while Black and Hispanic women were less likely to have used such services themselves or to know of cases in their social circles.[7] IVF remains a privilege that is not available to everyone. It is a treatment that is only possible with a certain degree of economic as well as reproductive freedom. In order to ensure better chances for a successful round of IVF, doctors need to produce more embryos than they can implant. Anti-abortion "personhood" laws decreeing that life begins at conception threaten treatments that rely on an excess of embryos in order to achieve a successful pregnancy; strict adherence to such laws would make IVF illegal because the procedure requires the ability to discard these embryos.[8] This is particularly true of PGD, which requires the ability to dispose of those embryos impacted by genetic disorders.

The class focused on the IVF process and there was very little discussion about pre-implantation genetic diagnosis. Evan and I would have to ask follow-up questions and consult the informational packets provided to understand the extra steps that would be required. I could tell that the others in the training session were not planning to have PGD. Their eyes glazed over when Evan or I asked about the procedure and the nurse tried to answer our questions. It would take some research to learn more about the history of PGD and debates that surrounded it.

Although many of my friends had undergone IVF, as far as PGD went, I knew no one. I had never heard anyone admit that they had undergone PGD or discuss their thoughts about the process. It was uncharted territory. Was I prepared to undergo the regular round of IVF—injecting myself with synthetic hormones to produce extra eggs, which would be screened for Pompe Disease and then harvested and fertilized with Evan's semen, which would also be screened? All of this so that an embryo that was not impacted with the disease would be implanted in my womb. I had waited for weeks to book this session. We could have come earlier, but hadn't. My pen dragged slowly, reluctantly, over the paperwork they handed to me. How badly did I want a child? How important was it to me to eliminate the risk of another Pompe diagnosis, another termination? The nurse talked on, and Evan diligently wrote down what she said, but I failed to take a single note.

Although often depicted in the media as a means for creating "designer babies," perfect children with ideal characteristics cherry-picked by their parents, PGD is often a last resort for desperate parents. Sociologists Sarah Franklin and Celia Roberts describe the "extreme ambivalences" that PGD generates among those people who decide to go through with it.[9] People who decide on PGD often feel, rightly or wrongly, that in the face of extreme genetic diagnoses, they have no other choice. They do not want to experience what Barbara Katz Rothman calls a "tentative pregnancy," in which they must wait thirteen weeks for amniocentesis only to decide whether they should abort.[10] It is rarely an á la carte option for elite couples, but rather, a hard decision made by people who believe they are making the right choice for their offspring. Ten years before we sat through the training session, PGD was still a fringe practice; now it was resolutely in the mainstream. My insurance provider was even willing to cover it. No one batted an eye when I said that I was considering it. And yet, I didn't know anyone who was talking about it. If others in my acquaintance had gone this route, they weren't sharing.

The others in the training session also seemed nervous, but I couldn't know the precise cause of their concern. The cost. The procedure. Parenthood itself. Though I imagined that my situation was different from theirs, I felt temporary solidarity with these people, sharing bad coffee and awkward humor as we each waded into the unknown.

The nurse held up a plastic square covered with synthetic skin. We would use it to practice injections. The mock skin was a tan color that I associated with women's hosiery. It might have been called "Natural" or "Barely There." Like the medical diagrams flanking the wall, the mock skin assumed white women and white babies as the default setting.[11]

The nurse was speaking loudly now to get our attention. She told us to take out the practice needles and she would show us how to give ourselves an injection. It might be easier if we would place the artificial skin on our backside to get a sense of the right angle.

Without cracking a smile, the nurse placed the square on her ass and twisted around to look at it while miming the act of jabbing a needle into its synthetic surface.

Seven people looked at each other uneasily and then, simultaneously, broke into laughter.

EVAN AND I waited in a sleek office in Tribeca. Everything was dazzling white as if to impress would-be patients with the exceptional hygiene of the practice. I would have been willing to undergo open-heart surgery on the immaculate carpet. It was not the first reproductive health clinic that we had visited. It had been six months since that first instructional session for IVF treatment. Life, of a sort, had intervened. The first fertility doctor that we met had suddenly switched practices. In the disorder that followed, we were a ball that got dropped. Then there was a mix-up with test results. We waited and waited until finally taking them again. On my end, it was all too easy to be distracted with a new job that brought with it an unending stream of reasons not to make the next appointment. Office managers called to book our appointments and I waited days to follow up. I was dragging my feet. The procedure felt so alien and hostile, the necessity so abstract, and we were doing all right, Evan and I. We could be the type of people who chose not to have children, who went on nice vacations, ate dinner at 9 p.m., and paid doting attention to our two hypothetical dogs. But even in these reveries, I felt that pang of future regret, a premonition that if we didn't have children, we would always feel the loss of it. What I couldn't see with any certainty was whether artificial reproduction was really the best chance we had.

The new doctor greeted us in the waiting room. She was a small blonde in a crisp white lab coat. We had already had one preliminary conversation over the phone, so she knew some of the backstory. It was a huge relief not to hash it all out again. I had learned to dread all the routine doctor's appointments when I would need to recite my litany of procedures. Even a dentist's visit was fraught with peril. On my last dental appointment, the chipper hygienist had looked at my file and smiled up at me brightly.

I see you were pregnant on your last visit. How is the baby?

I corrected her as humanely as possible. It was terrible to disappoint a stranger and I wished I could have produced baby photos for her sake.

But the new fertility doctor knew it all already. We could skip that step.

First things first, I'll need your urine.

For the umpteenth time, I found myself peeing into a small container labeled with my name and patient ID. I came back into the consulting room and the urine was spirited away by a nurse. The fertility specialist began discussing the procedure, the time-line, and the medications that I could pick up at the pharmacy after the consultation. After laying out all the details, the doctor left the room to look at the results of the urine test.

A few minutes later, she came back into the room with a quizzical look on her face.

Is there any chance that you are already pregnant?

Evan and I looked at each other. Yes, we admitted, it was quite possible. After six months of waiting and delaying IVF treatment, we had thought we might give it one more try: the old-fashioned way, consequences be damned. It was not so much a decision as an impulse. We had cast our lot with science and medicine, taking all the right steps to have the healthiest pregnancy possible; but there was still a part of me that was rebelling against it all—the forms, the appointments, the medications, the needles, the sterile containers of urine and semen, the crisp white paper on top of a gurney, and my feet in the stirrups. I had checked all the boxes that the doctors had put in front of me and scheduled all the checkups, but one night I'd said "screw it" and we did. Having sat on the fence for too long, we edged ourselves, ever so slightly, in a direction. We were not reckless people. We were not romantic about the idea of having a child "naturally." But we both might have wanted, even after everything we had been through, to let in a little space for the unexpected.

It doesn't look like you're going to need me right now. The doctor laughed, walking us past the gleaming waiting room and sending us out into the tumult of the street.

August was pleasantly cool in Amsterdam and a light rain fell on the canals, leaving pockmarks on the slow surface of the water. We arrived in the early morning and spent the day outrunning jet lag, visiting sight after sight to trick our minds and bodies into accepting a new time zone. We sat down only once we arrived at the Rijksmuseum and drank espressos in the museum café as our limbs began to slow down from the exertion of denying our bodies the sleep that they knew to be their due. We were not only outrunning the diurnal clock, but we were also waiting on news that would be coming anytime now. Before we left for Amsterdam to attend an academic conference, we had visited the hospital for the second CVS exam that I would undergo. This time, Evan was able to come with me and it was his hand that I held as the needle was inserted into my abdomen. We were told that we would find out the results in a few weeks, which happened to be the time we were planning this trip abroad. Should we postpone our trip? No, Dr. Patel said, she would call us in Amsterdam to tell us the results.

In the last year of doctor's visits, failed job searches, difficult conversations, and awful decisions, I had somehow published a book. It was a scholarly book based on my dissertation. The book had won a prize from an academic association and I would receive the prize at the conference in Amsterdam. It meant a great deal to me, this validation. I was no longer employed as a professor, but I was being recognized as a scholar. And the prize had paid for this trip.

With the fleeting jolt of energy from the espresso, we set out to look at the Rembrandt collection in the sprawling Rijksmuseum. At the end of a long hallway of paintings, we entered a large, open room covered in enormous canvases depicting Rembrandt's work for the guild associations. These commissions had once decorated the guild hall and commemorated these once-powerful professional associations. The enormous canvases managed to be dark and luminous at once, covered in resplendent blacks and reds with sparing flashes of white.

As you walk into the gallery, the first canvas you see, straight ahead, is *The Night Watch*. The painting shows a gathering of watchmen—Amsterdam's seventeenth-century police—armed with guns and long pikes as they set up to defend the city. They exhibit the tools of their trade with pride; these are the latest technology and are shown off for the viewer to marvel at their technical competence. The scene is dark with small sparks of color—a red sash, a white collar. But the brightest spot amid this darkness, and the figure to which the viewer's eyes instinctively turn, is a small girl who peers out from behind a watchman refilling his musket. She gazes over her shoulder and looks directly at the viewer. Dressed in a shimmering gold gown, the little girl stared at me. I was hopped up on caffeine and little sleep and her eyes—two brown spots of darkness—drew my eyes inward toward her preternaturally mature face. Her mouth was slightly open as if she were about to tell me something. Some secret that

only I could hear. What was she doing there, in this scene of guns and battle, this male realm of tools and trade? She comes from another place, another time—the past or the future—with a message. On her head sits a crown the same color as her golden hair and, tied to her waist, she carries a dead bird, its white wings tucked against her radiant dress. I leaned closer to the canvas to hear what she had to say. My knees wobbled a little and I told Evan that I would need to sit down. It had been a long day.

When we arrived at the hotel, we found that it was nicer than any we had stayed in together before, a real upgrade from the shabby Airbnbs and discount hotels that we usually stayed in when we traveled. The hotel mistakenly thought it was our honeymoon and sent us a free basket with champagne and stroopwafels. There were mints on the pillow named after Queen Wilhelmina, a sovereign who had maintained Dutch neutrality during the First World War and then fled the Nazis during the Second World War to lead the resistance in exile. The box of mints was white with blue lettering that resembled Delft china. The mints themselves were thick and chalky like squat Alka-Seltzer tablets.

As we unpacked our suitcases and our bodies called out for the sleepy warmth of the overstuffed bed, the phone rang.

Dr. Patel said that she knew it was late, but she wanted to try to catch us as soon as possible. It was good news. The baby would not have Pompe Disease. Evan and I had only passed along one set of the recessive gene, not the other. Those genes would continue to lie dormant in the tangled knots of the baby's DNA, not doing harm, but waiting to emerge only with an improbable match like ours had been.

It's a girl, by the way.

A week later, we would return to a city that had once been called New Amsterdam, carrying a child we would name after the mints left on our pillow the night that we learned she was safe.

Wilhelmina. Willie for short.

PART TWO

# MOTHERHOOD

5

# Tiny Earmolds

We enter the world in a peal of sound. A sharp cry that pierces the air as lungs fill. I heard Willie before I saw her, before she was placed in my numbed arms and I looked into her cloudy eyes. I pressed the slimy red creature to my skin. She was smaller than I could have imagined after months of carrying her around like an enormous watermelon under a series of ever-expanding dresses. She was both fragile and vibrant at once. She radiated the shimmering energy of a wild creature caught for a moment in one's arms before being let loose. She seemed to look in my eyes and I wondered what she saw. A blur, no doubt. A mother-like blur, perhaps.

A February snowstorm blew through New York City on Willie's first day in the world. We saw the snow gathering in the corners of our hospital window as the baby learned to latch on to my breast. It was a world of contrasts. The warm baby's head nestled against me and her cheeks flushed pink as I watched frost enlace itself around the window. My mother and sister had arrived with tiny clothes for Willie and warm socks with little rubber nubs on the bottom for me to wear around the cold linoleum floors of the hospital.

Willie slept on and off that first night beside me in the small cot they rolled into the room. She would cry every now and then— loud shrieks that set my heart racing—but was easily calmed with milk or a diaper change. She liked to sleep and we were told to wake her up every three hours to feed her or she wouldn't get enough nourishment. We ran hospital towels under the faucet and tickled the wet fabric against her cheek, her belly, her feet to try to wake her up with the cool wetness of the material. She gave reluctant little shrugs and tried her best to ignore us. The doctors and assistants came in and out, asking me to fill out innumerable forms, checking if the baby was latching correctly to my breast, taking our vitals. Toward dawn, a nurse came in to take Willie away from me for the first time. They would need to do a series of routine tests. I whispered to Evan to go with them. I didn't want her out of our sight. He watched the nurses in the exam room through a windowed hallway as they weighed Willie, listened to her heart and her lungs, pricked the bottom of her heel to take blood swabs, and put small earpieces in her ears to test her hearing. I was on edge while they were away. They had an elaborate system of identification—I wore a wrist bracelet with a QR code that synced up with a corresponding anklet that Willie wore. Nonetheless, my heart was short-circuiting my brain, full of the thought that she wouldn't be coming back to me. That someone would take her away.

She did come back. The nurse pushed her in on the rolling cot with Evan trailing behind. A pink-and-blue-striped hospital-issued hat covered her head, her forehead, her ears. Half of her face. Milky blue just-born eyes opened and looked around at a blurry world. Not yet a full day among us, her nose was squashed flat and her lips swollen and pursed from an abrupt departure out of an aquatic existence. Part fish and part child. A small mermaid tightly wrapped in a cotton tail.

It seemed incredible that they would let us leave the hospital with this tiny creature. Before we left, there was an elaborate procedure of signing forms—paperwork for the frightening bills that would soon arrive. We were insured, so the most horrifying numbers would appear on our bills with a line through them but still legible to remind us of what would happen if we were ever unemployed or uninsurable. The hospital required us to watch a video about shaking a baby. And then it was time to go home, out into the freezing air with this fragile infant whose skeleton was precariously balanced in our too-strong arms. How could we possibly take such a helpless creature into the windy 20-degree city? We prepared all the blankets we could find to wrap her up in layers and layers.

Before we left, a nurse came in with studied nonchalance.

They had gotten the test results back. Willie had failed the hearing test. It was probably just some fluid in her ears. That happened sometimes. We'd need to come back for more tests in a couple weeks.

Evan and I looked at each other. We knew that it was not fluid in her ears.


IN A DIVE bar in Austin ten years earlier, Bob Wills had been playing on the jukebox. Whether ironically or earnestly, it was unclear. It was swing music, not background music, but there was no dance floor and it was all a shade too loud. We were shouting to make ourselves heard over the fiddling, our faces lit by the neon light above the bar as Shiner beer bottles sweated onto the scarred wooden table. Classes were just wrapping up and a group of graduate students were meeting up for end-of-semester drinks. It was May and already crushingly hot in Texas. I wore a sleeveless green top that I hoped was dark enough to hide the pool of perspiration gathering under my arms.

Sorry, what?

I asked if you turned in your last paper yet.

Sorry, you'll have to speak louder.

At this, Evan gestured toward his ears. I looked more closely and saw a slender plastic wire connecting an earmold to a hearing aid behind his ear. It was easy to miss. The aid itself was covered by the arms of his eyeglasses. It was the same color as his thick hair. Dark brown.

This was the longest conversation I had ever had with Evan and I found myself leaning closer to him across the table to make myself heard as Bob Wills yodeled in our ears. I hadn't noticed Evan's hearing aids the first time we met. And not the second or third time either. Now we were sitting across from each other at a long table at a loud bar.

Do you want to go outside?

The night was dark and balmy. I'd been in Texas for two years and was just getting used to living somewhere where sundown didn't cool things off. We sat down in plastic lawn chairs on the bar's patio. Shabby chic with an extra dose of shabby. They were deep, reclining chairs and we had to scoot to the edges to have a conversation. It was quieter outside and Evan leaned forward intently as I started talking. He listened with his whole body. We'd seen each other around campus but we'd never taken a class together. He asked me where I was from, what brought me to Texas, and what I was researching. He paused after everything I said as if it was a matter of great importance. I asked questions in return and found out that he was one of the few graduate students in our program who was actually from Texas. He'd grown up in a military town an hour's drive from here. He had been married when he entered the program but he was separated from his wife now.

He had just returned from picking up his last things from their house in Waco. He said it was like visiting his own ghost. Under the eyes of his wife and her two closest friends, he put his stuff in boxes. Clothes, books, family heirlooms. Anything that was indisputably his. Looking down at the contents of one of these boxes, he didn't recognize the person who owned those things.

I asked if he really believed that he could have such an absolute break with his own self. Did he think that we shed identities like a snake sheds its skin?

Yes, he said. He didn't think of his life as continuous. It seemed more like a series of ruptures and breaks between different selves.

I didn't see it that way. I thought back to myself at eight years old and that little girl seemed to be very much still the same me.

Evan leaned a little closer. He wondered what that difference said about how we each see the world.

Suddenly I was aware that Evan was the most handsome man who had ever cared about how I saw the world.

He looked at me closely and intently when I spoke, absorbing every word with a care and attention rarely given by strangers, rarely even given by our closest intimates. He captured my words as if he were gently catching a butterfly in his bare hands. Softly, softly he cupped the creature, and only after peering at the patterns on its wings, the soft antennas on its head, did he carefully let each syllable go.

MAMA, MAMA, MAMA, the machine belted in an uncanny imitation of the human voice. It was 1862, and Alexander Graham

Bell was fifteen years old and his brother Melville was seventeen. Their father, Alexander Melville Bell, had set them on this task as a way of instilling the values of innovation and scientific rigor in his sons.[1] Can you make a machine that speaks?

Alexander the senior was a well-known elocutionist who was making a name for himself teaching actors, preachers, and the upwardly mobile of the nineteenth-century British Isles.[2] He had invented a language called "Visible Speech" that aimed to render the sounds of language into a system of graphic symbols. Unlike the English alphabet, which has a shaky relationship to sound—an "A," for instance, can be an "ah" or an "ay"—Visible Speech could be spoken by any language-speaker to represent any sound a mouth could make, from the tonal sounds of Chinese to the clicks of the Zulu tongue.[3] At the same time utopian thinkers were advocating Esperanto and other universal languages, Bell Senior was putting forward a system to record and transmit human speech across the barriers of language. He was arguing for the importance of speech in a time when the written word seemed dominant.

Bell Senior made his argument not only in prose, but also in verse, writing a poem called "The Tongue" (1846). The poem is an ode directed to the tongue itself, which Bell praises as "the organ of the soul!" He writes that it may seem strange to devote a poem to the tongue in a literary time when the printing press was dominating popular culture. In an age of newspapers and cheap print, the spoken word seemed to be an organ of the past, of those "remote and barb'rous times, / When men by manly sounds, much more than signs—/ The tam'd expression of the glowing soul—/ Were rous'd to gen'rous, or to daring deeds."[4] Here Bell argues that sounds are not "barbarous" or "primitive" compared to the written word, but rather, they signify action. Sounds are manly. Signs, including the written word, are tamed, domesticated, effete. They take words out of the active sphere in which they are spoken and fix them onto the page. To reawaken the virility and nobility of mankind, Bell Senior argues, we need speech. It was a secular as well as a religious vocation:

> For poesy and eloquence from thee
> Best shew their heavenly origin—their charms—
> Their power to call forth man's true nobleness,
> And fit him for the bliss of higher spheres.[5]

To be fit for heaven, mankind must speak, according to this professor of elocution. Poetry was one way for Bell Senior to advocate for the primacy of speech; technology was another.

When he tasked his boys with creating a speaking machine, Bell Senior gave them a pamphlet by the eighteenth-century inventor Wolfgang von Kempelen that explained how he had created his own speaking machine with a bellows that stood for the human lungs and scavenged instrument parts—the reed from a bagpipe and the bell of a clarinet—to imitate parts of the larynx and mouth. Von Kempelen's machine could produce only vowel sounds—a low, murmuring "ah." It was a gross simulacrum of speech that the Bell boys were intent on surpassing.

Alexander's father was an elocutionist and his mother, Eliza, was deaf. She was a talented pianist who felt her way through the vibrations of her instrument.[6] She was born with her hearing but began to experience progressive deafness later in childhood. Now here was young Alexander, a teenager looking to prove himself a scientific man like his father, creating a machine that called out to its mother. And what of his mother, who could not hear his calls? Did she sense the child's cries as vibrations disturbing the air? Did she stay close to her son through his baby years, her hand resting on his stomach as she slumbered? Or was she far away, playing her piano, seeking out the faint music her ear could still detect, oblivious to his need?

*Mama, mama, mama.*

The boys set to work modeling the vocal organs necessary to produce speech. Melville created an artificial larynx out of tin and rubber while Alexander set out to make a mouth and tongue modeled on a human skull his father had given him. He used latex to model the mouth, teeth, jaws, pharynx, and nasal cavities. For the soft palate, he stuffed a rubber bag with cotton and attached it with iron wires to a handle that he could manipulate up and down. Seven more handles were attached to seven sections of wood, all of which could be manipulated separately, serving a complicated set of maneuvers of the tongue. Instead of the bellows that von Kempelen used for his speaking machine, the boys decided their own lungs would suffice and created a mouthpiece through which they could blow directly into the machine. Melville put his lips to the machine. Alexander moved the handles. Out came a voice, or something like a voice.[7]

*Mama, mama, mama.*

In a peal of sound, a voice came into the world. Not exactly a human voice, but close enough for the boys to whoop in delight. Through careful study and industry, they had birthed it and it called to them. After toying with their new plaything, trying various permutations, they wanted to show it off to the world. But they were still boys. They decided to play a trick on their neighbors. They went racing down the hallways of their Edinburgh town house, into the common stairway. Melville put his lips to the machine. Alexander manipulated the handles.

*Mama, mama, mama.*

They blew louder and louder. The neighbors started to stir. Urgent voices raised in exasperation and alarm. Someone shouted out, "Good gracious, what can be the matter with that baby."[8]

Steps began to gather. Doors were opened. The boys looked at each other with stifled laughter. They gathered up the machine and snuck away. It was a game, but it was not a game. It would become a life's work.

Alexander had created a machine that could shout for its mother loudly enough that even his own mother would be forced to hear.

WILLIE'S LIPS PUFFED slightly as she slept with her cheek resting against the side of her stroller. She twitched and the movement disturbed the three color-coded cords attached to her head: a red cord secured to her right ear, a blue cord secured to her left ear, and an electrode attached to her forehead to monitor her brain activity. The audiologist stood up to check that the beige earpiece was still snug in her ear. We held our breath and hoped that she would continue to sleep. They needed an hour's worth of data while she slept before we could leave.

There is a hierarchy to hospital rooms. The delivery room in which Willie came into the world was large and light-filled, facing out on the Hudson River as if to welcome each new soul into an idealized vista of the city. The room where they led us now was on a much lower floor, hunkered near ground level where the sirens and honks of Broadway seemed to blast us directly. This would be bad enough on an ordinary visit, but we were in a room designated for postnatal testing and this was meant to be a follow-up hearing test. In fact, it was her second hearing test since we'd been released from the hospital. The first test was performed by a technician to qualify us for New York City's Early Intervention Program for children with disabilities. Then, we were handed over to an audiologist. Her name was Holly. She was in her late twenties and had come to NYC with her husband from Mississippi, where they would return to at the end of the year. She wore her hair in short blond curls and had precise, elfin features that were softened by her slight drawl. Her office was no bigger than a closet and huddled with children's toys, models of the human ear, and promotional materials from hearing aid companies.

On our first meeting she told us that she was afraid we'd have to run the test again.

Why? Didn't they already get the information they needed? A week after we were released from the hospital, we'd come back to have our baby hooked up to cords. The technician showed us a graph. She confirmed that Willie had inherited congenital deafness and would qualify for city services, which included free hearing aids and speech therapy. What more did they need to know?

There was something Holly didn't like about the results. She hinted that they were not successfully completed by the previous technician. They would need information from this test to determine the settings for Willie's first pair of hearing aids and she wanted to get it right. She would be more comfortable running her own test.

So back we came, hoping that Willie could once again sleep through the test for Holly to record the information she needed. If Willie woke up, Holly would have to pause the test and wait until she fell asleep again. Any noises that Willie or we made would interrupt the flow of data they were collecting from her brain. The test was called an auditory brainstem response (ABR). The earphones inserted into Willie's ears were emitting various clicking sounds. As the earphones clicked, the electrodes were measuring Willie's brain activity to record any response. It would take a full hour for Holly to get the information she needed. A car horn honked. The midday light streamed directly through the flimsy blinds. At least she was a good sleeper.

There was very little to look at in the bare room where the test was being performed, so I found myself studying a diagram of the ear. The diagram showed a bisected ear, cut in half and exposed to the spectator as it could never be in real life. On the far left of the image was the outer ear; this is what we picture when we talk about ears. This seashell of cartilage and flesh captures sound waves and funnels them along down their passage to the eardrum. The passage of sound through the ear resembled nothing so much as a knight's journey fraught with obstacles. First the knight rides his trusty steed to the entry of a cave where he passes through a long cavern until he reaches his first test—passage through the eardrum. To continue on his journey, he must bang this taut membrane and convert the sonic waves into vibrations. If the eardrum is broken—a football injury, perhaps, or a boxed ear—then our knight's journey will end or falter. If he succeeds, he will gain passage to the middle ear, trading in his horse for a donkey to clomp along as mechanical vibrations through a forest of tiny bones that will rattle as he passes, sending word of his arrival down the air-filled chamber. From the forest of bones, the knight must then gain passage to the cochlea of the inner ear where he will trade the donkey for a boat, traveling through an aquatic sea. In this sea are tiny hair follicles that move with the fluid and that transfer the vibrations to electrical signals. This may be where Willie and Evan encounter some kind of mysterious obstacle, an unknown miasma that interferes with the hair follicles and blocks our knight's passage. Out of the cochlea, the knight trades his skiff for a dragon, traveling through the auditory nerve as electrical energy until he reaches the brain stem, where he passes through a series of stations along the auditory pathway until he finally blows his trumpet and the journey ends. Only then do we experience what we think of as sound.

Willie was awake as Holly explained the results to us. There were graphs and bell curves and long lists of numbers. She showed us at what point Willie stopped responding to the clicks and what that might suggest about her ability to process sound and, later, language. As soon as possible, she would need to start wearing hearing aids during all waking hours to have a chance to get the receptive language she needed if she was going to learn to speak. We were taken aback. Despite the fact that congenital deafness ran in his family, none of Evan's relations that we knew of had worn hearing aids as infants. Nor, for that matter, did any of them have trouble learning to speak.

Holly looked at Evan. She told us softly that we cannot yet know whether her hearing loss is the same. We would need to learn more.

As EVAN AND I drove through central Texas on our first trip together since we'd started dating, the landscape was long and flat with huge stretches of unbroken sky. I was used to flatness, but the flat landscape of my Midwestern youth was pastoral green, broken up by fields of corn, red barns, and industrial grain silos on the long drive to my grandparents' house in Iowa or to visit my sister and cousins at college in southern Indiana. Here the vistas were arid, colored a dusty orange from the mild winter to the scorched-earth summer. Only now, in the early spring, were they spotted with the occasional patch of bluebonnets; families pulled off the road along the way to set a chunky toddler in a wave of blue for a family photo. As we neared Houston, the

landscape started to change, opening up to the semitropical Gulf
seascape that would accompany us to New Orleans.

We talked through graduate student problems. I was stuck in
a difficult chapter of my dissertation. I'd been writing it for too
long and it wasn't budging. I was trying to understand something about the Irish poet W. B. Yeats. I wanted to know whether
the invention of radio had changed the way he thought about
poetry as a spoken art. Did he write differently when he wrote
for the radio? Did his poems sound different? It was the kind of
esoteric question that lent itself to a dissertation chapter. And
now I needed to try to answer it.

I asked Evan if he'd listen to it again. Tell me what he thought.
He was a captive audience; we wouldn't reach our destination for
hours. The poem was called "Sweet Dancer" and Yeats had written it in 1932 for a BBC broadcast. When Yeats wrote the poem,
he was sixty-eight and had recently ended a fling with a much
younger woman named Margot Ruddock. He was experiencing
what he called a "second puberty," reinventing his youth in that
old cliché of a May–December romance.[9] Margot was a poet
herself and suffered a nervous breakdown and was institution-
alized after meeting Yeats. It was a period of Yeats's career when
he wrote some of his most powerful lyrics and, yet, in which he
was the most politically repugnant. One of his foremost late-life
passions was eugenics and, like other leaders of 1930s literary,
artistic, and political culture, Yeats began promoting the popular
pseudoscience. Among the various responsibilities of the artist,
according to Yeats and his ilk, was to sound the alarm about the
devolution of civilization through the improper breeding of "the
best." This poem was, mercifully, not one of his eugenicist poems.
It happened to be a love poem. It was not one of Yeats's better
poems, but I kept coming back to it, wondering if there was some

clue in it that might help me unpack what new sound technologies, like radio, meant to poets who were encountering them for
the first time.

Evan was driving and kept his eyes on the road as we talked.
When I read the poem out loud, what he noticed first was the
repetition—the obvious parts like the end rhymes and the re-
frain, "Let her finish her dance,/ Let her finish her dance," but
also those moments of internal rhyme and repetition such as
Yeats's description of the dancer having "Escaped from bitter
youth,/ Escaped out of her crowd/ Or out of her black cloud." [10]
The "crowd . . . cloud" rhyme reminded Evan of William Wordsworth's poem "I Wandered Lonely as a Cloud":

> I wandered lonely as a cloud
> That floats on high o'er vales and hills,
> When all at once I saw a crowd,
> A host, of golden daffodils[.] [11]

They were both poems about artistic isolation, about feeling
apart from mankind and seeking solace in the natural world.

Evan has an incredibly good ear for poetry—a particular
sensitivity to its meter and rhythm. He has a fondness for poetry
on the page for which his imagination provides the sound, an
inner voice that mediates between poet and reader. The sound of
poetry, for Evan, does not depend on the abilities of an anatomical ear. He came to graduate school interested in working on
the Romantic poets of the nineteenth century—Wordsworth,
Coleridge, Shelley—but had shifted back to the eighteenth
century when he started learning more about a group of poets
from the Age of Enlightenment who fascinated him. I found
myself thinking about his talent for reading poetry. Poetry often relies on the writer and reader hearing an inner voice—a

subvocalization that is not audible, but rather a product of the imagination.

Since the days of the printing press, much of the poetry we read has a fictive relationship to sound—we hear only the ghost of sound in the words of the poet. One of Yeats's great desires was to make poetry oral again—to bring it back to the days of Homer or the Irish bard Aogán Ó Rathaille—and he saw new sound technologies like radio as an opportunity to revive these lost arts. New technology could, paradoxically, allow him to bring literature back to its roots in oral tradition. For Yeats there was no question that the spoken word was more direct and authentic than the secondhand signs of writing. Like Bell Senior, he also thought it was more manly. Evan came from a different tradition than this, a working-class tradition of the strong silent type, but in his family, silence could be quite literal.

Evan's phone rang from the cupholder between us. It was his dad, Dale. We had plenty of road in front of us and so Evan picked up the phone. Suddenly the car filled with a voice I had never heard before. Evan was talking to his dad in a new voice. It was very loud, and it was very Texan—an accent that melded the migrations of two peoples, the southerners of the East Coast moving westward, taking with them their lilting drawls, and the hill people of the Appalachians moving southwest, bringing their Irish-inflected twanging vowels. Mix these with German and Czech migrants, alongside a willful refusal of the Spanish and Native American languages of the occupants of the land, and you get a Texan accent. I looked over at him in surprise. His eyes laughed at my expression as he listened to his dad on the other end. It was not a long conversation. Someone had bought a car from someone else. The grandkids had just left town after a visit. The spring was looking too dry. The town reservoir was way down. A bad start to the season.

When Evan got off the phone he laughed again at my reaction. Did you forget you were dating a boy from central Texas?

I didn't think that I'd ever been properly introduced to that boy.

Evan explained that his dad's hearing seemed to be getting worse. After a lifetime of not wearing hearing aids, he was struggling more and more to keep up. When he spoke up so his dad could hear, the years seemed to peel away from him and he channeled the voice of his youth.

I asked why his dad had never worn hearing aids.

He was a mechanic. All that automotive sound was unbearably loud with hearing aids in. He could never get used to taking them out and putting them back in. Even in conversational settings, the hearing aids were never quite right. He'd gotten along so long without them that he could never get used to them.

Was he always hard of hearing?

Yes. So were his brother and his father. They had all gotten along well enough, been able to do jobs that paid good wages—mostly agricultural and mechanical labor—and didn't feel they were missing out on the important things in life. There were a few cousins still out in rural Tennessee who were considered deaf, but it was a side of the family that hadn't stayed in touch. It was a family without a tree, that receded quickly into the unwritten history of rural life. Dale had left when he was a teenager, fleeing an abusive household. He and his mother came to Texas to start a new family, still trailing some of that past with them.

I thought about what kind of past we would trail with us into our future. There was definitely a "we" here. There was definitely a future here.

ALEXANDER GRAHAM BELL met his future wife, Mabel Hubbard, when she came to him as a student. Alexander was now following in his father's footsteps, making a name for himself as an elocutionist in America with incredible claims that he could use his father's system of Visible Speech to teach the deaf to speak. Mabel was the daughter of a prominent Boston family. She lost her hearing to a bout of scarlet fever when she was five years old. Her father, Gardiner Greene Hubbard, wanted the best for his daughter. The best, as he saw it, meant giving her the means to pass as a hearing woman. He surveyed the scene in Boston and found nothing to his liking. He visited the American Asylum, which had been founded as the first school for deaf education in 1817. Its first president was Thomas Gallaudet and its first head teacher was a deaf man named Laurent Clerc. Together, they established the foundations of American Sign Language. Hubbard was not impressed with the sight of students communicating with their hands. He contemptuously compared what he saw there to the languages of the Indians or the Hottentots.[12] It would not do for his civilized daughter. He found financial backing from the philanthropist John Clarke and lobbied the Massachusetts legislature to found the Clarke School for the Deaf, which would instruct deaf students in speech, not sign language.

Thus began an ongoing conflict in American deaf education between the manualists (proponents of American Sign Language) and the oralists (proponents of speech). American Sign Language was thriving in the deaf community in the mid-nineteenth century, allowing people who society had once written off as "deaf and dumb," subhuman even, to make their intelligence understood. In the residential schools where sign language was taught, deaf students discovered a sense of community and were able to learn the same subjects as their hearing peers—literature, math, and science—as well as prepare themselves for trades where they could make a livelihood and support families. They could meet other deaf people and marry someone with whom they could communicate with ease. But for people like Hubbard, sign language did not allow for the most cherished goal of parenthood—giving his daughter a "normal" life. A life that fit into his. He hired a young woman named Mary True who, though not formally trained, shared his belief that Mabel could speak. She took the girl on long walks and pointed to things they saw. She pointed to her lips as she talked. Like this. No, not like that. This.

Despite years of instruction in oralism, Mabel still struggled to make herself understood in spoken English. In 1873, her father introduced her to a bright new teacher named Alexander Graham Bell. In the intervening years, Bell had traveled from Scotland to Canada to Boston, touting his father's method of elocutionary instruction to schools for the deaf, which were trying and often failing to educate their pupils in oralism. On the side, he continued to dabble with electronics, moving from his childhood experiments with speaking machines to a developing interest in hearing machines—devices that might transmit and record sound across distances.

When Alexander met Mabel, he was twenty-six and she was sixteen. He saw in her a bright student, well-read, well-traveled, and eager to know more about the world around her. It's possible that he might have seen a little bit of his mother in her as well: a proud, undeterred deaf woman in a society that made few accommodations.

Within three years they were engaged to be married.


OVER THE FIRST three months of Willie's life, I crisscrossed the city with her snug in a carrier strapped to my chest. I had a maternity leave that was, by U.S. standards, generous. After three months, it was about to end and I was trying to squeeze every moment I could from this time. Willie had grown from the lean, vulnerable infant that I kept under guard against the winter cold to a robust baby with Michelin-Man rings around her legs and arms. In her carrier, she liked to face outward so she could see the world. According to the websites I routinely checked, her vision was not yet fully developed. She could see an object clearly only if it was within eight to fifteen inches; everything else must have seemed a psychedelic blur of color and motion. I imagined that the city looked to her like a vast kaleidoscope changing moment by moment.

The weather was starting to warm—our first day without a winter hat. I peered down at the bald head bobbing along as I walked. Two flashing lights winked back at me. Willie was wearing her first pair of hearing aids. We had completed the voluminous pile of paperwork required from NYC's Early Intervention office and were passed on to a case manager named Gary: a fast-talking Bronx-based social worker. He was a whiz at paperwork—sending me documents covered with yellow highlighter. Sign here. And here. And here. He filed papers and then texted, emailed, called until everyone had done their part. Nothing was ever missed and no phone call lasted longer than necessary.

Are the hearing aids in yet?

Yes.

All right! Give that baby a big kiss.

Will do.

Phone clicks.

Even with the hearing aids in, I was never sure how much she could hear my voice. When she woke up crying, I would cradle her in my arms and sing a lullaby. Was it the feeling of my arms around her that comforted her or was it the sound of my voice singing one of the few lullabies that I could remember? As long as I was able to quiet those gasping sobs and watch her face soften, I did not care what worked. She understood that I was there and that everything would be all right. And that was all that mattered, at least for now.

Out of pocket, each hearing aid would have cost $3,000. In New York City, the Early Intervention Program covered the hearing aids and related costs for her first three years. After that we would be on our own. They also covered speech therapy, which was where we were now going. I would need to take the crosstown bus twice a week to the Upper East Side for a thirty-minute appointment. To cross two miles of Manhattan, it would take an hour. Speech therapy was at the Clarke School—a New York City offshoot of the institution that was founded by Mabel Hubbard's father. Since Mabel's time, oralism had developed from what was little more than a naïve belief that speech was best into elaborate systems of instruction that had become inextricably linked to technological development. This too was the legacy of Alexander Graham Bell. According to Clarke's website, "A child's capacity to talk and be understood starts with technology that gives them appropriate access to the sounds of speech. Once they have access, a child can be taught to *listen,* with the guidance of professionals." We were using Clarke's outpatient services, but they also had a school for children through preschool. All the children wore devices from hearing aids to cochlear implants.

It was a long bus ride and then a half-mile walk to get there, but at least the weather was nice. We rode the bus through Central Park, feeling the urban asphalt give way, momentarily, to lush green, before reemerging on the East Side with its well-regulated residential buildings. We got off the bus and started down the last block, where students in uniforms rushed into the unassuming front doors of elite private schools. Blocks away from our destination, I looked down at Willie's bobbing head. Only one light blinked back.

My heart raced. Where was the other hearing aid? I felt around in the pocket of the carrier. Nothing. Willie looked up at me with a puzzled expression. Think, think. Was it on while we were on the bus? I couldn't say for sure. My mind leaped three steps forward. If it had fallen off on the bus, there was no way I'd see it again. How many feet would trample it before it fell out on the street and was pulverized under the wheels of another bus? I thought of the call I would have to make. Would Gary be able to get us a new one from Early Intervention? Would we have to pay for it? But no, maybe it had fallen off after the bus. If I walked very slowly and kept my eyes on the pavement while retracing my steps, perhaps I would see it. If only it wasn't gray. The same gray as the sidewalk.

I shuffled slowly along, scanning each inch of the sidewalk below me. There were mercifully few people around. Willie wasn't fussing yet—no need for a diaper change or feeding as I searched, exposed and anxious, along Eighty-Sixth Street. Willie gurgled. She must have noticed we were at a different angle than usual. Her head titled slightly closer to the ground as I walked, stooped toward the pavement. She must have felt my heart racing faster against her back.

And then, nestled in a crack, a small light winked at me. It was there, waiting to be picked up. Untrodden.

We were about ten minutes late for speech therapy. It could have been much more, but I was still irritated that we had spent an hour getting to what would now be a twenty-minute appointment. In order to get to the therapist's office, I needed to get through the security at the front door and then past the two classrooms, each arranged with overstuffed pillows in a ring for circle time, shelves teeming with hard-nibbled cardboard books and past the black-and-white tiled bathroom with its miniature toilets and low sinks.

Willie's speech therapist was named Emma. She was the first of six speech therapists we would have in Willie's first three years. But we didn't know that yet. Whenever we arrived, Willie's eyes went straight to the bookshelves to look for a stuffed bear that Emma would pull out for her. Willie grunted in satisfaction when the bear came toward her, opening her arms to embrace the plush brown fur. In our twenty minutes together, Emma would work on rehearsing "Ling Sounds"—the six basic sounds that comprise the range of frequencies of human speech. Each sound was represented by a different toy and Willie was meant to learn to associate the sound with the toy.

"Aaah" for the plane.

"Oooo" for the ghost.

"Eeee, eeee" for the mouse.

"Ssss" for the snake.

"Shhh" for the sleeping baby.

"Mmm" for the ice cream cone.

Both in speech therapy and at home, we needed to drill Willie into associating these sounds with these toys. This would become the basis of the sound checks that the audiologist would perform to calibrate her hearing aids before she could speak. If she heard the "mmm" and looked at the ice cream cone, they were working. If that "mmm" eluded her, she might not be getting those low tones. Like Evan, low frequencies were the hardest for Willie. Higher frequencies—the "ssss" for snake or "shhh" for the sleeping baby—were easier for her to catch. Even without her hearing aids, a high whistle would often attract her attention, startling her through the muffled quiet of her unaided world.

Emma would cover her mouth when she made the sound so

that Willie could not match the mouth shape to the object. It had
to be sound alone.

"Ssss."

Willie flashed her eyes toward the snake.

Emma clapped her hands. She told me I was doing a great job
keeping her hearing aids in. Good mom. Good baby.

At the end of our session, I asked her if she had any resources
that she could direct me to for learning sign language. The same
question that I had asked Holly the audiologist and Gary the social worker. There are resources online, she said vaguely. But she
wanted to make sure that I was prioritizing speech. Willie's coming along so well, understanding so much. Emma didn't want
us to regress. I was learning that, while they might go by different names, the oralist versus manualist distinction was still very
much alive. In choosing Early Intervention and hearing aids, I
had picked a lane without realizing it.

I thought back to first meeting Rachel, an acquaintance from
graduate school, who was serving a term as Miss Deaf America while studying in our program. During our third year, she
was invited to travel from Austin to Indianapolis to sign the national anthem at the Super Bowl. A group of us gathered for a
Super Bowl party and waited for her to appear. Kelly Clarkson
took to the microphone to belt out "O Say Can You See." The
camera never panned to Rachel. The anthem went un-signed for
audiences at home. From Rachel, I first learned that there was a
distinctive Deaf culture defined by a shared language, history,
and traditions. She capitalized "Deaf" with an uppercase "D" to
highlight her Deaf identity. The uppercase D defined not a medical diagnosis but, rather, a sense of belonging within a group
that shared a language and a culture with its own literature and
arts and customs. I regretted not being able to sign with Rachel,
but I learned a great deal from her nonetheless. I often thought

about whether Willie would think of herself as deaf or Deaf—if she would see herself as someone with a medical condition or a proud member of a minority culture. Rachel came to my mind often as I asked Willie's specialists whether I ought to be learning American Sign Language. If there were resources available that had been developed by deaf or hard-of-hearing people, then why weren't these ever mentioned? Why were none of the specialists we encountered deaf or hard of hearing themselves? And which was Willie? Was she deaf or Deaf or hard of hearing? Where did the line of demarcation fall?

Emma was bright and spirited, a natural with children. She was evasive about sign language but not hostile to it, as we would find with later speech therapists and audiologists who would tell us bluntly and without providing supporting evidence that sign language would delay Willie's development. The priority, according to the experts we consulted, was to make sure that Willie met developmental milestones for speech; it was our job to fit Willie into the norms, not to question those norms. To these experts I would ask whether it was any different than wanting a child to be bilingual in English and Spanish. Wasn't it good to have more resources, to know more languages? To which they would respond, but you don't speak Spanish at home, do you? The answer was no. I felt adrift trying to learn a language on my own. I believed myself to be a poor student of languages—I blamed self-consciousness, the inability to dive into something new and allow myself to look foolish at first. I made use of my time at home to watch "baby sign" videos with Willie on YouTube. Rachel Coleman was the foremost YouTube sign language children's programming celebrity. She was not deaf herself and had started her career as a Christian rock singer before giving birth to a deaf daughter and devoting her musical talents and missionary zeal to sign language instruction. Her songs were ridiculously catchy. At home during long winter days, Willie and I learned the alphabet together, the colors, the emotions. Rachel Coleman wore colored tape on her fingers to help big and little people recognize her finger positions. She wore her hair in an exaggerated flip. Her daughter and nephew were the stars of the show, and the theme song—"It's signing time with Alex and Leah!"—would pop into my head in random waves throughout the day. But I still couldn't put together a sentence. And now, maternity leave was nearly over and I knew that I would barely be able to keep my head above water between work and parenting.

When Willie and I left the Clarke School that day and headed back to the crosstown bus, I checked compulsively for the winking lights of her aids. She fell asleep on the bus, as she always did after speech therapy, exhausted from the effort of listening. I pulled out my phone and ordered a pair of ear clips to attach her hearing aids to the back of her shirt: they were bright yellow and tied by a string to a bumblebee at the base of the clip. Impossible to miss against the pavement.

I WAS NOT prepared for Evan's sadness when Willie was diagnosed with hearing loss. We had always known it was a distinct possibility. When we mapped his family tree with the geneticist, it became clear that it was a dominant trait. A fifty-fifty chance. But the news itself, confirmed yet again by Holly after Willie's third hearing test, knocked him down. It was the first time that I realized the great toll it had taken on him. Twenty years of passing as hearing. Another twenty years of maintaining expensive and finicky hearing aids in order to keep up with a world that did not want to slow down, face you, and repeat itself. The stillness he needed to thrive was only ever on the page or in the quiet of our apartment, a newborn baby lying between us, gurgling softly to our ears alone.

Evan was not diagnosed with congenital deafness until kindergarten. One day his teacher, Mrs. Graves, lined up all the kids to take their turn in a mysterious booth that had been set up in the common area. The first graders were finishing up and child after child filtered out in five-minute intervals holding green cards in their hand.

What do you do in there?

You just listen and raise your hand when you hear a beep. It's easy.

Evan's little brow furrowed. He would like more information, but it sounded easy enough.

He went in the booth and waited for a very long time for a beep. When he heard the first beep, he raised his hand. After a few more, the man in the white coat told him he was finished and handed him a card.

It was red.

The children stared at him as he walked out of the booth.

What had he done wrong?

He was referred to an audiologist and his parents dutifully took him to the appointment where they confirmed that he had sensorineural hearing loss. The audiologist asked how he was doing in school. He had taught himself to read at age four, his parents boasted. Teachers loved him. So attentive in class, they would say. Just wait and see if he starts struggling in school, the audiologist told them, then they might consider hearing aids. Evan's older sister Tanya had been diagnosed seven years earlier and she was making straight A's. As long as everyone was doing well in school, they could avoid unsightly and expensive hearing aids. Dale got by without them. The kids would be all right.

But the kids were already heading into a different life than their parents had known and getting by would not always be enough.

Evan sat in the front row of class and watched his teacher carefully. He paid close attention to her lips as she spoke and if he lost a lot of the information, he looked for contextual clues to try to fill in what he missed. If she turned her back while talking to write something down, he waited till he could understand her again. Her speech, for him, was full of gaps, ellipses, half-uttered sentences. He would need to fill in those blank spaces with what he could infer or learn on his own. As he got older, he would read every page of the textbook and take reams of notes in careful handwriting. By the end of each day, he collapsed into bed, exhausted.

Once he got to college, Evan began wearing hearing aids and reading poetry. The two experiences emerged together, opening up new ways of being in language. On the one hand, he could now hear more language more clearly. The hearing aids helped a great deal, but they came with their own complications. They sometimes amplified more than he wanted—the sound of a blaring siren, a neighbor thumping in the dorm room above, a radiator drip, the roommate paring his toenails. Other times they failed, running out of batteries in the middle of class or cutting in and out unexpectedly. To make matters worse, his hearing loss did not fit the usual pattern—for some reason, in his family, they lost more low frequencies than high frequencies and standard settings were not designed with this in mind. He was also much younger than the average hearing aid user. All of the marketing and features were geared toward the largest demographics of hearing aid users—the elderly. If he needed a reminder that hearing aids weren't designed for him, he needed to look no further than the brochure that came with that first pair, on which an eighty-year-old man boasted that he could now hear his grandson's piano recital.

Neither of Evan's parents went to college. This could be liberating for Evan in some ways. If they had little guidance to give him on navigating the college experience, they also had few expectations about what he should major in or what classes he should take. When he decided to major in English, they were pleased enough. He might go on to get a law degree or something like that. They didn't foresee that what he was discovering in his English classes would lead him away from the more practical or lucrative career paths that a college education signaled for his family. Instead, what he discovered in his classes was a deep understanding and love of poetry—an ability to interpret the sound and rhythms that poets inscribed on the page and that were not muddied by the troubling intermediary of voices and ears. Whereas Yeats believed the written word was merely a faint echo of the embodied sound of the bardic voice, Evan heard more on the page than he could hear in the world. The writer Gerald Shea describes his own experience of partial hearing as a "language of lyricals"—a poetry of "false phrases that stir the imagination with their nonexistent places and imaginary people."[13] He compares his experience to the language experiments of James Joyce's *Finnegans Wake* with its nonsense phrases, nearly-there syntax, and comprehensive incomprehensibility. To the extent that *Finnegans Wake* has a story, it is a tale of the fall of a man who goes by many names, including Humphrey Chimpden Earwicker. "Impalpabunt, he abhears. The soundwaves are his buffeteers; they trompe him with their trompes; the wave of roary and the wave of hooshed and the wave of hawhawhawrd and the wave of neverheedthemhorseluggarsandlisteltomine."[14] It is a book that pushes language as far as it can go toward incomprehensibility while still keeping one toe grounded in the sounds, patterns, and rules of written and spoken language. Shea goes on to write, "I envy Joyce and other writers the luxury of their deliberate wordplay, for the lyricals of the partially deaf are not conscious poetry, and when they arise in the commerce of necessity they can be a hellish experience. They make of our lives a constant unscrambling of language, punctuated by masquerades of understanding."[15]

For Evan, poems were full of movement, but their movement was contained—they stayed still and let you take your time to understand and know them. You could read and reread a poem until its meaning unfolded for you—a meaning that became richer for the time it took to hear it.

LIKE HIS FATHER, Alexander Graham Bell dabbled in poetry, writing youthful lyrics about the sounds of the blackbird and worshipful odes to Queen Victoria. He liked to pun on his name—bell—as a clarion call to his fellow man. His poems commemorated the passage of time and significant events that passed: a dutiful sonnet to his father in celebration of a birthday and a heartbroken elegy after his brother Melville's early death. In an undated notebook, he composed a short piece called "The Poet":

The Poet is the man
Who feels Nature reflected in himself,
And yearns to give her utterance.
He grieves with the sorrowful;
Rejoices with the glad;
The hearts of others
Beat within his bosom.
The poet's strain sets *mind* to music.[16]

The ideal poet that Bell imagines is very much like Alexander Graham Bell himself. Like the boy creating a speaking machine, the poet wants to make silent Nature speak. He is empathetic, caring for his fellow men so deeply that it veers into a kind of co-opting of their experience as the "hearts of others / Beat within his bosom." He ends with a final suggestive line: "The poet's strain sets *mind* to music." The use of the word "strain" is unexpected here—Bell uses it to refer to the musical strain, a term that comes from the physical act of pulling a stringed instrument taut. It is the physical exertion that allows for the correct musical sound. But by the nineteenth century the more common usage related to heredity. Eugenicists would refer to a noxious strain in the family line: a Jewish strain; an imbecile strain; a deaf strain. A strain was something that could be beautiful, as in music, but even its beauty suggested exertion and struggle. Struggle allows the poet to translate the internal to the external, making sense into sound. "The Poet" is rife with all of Bell's contradictions. It asserts that the great man, inventor or poet, can make silence speak simply by exerting his enormous will.

Seven years into Alexander Graham Bell's marriage to Mabel, after the birth of their two daughters, the now-famous inventor of the telephone sat down to write his *Memoir upon the Formation of a Deaf Variety of the Human Race* (1884). This book brought together Bell's long-standing advocacy of oralism with his emerging investment in eugenics. In it, Bell argued that the marriage of deaf people threatened to produce a new deaf race that would eventually overtake the hearing population. He based his conclusions on a survey of deaf residents of Massachusetts that purported to show deaf men and women having more children than their hearing peers. Bell blamed this tendency of deaf men and women to marry each other on manualist education—deaf students met at school, spoke sign language with each other, and fell in love within the deaf communities that formed around signing. This was, for Bell, a calamity that threatened the human species. The only solution was oralism. If deaf children could be taught to speak and mix with hearing children, they would not marry each other and any recessive genes carrying deafness would dissipate into the general population. It was an argument that capitalized on the scientific sheen of eugenics and tapped into the momentum of similar movements against immigration and miscegenation—the fear that a beleaguered, often white and middle-class population would be overrun by masses of others.

How did a man who was born to one deaf woman and married another end up arguing so forcefully against the propagation of deafness? For one thing, Eliza and Mabel had special status—both were postlingually deaf and were able to speak, even if speech was often difficult. Neither bore the taint of hereditary deafness; they were both deafened by childhood illnesses. And, in any case, Bell's *Memoir* promoted intermarriages such as his and his parents'—the marriage of a hearing man and a deaf woman was, according to his logic, a means of saving the human species and bearing more hearing children, like his and Mabel's two girls. Bell's biographer Katie Booth describes Bell's blend of saviorism and eugenicism as a failure of the imagination: "He got so caught up in the feeling of sympathy that he never veered into empathy; his imagination didn't stretch enough to understand, or even ask, what the deaf themselves wanted; and in the face of rejection and failure, he pushed harder, dug down deeper, argued ever more from a single, fixed point."[17] Bell's melding of oralism and eugenics would have far-reaching consequences, inaugurating an era in American deaf education in which deaf children were forced into endless speech lessons to the detriment of their learning of other subjects, children caught signing were physically punished, and those who could not speak were deemed failures and ostracized by their teachers and speaking peers. Even today, the name of Alexander Graham Bell remains shorthand for oppression and bigotry for members of the Deaf community. If, as he wrote in his poem, the hearts of others beat within his bosom, then this version of sympathy would prove itself to be a cage for many deaf men and women.

I WAS ONE of the lucky few who could take a baby to a museum with no fuss. Willie, wide awake, was observant and interested— watching the colors swirl before her eyes. Willie, asleep, was lulled by the motion of step, step, stop: the anapestic meter of feet shuffling from piece to piece.

Jane flew in from Chicago to see the baby and we were taking cautious sips of the city while she was in town. We had been friends since the days of slap bracelets and scrunchies, both of which were making a comeback. In those days, I was the storyteller and she was the scientist. Our lives, to a remarkable degree, had stayed on course and she was now a gynecologist. Art museums were less her thing, but I thought she might like to see a show at the Cooper Hewitt Museum, a branch of the Smithsonian devoted to design, which was located in a stately former mansion once owned by Andrew Carnegie, facing out onto Central Park. The exhibition was called "Access + Ability." The exhibition focused on adaptable design for people with disabilities. It promised to bring together science and art, which seemed like a promising fusion of our interests. And so Jane, Evan, and I crossed town together to walk through the cool halls of the museum with Willie snuggled tightly into her carrier.

It was a popular exhibition and the crowd seemed to move us from piece to piece at its own pace. First, we glanced at a racing

wheelchair with large back wheels and a sleek body for max-
imum speed. Next, a pair of Nike Velcro shoes designed by a
teenager with cerebral palsy so that he would not need assistance
with the laces. They reminded me of the kind that my brother
Alex liked to wear. When Diesel released a pair of Velcro shoes
for adults in the early 2000s, our mom had bought three pairs,
knowing that it was a fleeting trend and they would disappear
from the stores again soon enough. It was funny to see something so mundane in a museum. All of the objects on display,
from clothes to hardware, were designed in futuristic styles with
metallic chrome details and the smooth, angular features of Ikea
furniture.

The smallest items in the exhibit, where the crowd would
momentarily pause, squinting to make out the text descriptions,
were devices for the deaf. There was a minuscule hearing aid designed to be nearly invisible, followed by a bedazzled hearing aid
covered with Swarovski crystals. The objects raised more questions for me. Was the goal to make hearing aids invisible or to
make them aesthetic objects in their own right? I looked down
at Willie's current pair in their utility gray. What kind of hearing
aids would she want to wear as she got older? Evan tended to
like his on the invisible side—choosing brown aids that hid in
his brown hair. We would soon be able to pick the first pair she
would own. The next pair could be a neutral, camouflaged shade
or a bright color. I planned to split the difference, choosing a
rosy pink that complemented her skin and a glittery ear mold—
just a bit of bling. This was going to be the last pair I picked out
myself; as she gets older, it is likely that Willie will have other
ideas entirely.

The last object we saw at the museum was called a "Sound-
Shirt"—it was a dark blue figure-skimming shirt with light blue
geometric designs on a female mannequin. The placard boasted

that it was embedded with sixteen "micro-actuators," or sensors, that allowed whoever was wearing it to "feel" music. Each of the sixteen sensors corresponded to a different instrument in the orchestra. It promised to allow deaf and hard-of-hearing people to feel a symphony.

I thought of Eliza Bell playing her piano with her ear pressed to the instrument. I thought of her son creating a speaking machine. Our machines were getting better and better, it seemed. But everything in the exhibition looked expensive and, in many cases, difficult to maintain. I wondered who would pay for these devices. Who would mend them when they broke and comfort a frustrated child when they weren't working properly? I thought of the raw materials buried precariously deep in mines, fueling more and more devices. And what was the end goal? Was it to make a deaf person more like a hearing person—or was it to make deafness more aesthetically pleasing? For whom?

We finished up the exhibition. It was getting warm enough to sit outside and so we found a café overlooking Central Park. Willie started to fuss in my lap and so I unzipped the side of the sweater that I had bought for nursing. It was a piece of adaptive technology in its own right, with long zippers down the torso and a loose flap of fabric over the top to discreetly free a breast in public. Willie latched on as I sipped on my tea. The sun warmed my face and the park was showing traces of green buds about to burst forth. Jane was leaving the next day and maternity leave would be over soon; I sipped my drink slowly, wanting this moment to stretch out as long as it could.

WE NEVER TOOK plaster imprints of Willie's feet or hands—the kind that you can frame or turn into an ornament or collect over the years to remember how tiny your now-grown child once

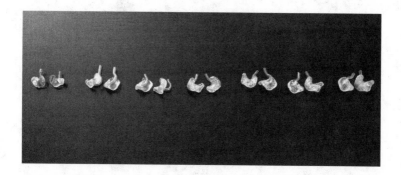

was. Instead, I kept her earmolds. Every time we went to see the audiologist, Holly and her successors would make a new impression. The audiologist filled a large syringe with a pliable green foam, like the kind you use to make a dental impression for a mouth guard, and would squirt it into Willie's ear. I knew from Evan that it was a strange, blocked-up sensation but not painful or uncomfortable. Holly and the other audiologists would send this impression to the hearing aid company, which would send back a clear mold that fit perfectly into Willie's ear. She was growing so fast that she needed new molds every three months. Over time, we had a collection of growing earmolds, each the exact shape of our daughter's ear canal. Look how small she was, I say to Evan as I pull them out and arrange them, one by one, on the table. Look how much she's grown.

As she leaves early infancy, Willie's eyes lose the sky-blue color that awoke to me when she was born and take on the gorgeous, enigmatic hazel of Evan's eyes. As she plumps up, we notice a little dimple appear in her chin, just like Evan's. What little hair starts to sprout is the same towhead blond that he once had. She has her father's eyes, her father's chin, her father's hair. She has her father's ears. There is so much poetry in these repeated lines that I must say them again, quietly, to myself. She has her father's ears.

# 6

# Sweetness

We took pictures of Willie's first taste of solid food. It was a thin gruel of rice cereal. Her pediatrician, Dr. Blanchet, recommended we mix it with a little breast milk to get her started eating solids. She took a bite and gave me a quizzical look. The stuff on her tongue was different than the breast milk she was used to. Grittier and more viscous. It was disappointing, but she did like the feel of the cold spoon on her teething jaws. The wooden bowl in which we served the cereal had an even more interesting texture; she chomped down on its rim, not caring to try any more of the gruel. There were other, more exciting flavors and tactile sensations to explore. The whole time my phone's camera went *click, click, click*. I took so many pictures that I can flip through them rapidly and see her staccato movements like a scene from a stop-motion animated film.

I looked at the pictures while I was at work, more often than I cared to admit. I was there and not there. The workday—with its to-do lists and emails and meetings and events—was overlaid above the mental and physical calls of parenthood. I would drop off Willie at day care on my way in to work, sit down to my computer, and, before I got far into the tasks at hand, my breasts would start to swell and sting and I would need to pump.

The university provided a private space for breastfeeding mothers that was trying its best to feel cozy. I spoke to friends who pumped in closets and bathrooms and knew how fortunate I was to have this space. Some friends gave up breastfeeding entirely when they went back to jobs that didn't provide rooms like this or the luxury of time to step away. We shared stories about trying to pump at work, one hand on a pump and the other typing at a keyboard. Only the lucky ones had a door to shut out intruders. I heard about half-filled bottles, balanced precariously on a lap, falling to the floor of bathroom stalls. I heard about unforgiving schedules and painful blocked milk ducts. About milk supplies that were too low or too high—hours spent at work trying to pump a single six-ounce bottle or an oversupply of milk that soaked through shirts in the middle of meetings or while teaching a class. We talked about a work wardrobe that no longer fit and the costs of clothing a body that seemed to resist button-down shirts or professional-looking fabrics. I counted my blessings that work provided me with a Lactation Room in the law school and gave me a code to sign up for a given time each day. It included a hospital-grade pump, a comfortable pleather chair, a mini fridge for storing pumped milk, and a corkboard where someone had thumbtacked photos of their baby. Three other phantom women used the space and I knew them only through the yellow-white bottles of frothing breastmilk they left in the fridge and the tangling coils of their pumping equipment. I wasn't sure if the corkboard baby belonged to one of these women or was a remainder from a previous occupant. I thought about this woman as I pumped, staring up at her baby. She may have been having trouble producing milk at work. The picture was there to cue her body to another's need, to remind her that, chimera-like, her body was both hers and another's. Did the picture do the trick, or did she shed tears of frustration, breasts stinging, pumping empty air into the expectant lid of the bottle? Did she go home at night with empty bottles, taking long, hot showers to ease the pain of her blocked milk ducts? I had it easier than this spectral woman; I could steal away from work to spend twenty minutes with plastic cups rhythmically sucking milk from my breasts into a storage bottle and leave with bottles filled. I would pull out my phone and scroll through social media to the *whirl, whirl* sound and someone else's baby smiling down at me. Then I would snap my nursing bra back in place, button my shirt, check for leaks, and go back to work.

It had been six months of breastfeeding and pumping and, despite how much better I had it than most, I was ready to stop after one year. I was sick of lugging around a bag of pumping supplies and ice-packed milk, frustrated with the extra time I needed to carve out in my day to keep the milk coming. I was willing to do it for another six months so we could make it to her first birthday. In the meantime, we were introducing an expanding range of solid foods. During work, I scrolled through websites. I read blog posts about "baby-led weaning" that encouraged me to cut pieces of fruit and vegetables into non-choking sizes, perfectly geometrical slivers of grapes and spears of banana, so that my growing baby could try things out and decide what she liked. I loved the pictures of the meticulously plated fruits and vegetables, gleaming on BPA-free nonbreakable platters. Less appealing were the long scrolls of text that followed the beautiful pictures and the rancorous chats that ran on and on below. There was a familiar intensity to the conversations surrounding babies and food. Everything was at such a high pitch: you absolutely *must* introduce peanut butter at a certain age to prevent life-threatening allergies; you should *never* give a child under one year of age honey or they will get botulism. The rules were as baroque and all-encompassing as the pregnancy rules I had half-heartedly followed, cutting out my favorite things like sushi and soft-boiled eggs. I skimmed the baby food blogs and learned just enough to be informed without sinking into a parenting abyss. It reminded me too much of adult diet culture—the rules of good fats and bad fats, carbohydrates and proteins, Whole30s and ke-tones. I had somehow made it through my twenties and most of my thirties without obsessing over my diet and I very much wanted to raise a child who didn't feel the need to obsess over hers.

Willie spent the days at Mother Goose Daycare, which we chose from a vast spreadsheet of childcare options that we got from the university's Office of Work-Life. The day Evan and I went to check it out, a woman answered the door, short and squat with frizzled curls. She looked like she could have been a long-lost aunt. A mezuzah was tacked in its characteristic slant on the doorframe. Before we knocked on this particular door, we had visited a number of other day cares dotting the Upper West Side and Harlem. We felt like Goldilocks dismissing this one as too big, this one as too small, this one as too corporate, this one as too hippy-dippy. Willie was six months old. I had taken three months' parental leave and Evan had taken the next three months' leave, but now we were out of time and needed a plan.

Mother Goose Daycare was an in-home day care, which in New York City meant that the proprietor was huddled together cheek by jowl with her assistants and her charges. The apartment was made up of five small rooms: first a messy kitchen piled high with Tupperware and dishes, which we were quickly guided past; then a playroom of no more than 400 square feet where seven small children played with three teachers; and then, at the back, Mother Goose's private space—a living room, bedroom, and bathroom. The children's playroom, the room that mattered the most as far as we were concerned, was spartan except for a smattering of toys being passed among the children. We were not allowed to linger in this room. It was, evidently, a privilege to be reserved for serious applicants. Instead, we were shown into Mother Goose's private room. This room was as fussy and ornamental as the playroom was functional and spare. Chairs were Victorian in vintage with spindly legs and coarse, velveteen cushions. Each chair was piled with embroidered pillows conveying woodland scenes. Traffic from the street below rattled the decorative china with pastoral scenes, making their shepherds quake before their sheep. She told us about her love for musical theater. She dug out the fact that I was Jewish and Evan was Christian and went into great detail about her love of *Godspell*. She showed us her record collection, talked about which shows she had seen in their first runs. She'd started the day care to support herself and her son after her deadbeat husband left them high and dry. Her son was in medical school. He was going to be a doctor. Raised by a single mom in the city. And look how well he turned out. He was going to be a doctor. She repeated the fact, offering it as a reference.

We made calls afterward, did our due diligence, but I liked her protectiveness, her quirky, musical-inspired ecumenism, and, mostly, her maternal fierceness. It seemed as good a spot as any we'd seen. From Monday through Thursday, that's where Willie would go, playing side by side with other babies as they stacked blocks and learned to babble to each other. To ensure that the other children wouldn't pull at her hearing aids, we dressed her in snug little bonnets that made her look like a nineteenth-century Quaker. It seemed like we had a plan. We thought it might even last.

HAVE YOU NOTICED anything different?

Drop-off at Mother Goose's was always rushed, with the handful of parents in the crowded hallway jostling babies out of jackets and shoes, handing over diapers, pumped milk, and cubes of pureed pears and sweet potatoes. We had made it past Willie's first birthday and I was no longer pumping milk, so drop-off was smoother now, without the need to hand off ice-packed bottles of breastmilk. Otherwise the routine remained the same with variations for the seasons. Winter boots subbed in for jelly sandals. Willie was riding the tail end of a bad virus of some sort. She came down with a terrible fever on her birthday and we had taken her to the doctor; she recovered quickly and now just had the run-of-the-mill kid-in-day-care runny nose that she couldn't quite shake. But that wasn't what I was concerned about. Something else was not quite right. I wanted to know if anyone else had noticed.

I told Mother Goose that Willie was coming home very thirsty and overnight she was soaking through her diapers. Mother Goose looked taken aback. She hadn't noticed anything. Willie seemed fine. She shook her head as another child was handed to her. It wasn't happening during the day, she told me. Her diapers were normal and she wasn't drinking more than usual.

I went in to work and asked the same question to a new colleague. She had a young son Willie's age and always seemed to know more than I did. Her mother had recently moved from West Africa to help with the childcare. I knew that they had challenges of their own—not enough space and a husband working his way through a challenging graduate program—but I found myself idealizing their arrangement and wishing for a family member at home helping with Willie's care, even if we would end up nipping at each other's heels all the time. When Willie was sick, my new colleague came to work with homeopathic drops of peppermint, juniper berry, and eucalyptus for me to scatter on the mattress of her crib and help her breathe.

I asked if her son ever soaked through his diapers.

She told me that he never had. Maybe Willie had grown out of her current diaper size? What if we went ahead and bought the next size up? See if that helps? Her voice was reassuring but her eyes looked worried.

That night, I woke up at 3 a.m. unable to sleep. I pulled out my phone and opened up WebMD's symptom tracker. I selected Willie's age—one year old, the smallest integer I could select—and her gender.

I selected the symptoms from a drop-down menu. Needs to pee all the time. Pees a lot overnight. Increased thirst.

Looking through the possible symptom matches, I started to rule them out in my head. A urinary tract infection came up as a "fair match," but that wouldn't explain her thirst. She did not seem sick enough for it to be appendicitis (another "fair match")—she was not nauseated or vomiting or refusing to eat. If anything, she was hungrier than usual.

There was one match that lodged firmly in my mind and that I was not able to shake off or dismiss.

Diabetes Mellitus. Moderate Match.

I scrolled through the description with a ringing in my ears. Symptoms included extreme thirst, dry mouth, and frequent urination. Willie had seemed tired lately, but she was also getting over a cold and it seemed like a normal reaction to a normal sickness. The bad virus that had struck her on her birthday had since passed. On that day, we had invited family members and friends to come celebrate, but our guests ended up socializing without her in a sad multipurpose room in our building, eating the brisket and sides that we had bought for the occasion, while my mom, dad, Evan, and I took turns sitting with her, taking her temperature, and pushing fluids between long, labored naps. But, since then, she seemed to be back to her usual energy level. She was not cranky or out of sorts. She had always been a good sleeper and continued to sleep well. Was it fatigue that made her such a good sleeper? She did look thinner to me, but she was also morphing from babydom to toddlerdom, pulling herself up more often, walking a few steps at a time while clinging to an outstretched hand. She had taken some of her first steps that month and was getting around on her feet more often, shuffling from my leg to Evan's arms with more confidence. All that up and down and here and there could have accounted for losing the butterball roundness of her baby shape. Wasn't this a normal part of growing and moving more? I tried to fit "diabetes mellitus" into the narrative I had built around her changing shape. Was I paranoid, or did her face look slightly wan; not just thinner, but perhaps a deeper hollowing out that I should have noticed before? I could dismiss other symptoms: her breath did not, as far as I could tell, smell fruity—a sign of accumulating sugar in her bloodstream—nor was it heavy or labored. And yet, I couldn't shake the idea that she might have diabetes, far-fetched as it seemed. Why else was she so thirsty? Why else was she urinating so much? The word "diabetes" continued to ring into the night as an internal alarm that I could not dismiss. From WebMD, I followed a tortuous path from website to website looking for confirmation. The Mayo Clinic. Cleveland Clinic. The NIH. The CDC. When I saw Evan's eyelids begin to flutter at 6 a.m., I woke him up.

We need to take Willie to the doctor. Today.

Dr. Blanchet was as unflappable as usual when I took Willie to see her that morning. Evan was supposed to be teaching that day, but he asked if I wanted him to come with me. I said no. I was embarrassed by my own fear and the distinct possibility that I might be overreacting, succumbing to maternal paranoia. As worried as I was about Willie, I was also afraid of becoming one of those hysterical moms, the kind who calls the doctor's office late in the night over imagined symptoms. If I admitted that I wanted him to cancel his class, I would be accepting this as the emergency that some deep part of me knew it to be.

When Dr. Blanchet saw us and I told her my theory, she was skeptical. She asked for Willie's symptoms and all I could say was that she was thirsty and wetting her diapers. Dr. Blanchet spoke with a Parisian accent that was both reassuring and maddeningly cool. Willie was very young for diabetes. It is very unlikely, she tutted, especially with no family history. Children at seven, eight come in with diabetes. But thirteen months, no. And those who do come in young are very, very sick. Willie is well, is she not? I looked at Willie playing with the stethoscope that Dr. Blanchet had handed her. She pressed the stethoscope's cool metal diaphragm to her cheek and let out a small coo of surprise. She doesn't seem sick, I agreed. It is very unlikely, Dr. Blanchet repeated, but she would test her.

And here is how I remember the next moments.

Dr. Blanchet is opening the door briskly. I know by the abruptness of her entry that it is not good news. She is telling me that I am right. Willie has diabetes. I ask if she is sure. Yes, she is sure. We need to go to the emergency room now.

I am standing on the corner of Broadway and Eighty-Sixth Street with Willie in my carrier trying to hail a cab. No one is stopping. I hate this city. I hate it. I am angry at the pedestrians who pass in a hurry and don't give a damn. At the cabs that don't stop. At myself for being here at all.

I do not cry.

I am very, very angry.

We arrive at the hospital and I tell the receptionist that my daughter was just diagnosed with diabetes. She looks at me askance. How old is she? Thirteen months. What she sees is a mother coming at her like a comet with a healthy baby in her arms. Okay, she says, slowly, we need to take a blood test. They show me to a nurse who takes one of Willie's tiny fingers in her hands and wipes it with a small square of an alcohol swab. She pinches the tip of Willie's finger to warm it up and get the blood to rise to the surface. Then she takes out a small lancet and pricks her finger. Willie doesn't seem to mind but watches intently as a small bubble of blood rises to the tip. The nurse touches a test strip to the blood bubble and it soaks the small surface. I look at the meter. It lights up in red. The number is 557. The number means nothing to me, but the red light tells me everything that I need to know.

Suddenly everyone around us is moving fast.

I don't remember anything else about that day.

THE EARLIEST WRITTEN descriptions of diabetes appear in Greek texts from the second century A.D. Ancient physicians documented the extreme thirst and constant urination, which were the first signs of the fatal disease. After these first signs, the patient would begin melting away—losing weight while remaining insatiably thirsty, letting off a sweet odor, and eventually succumbing to a fatal coma. The word "diabetes" derives from the Greek for "siphon," and the Greek physician Aretaeus of Cappadocia described it as a "mysterious illness" in which "the flesh and limbs melt into urine."[1] From that point, until the early twentieth century, physicians, patients, and family members could only watch passively as the disease ran its terrible course. Through the nineteenth and early twentieth centuries, physicians were able to keep diabetics alive for a few more years at most by severely limiting their diet. Pre-insulin diabetic diets included an oat cure, a milk diet, a rice cure, potato therapy, and others.[2] Medical historian Michael Bliss speculates that there "may be a direct link between these early fads in diet therapy for diabetes and popular fad diets of the late twentieth century."[3] The most effective diet was the "starvation diet" developed by Frederick Allen at the Rockefeller Institute.[4] Images of diabetic patients in the pre-insulin era are gruesome. Skeletal children who were deliberately underfed because it was the only way to keep the disease at bay: withholding food from a starving child to maintain a weak pulse of life. This hideous treatment would buy a patient a few more years at most while they subsisted on small rations of thrice-boiled vegetables, flavorless rusks, dairy, and meat.

In one of the photographs from the pre-insulin era, a dark-eyed mother holds her emaciated son in her arms. His face is a mask of pain, head tilted upward, eyes squinting, and mouth open in a silent cry. His age is impossible to tell, but judging by his length, he may be three years old. One slim hand is wrapped around his mother's neck. The other seems to clasp her wrist. He wears only underwear and you can count the ribs on his body, see the sharp elbow bone that cuts into the blank space of the photograph. I imagine this mother tasked with weighing all the food that she will feed her son to make sure that her dying child does not eat an ounce more than the doctor prescribed. I hear the child's pleas in her ear, asking for more, and her voice—the voice of a good mother—telling him no. Her dark eyes stare directly at the camera; there is a flash of fear and, behind that fear, an almost imperceptible fury.

It was not until the late nineteenth century that scientists first identified the pancreas as the organ responsible for diabetes. They removed the pancreas from a dog and discovered that the dog immediately became diabetic.[5] From there, it took extensive further research to locate an internal secretion in the pancreas, in mysterious cells that a German medical student had discovered twenty years earlier and named the Islets (Islands) of Langerhans.[6] In the twentieth century, endocrinology was emerging as a new specialty as doctors began to better understand the role of hormones in the body's various functions, from digestion to reproduction. These breakthroughs led two scientists at the University of Toronto, Frederick Banting and Charles Best, to identify insulin as the missing hormone responsible for diabetes and to begin working with pharmaceutical company Eli Lilly and Company to make it commercially available for diabetic patients in 1922.

Insulin functions like a key that opens the blood cells so that glucose can enter the bloodstream and provide bodies with energy. Without this key, the body cannot metabolize food. Unused glucose accumulates in the bloodstream and is passed in the urine without being used by the body. In order to produce insulin in the quantities that would be necessary to treat diabetics throughout North America, not to mention around the world, the University of Toronto partnered with the Indianapolis-based Eli Lilly. The contract gave Lilly a temporary exclusive contract to produce insulin, during which time it would sell it at cost.[7] In the years since this agreement, the cost of insulin has skyrocketed in the United States, rising more than 300 percent over the last twenty years.[8] A recent study found that 14.1 percent of diabetics experienced "catastrophic spending," meaning that they devoted 40 percent or more of their family income on the drug alone.[9] Recent measures to cap prices have brought needed relief, but the cost of insulin continues to be a global concern.

At the hospital, we were handed a child's activity book explaining diabetes. Willie was too young for it, but I leafed through the glossy pages. It was published by Eli Lilly in collaboration with Disney and features a jaunty monkey named Coco who loves to play soccer and who, after being diagnosed with T1D, must learn to manage her diabetes. On one page, Coco holds a giant key that is labeled "Insulin" and explains that this key unlocks cells that allow our body to turn food into energy. Coco is a very energetic monkey. She is a good little monkey who eats healthy foods and keeps track of what she eats. She takes her shots without complaining because she knows they help give her energy. With insulin, exercise, and a proper diet, Coco can do anything she wants to do. Coco plays soccer. Coco scores the winning goal. Mickey, Goofy, and Pluto celebrate the win. Go, Team Coco!

It was meant to be uplifting, but I couldn't help feeling sorry for that little monkey. I was glad she scored her goal, but I wished for a missing page in the book, on which she could tell Mickey that sometimes she felt bad, that she and her family worried about how they would afford the insulin that she would need to live out the rest of her life. I wondered if, looking ahead to her teenage years, she would feel trapped and scared and angry. And who would she confide in then? Could she tell her monkey-mother that sometimes she was still really, really angry? And would it be possible for her monkey-mother to hold her in her arms and whisper back that she too carried a tight ball of anger in her chest and that it was never going to go away?

ON THE WAY to the ER, I called Evan and he ran out of his class and joined me as fast as he could. After a few frantic hours in the ER, we were taken to another hospital room in New York-Presbyterian.

It was like birth in reverse, returning to the same hospital where Willie was born. I had failed her and now we were back to try all over again. It was impossible to be gentle with myself: I had failed the most basic part of parenting, keeping a child fed and healthy. The food I had carefully researched, prepared, and packed for her every day was leaking into her blood, filling it with sugars that her body could not use. She was starving and I, her mother, hadn't noticed. We were back at the hospital where she had been born a year and a month ago. As then, we arrived in a rush of panic, but now there was also a deep sadness beneath that fear. In the intervening time, I thought I had learned how to take care of this child, but now I was starting all over again. We were placed in a room with no view that we shared with another family; the two parts of the room were divided by a flimsy curtain. The hospital crib was enormous—nothing like the small bassinet that the nurse had wheeled close to my hospital bed when Willie was born. This crib was large and foreboding and Willie looked tiny tucked up on her side, snoring softly. She wore a blue hospital sock on her arm to keep her from pulling out the needles that were piercing her skin, supplying her body with hydration. I thought back to how she'd looked when they first handed her to me—so small and red and fiery. And now we were back.

Willie still had a cold when she was admitted and was considered contagious, so they put us in a room with another girl who was contagious with something or another. There was a big sign on the door with the word "CONTAGIOUS" emblazoned across it. Two endocrinologists came in wearing layers of protective gear: masks, face shields, gloves. Their names were Dr. Stein and Dr. Ferreira.

We were very lucky, Dr. Stein told us. It is very rare for a baby to be diagnosed with Type 1 Diabetes. The median age of diagnosis is a full decade later—around twelve years old—and some

Type 1 diabetics do not show symptoms until they are in their thirties or forties. This wasn't the lucky part, of course. The lucky part was that she was not in a coma. Did they know what caused it? They did not, but genetics and environment each played a role. An individual who becomes diabetic must first have a genetic predisposition for the disease, but the disease itself is triggered by the body's immune system attacking its own beta cells as a faulty response to a virus. The kind that Willie had on her first birthday. Usually when a child this young comes in with diabetes, she has already sustained major damage to her body. We usually don't know that they are sick until they are critically ill.

They handed Evan and me a thick binder. We would need to stay in the hospital for about a week. They would not let us leave until we were ready to manage her diabetes on our own. We would need to read and understand everything in the binder before we could leave.

Dr. Stein was impressed that we both had PhDs, even if they were in the humanities. We seemed smart, like we'd be able to pick this up, but it was a lot to learn and it would take time.

Evan and I studied the binder like we were preparing for an exam. The binder included tabs labeled: "Overview," "Insulin," "Nutrition," "Logs," "School," "Exercise," "Family life." It began with an introductory page: "In order to manage diabetes we will teach you how to check your blood glucose, count carbohydrates, and take insulin by injection." From there, the binder got into more technical detail with the names of the different types of insulin and their role in regulating blood sugar. We would give Willie a shot of long-acting insulin once a day to keep some insulin in her system throughout the day, while we would need to give her rapid-acting insulin every time she ate to respond to the glucose in the meal. Between the two types of insulin, we would be replicating the functions of a working pancreas, keeping a base level of insulin in her system at all times and also producing quick bursts of additional insulin to respond to her food intake. The binder included explanations of where to give insulin—fatty spots like the belly and back of the arm—and how to properly dispose of used needles. There were food pyramids and annotated diagrams of nutrition labels; resources for measuring food and suggestions for healthy snacks; handouts for support groups and clinical studies; advertisements for medical alert bracelets and diabetes camps; templates for school medical plans and babysitter instructions.

A separate page included a checklist for toddlers with diabetes. The checklist instructed us that a "caregiver is to perform all diabetes-related tasks for the toddler." At the hospital, we were meant to learn those tasks. Someday we would teach them to Willie so she could do them herself.

Every three hours, we would call for the nurse, who would walk us through our new routine. First, we needed to test her blood sugar. We found out that Willie preferred us to prick her toes rather than her hands. We set the lancet to its lightest setting—1, as small a prick as possible for toes that were impossibly tiny. We took her readings every three hours, including overnight. The hospital was so cold at night that sometimes blood would not rise to the surface of her toes when we pricked them. We raised the setting—1, 2, 3—and finally, a bubble of blood would rise to the surface. Sometimes she would sleep through the prickings and sometimes she would not, waking with a howl of surprise and betrayal.

If the readings revealed that her blood sugar was low, we would give her juice so she wouldn't become hypoglycemic. Sometimes it was very low and I would shout for Evan to grab the juice. The little straw with its needlelike point had a way of being impossible to insert quickly when it was most needed. If her blood sugar was high, we would give her more insulin. The nurse watched patiently as we learned to wipe the insulin pen with an alcohol pad to ensure it was sterile. We would then twist a needle onto the top until we heard a slight click. Each time we prepped the needle, we were told to discard two units of insulin to make sure there were no air bubbles in the syringe and to make sure that the pen and needle were working. We watched spray after spray of expensive insulin go down the sink. Willie was sometimes patient with the shots. We discovered that she preferred them in her stomach or the fatty pad at the back of her upper arm. If we tried to give her one on her bottom, she shrieked and twisted away. One of us would hold her in our lap, distracting her with a toy or a queued-up video on our phones. The other would squeeze the fat on her tummy between our finger and thumb and gently, quickly, press the needle into her skin. Within a few days her stomach and arms were dotted with puncture marks. She needed around five shots a day. She would continue to need about five shots a day. The shots would not end when we left the hospital. The shots would go on and on and on. What we were doing at the hospital was not the exception, it was the new routine; we would need to do this every day when we got home. Finger sticks every three hours. Pumping her with juice to ward off disaster. Prepping needle after needle. Giving shot after shot.

I had to relearn my child's body language, interpreting her cues to understand a body that was not my own but that I needed to respond to as if it was. Willie showed almost no outward signs of hypoglycemia, which, we were told, involves sweatiness, dizziness, and irritability. At one point, we gave her a finger-stick test that revealed her blood sugar was dangerously low. We ran for a juice box and prayed that she would suck it down as fast as possible. She looked up from her toy, a brightly colored pop-up box that played music when she pressed a button and a small plastic monkey, lion, hippo, or elephant launched out. She squealed with surprise and glee when she saw that she was getting juice. According to her glucose reading, she should have felt very weak and exhausted, nearing the point of passing out. She blinked at me with merry eyes, thrilled to be getting an Elmo-themed box of fruit punch. Sometimes she was tired or cranky and her blood sugar came back high or low and we could retroactively imagine this had affected her energy and mood. But that was rarely the case.

"You're tough stuff," I told her, cradling her in my lap as Evan disposed of the used needle in the hospital sharps bin. But I also wondered when this incessant poking and prodding was going to wear her down. It was already wearing me down. She could not tell me how she felt in words, but only in the eclectic language of one-year-olds: unexpected fussiness or refusal to do something she otherwise enjoyed.

My mom arrived at the hospital within two days. She was big-eyed and edgy, eager to study everything there was to know and refusing to be overwhelmed by the enormity of the task. She wanted us to explain everything—what does this do, and this, and this. She counted every carbohydrate with us and helped prep the needles to give her granddaughter the insulin she needed to live. She woke up every three hours for Willie's finger-stick tests even though I told her over and over again that she didn't have to. She drove me crazy. I saw that she was channeling her nervousness into mastering all the minutia, into getting it right. The mom instincts were firing on all cylinders and she was trying to master every detail as a way of caring for Willie and caring for me. It annoyed me in part because she made me see that I had been doing the exact same thing. She was simply two days behind me in her obsessive reading of the binder, in her ambition to calculate mealtime math and proper dosages like there was an exam coming up and she would get an A+. Seeing her doing all the things that I was doing made me frustrated with her and myself. There was no test at the end of this all. No one was going to pat us on the back for being so quick and clever.

In quieter moments, we talked about what it was like being a parent with a child in the hospital. She asked me if I remembered Alex's scoliosis surgery when he was sixteen. I told her that going to visit him, when I was six, was one of the clearest memories of my childhood. I remembered the cartoon characters on the wall of the children's ward and the boxes of rooms with sad children and sadder parents who were too wrapped up in their own pain to notice anything else. Alex had almost died in surgery. He was scared in the hospital, which manifested as anger, and he bit his own hands so hard that he drew blood. And yet now, he talks about his time in the hospital with great fondness—he is proud to have had surgery and stayed at a hospital. He reaches over his shoulder and gestures toward his back where a deep pink scar runs like a jagged canyon across the freckled landscape. But I remember it as a time when one of us went over into an unfamiliar world and came back different. My mother remembers it through the pain and fear and panic of a child's near death. Speaking of Alex's surgery, it was the first time we realized that our experiences of motherhood were going to be more alike than we could have imagined. Like her, I would have to fight for every moment, holding disaster at bay like the Dutch boy with his finger in the dam. I would also need to wrestle the sentries of bureaucracy to keep up with insurance, medications, appointments, and, eventually, school medical accommodations. Like her, I would probably struggle my whole life trying to master something that was, at its core, insurmountable. It was a sad way to realize that I had, against all odds, become very much like my mother.

Dr. Stein promised that this would soon feel like a normal part of life for us and for Willie.

It was meant to make us feel better. It was a life sentence, but it was also a life. Without the insulin, Willie would not have had that. I tried to be grateful, but no gratitude could withstand the cruel pressure against my daughter's soft skin as I punctured it with the needle that would let her live.

WITH THE DISCOVERY of insulin treatment, diabetes transformed from an acute to a chronic illness. People no longer needed to die from it—at least, they didn't die right away. If they had access to insulin and carefully managed their diet, they could live a long life with the disease. But this miracle came with strings attached. In Chris Feudtner's study of the first generation of insulin-dependent children, he writes movingly about the personal, social, and financial costs of managing diabetes. Feudtner describes the "bittersweet consequences of this transformation," as diabetes management turned into a constant battle against a fresh set of symptoms that emerged once diabetes became a chronic illness.[10] Now that diabetics were living longer, they were also experiencing terrible side effects from a lifetime of elevated blood sugar, including blindness, kidney failure, limb amputation, heart failure, and stroke. Compounding these existing risks, pregnancy for Type 1 diabetics was a life-threatening ordeal for both parent and child. The miracle elixir itself was potentially fatal; too much insulin produces hypoglycemia, leading to confusion, shakiness, nausea, and, if untreated, seizures, coma, and even death.

The origins of diabetic management in America began in the offices of Dr. Elliott P. Joslin in Boston, Massachusetts. Joslin instructed patients and their families that they must carefully manage their diet, weighing and measuring everything they ate and calibrating their insulin to their food intake. A New England puritan at heart, Joslin urged patients to adopt a fastidious and controlled diet, and to inject themselves with carefully calibrated doses of insulin multiple times a day. This is still, by and large, the dominant method for diabetic management.[11] Three key terms developed in the medical discourse surrounding diabetes: management, control, and responsibility.[12] Feudtner describes the social costs of this approach: "All these methods to manage diabetes have entailed work—unremitting labor that has come in many forms for patients and family members alike, shaping their days and molding their interpersonal interactions."[13] For very young children with diabetes, this labor is performed by parents. In many households, this medical care work falls disproportionately on women.

How did this happen to Willie, and why had it happened when she was so young? I both wanted and didn't want to know the causes. Willie's diagnosis, Type 1 Diabetes, also known as juvenile diabetes or insulin-dependent diabetes, generally begins in childhood and involves the sudden and complete failure of the pancreas to produce its own insulin. Type 2 Diabetes, on the other hand, more often occurs in older people and is caused by the pancreas's eventual inability to produce enough insulin. It happens when the pancreas can no longer meet the body's needs for insulin production. And yet, despite this definition of two types, there is really a broad spectrum of diabetes, including gestational diabetes, which can be triggered by pregnancy, and other, less well-understood forms of diabetes that are monogenic rather than polygenic (they represent a mutation on a single

gene rather than multiple genes)—these are called neonatal diabetes mellitus (NDM) and maturity-onset diabetes of the young
(MODY). Without further genetic testing, the doctors could not
rule out that Willie might have one of these rarer forms of diabetes, given her young age. Her antibody test came back, im-
probably, negative; testing the blood, they did not see the telltale
signs of an elevated immune response. I asked if it was possible
that she didn't have diabetes at all, that her high glucose level
was just a fluke or related to something else. No, I was told, she
had diabetes—that much was clear—and no matter what kind of
diabetes she had, we would be treating it with insulin.

As Willie's endocrinologist had told us, the main causes for
Type 1 Diabetes were genetics and environment, but this didn't
help me understand what had triggered the disease in Willie. Dr.
Stein seemed reluctant to speculate about causes—she wanted
us to focus on the more pressing issue of managing the disease.
So, of course, I went online where I found a range of theories
for causation and speculations about why more very young children seemed to be diagnosed now than ever before. Every piece I
read, no matter how half-baked or conspiratorial, pricked me in
a sensitive place. There were so many things I might have done
wrong. One controversial theory was that introducing cow's
milk too early might trigger the body's autoimmune response
due to the child's body responding to the insulin from the cow
as a foreign threat. It was the kind of theory perfectly poised
for maternal guilt; every hesitation I had experienced about my
decision to stop breastfeeding came soaring back into my mind.
Even though Willie was a year old by the point that I stopped
breastfeeding and introduced cow's milk into her diet—not under six months, like the subjects in the studies I read—it still
made me feel like I had made a fatal mistake.[14] I had replaced my
breastmilk with a foreign milk. Here was an article staring me in

the face telling me that I might have made a catastrophically bad choice. Even worse were the articles that attributed the rise of babies and toddlers with diabetes to the fact that they might be experiencing too much good hygiene.[15] All the efforts that we, as a society, had put into keeping our babies healthy had backfired and foreign viruses were wreaking havoc on immune systems that were no longer prepared for them. It was an ironic punishment for all those good, middle-class mothers who fought so hard to ward off infections and to keep their kids healthy and safe. The babies were now too healthy. Good health and too much care was making them sick.[16]

In her study of diabetes and race in America, Arleen Marcia Tuchman argues that when the rates of diabetes first began to rise in the twentieth century, it was considered a scourge of modernity, a product of urban comforts and middle-class lassitude. Diabetes was first labeled a *Judenkrankheit,* or "Jewish disease," and used to stereotype Jews as obese, lazy, and undisciplined. Dr. Joslin argued against a genetic basis for diabetes in Jews but, instead, attributed the prevalence to what he saw as an indolent lifestyle: "The Jew, in my opinion, is not prone to diabetes because he is a Jew, but rather because he is fat."[17] Later, this stereotype would morph into an insidious typology for understanding the prevalence of diabetes among Black, Hispanic, and Native American men and women. Tuchman argues that we ought to consider diabetes as a spectrum of disorders rather than a disease with two discrete types, and that the categorization of different types of diabetes often reflects American attitudes toward racial difference.[18] Among parents of children with diabetes, perhaps particularly white, middle-class parents, there is a quickness to distinguish a Type 1 diabetic from a Type 2 diabetic. Now that Type 2 Diabetes is on the rise among children, this tendency to differentiate has become stronger. T1D is both the "bad," most unforgiving form of diabetes but also, through a moralistic lens, the "good" type—the type that happens to good people who have done all the right things. I noticed this tendency in myself. I wanted to remind people that Willie is a *Type 1* diabetic and explain that I hand-pureed organic fruits and vegetables for her, that I gave her perfectly portioned spears of cucumber and melon so that she wouldn't choke. But if the "hygiene hypothesis" is correct, then it is this very tendency to control against danger and risk that created the conditions for a backfiring immune system. If this is the case, then the parents whose children have Type 1 Diabetes and parents whose children have Type 2 Diabetes are equally products of our environment. Whether we live in a food desert or buy organic groceries, our environments trigger the disease. I was never told that I did something wrong, the way that parents of children with Type 2 Diabetes are often made to feel responsible for childhood obesity or other factors that contribute to this type of diabetes in children. I was not shamed for the way that I cared for my child; in fact, I was lavished with praise for catching the disease as early as I did and insisting on getting Willie tested. And yet, I do not believe that I was any more or less responsible for having a child with diabetes than a parent of a child with Type 2 Diabetes; we were all in the same leaky vessel, even if we rarely recognized each other.

Dr. Stein reassured us that we did nothing wrong. She praised us for catching it so early. Usually when a child comes in at this age with diabetes they are already in the late stages of diabetic ketoacidosis (DKA). They give off a fruity smell like rotting apples and their organs have already begun to fail them. We were vigilant. We were lucky. The week at the hospital was ending and I took Dr. Stein's card and added it to the file of our ever-widening array of specialists that would make their rounds at the hospital to introduce themselves (endocrinologists, educational nurses, dieticians, and geneticists). We would add these specialists to our pile of doctor's cards alongside the audiologists, speech therapists, dentists, and pediatricians.

Handing us the binder of information with graphs and cartoons and instructional captions explaining the disease and its management, Dr. Stein turned to us confidentially and with added emphasis. She told us that it was most likely that one of us would need to quit our job to manage Willie's care full time. When Willie turned three years old, she would be eligible for services through the schools, but she was not old enough yet. Unless we could afford a full-time nurse or nanny who could be trained in diabetic care, we would not be able to keep her in day care and would not be able to continue working.

She looked from Evan to me. Her look rested for a fraction of a second longer on my face than on his.

We moved to an empty room that had freed up on the floor below. More specialists came in with more options for us to consider. Two geneticists pulled up chairs next to Willie's crib. They were interested in whether Willie might have one of the rarer forms of diabetes. They wanted to do a full genetic workup. They explained that it would be very simple. They would just need some blood. Suddenly the two figures wrapped in white jackets, the one tall and pale, the other short and dark, appeared like stalking vampires before my eyes. Blood, blood, blood. They told me that the additional blood work would help them know more about Willie's genetic profile. They wondered if there was a link between her hearing loss and her diabetes. I explained the prevalence of hearing loss in Evan's family and the fact that no one we knew in either of our families had diabetes. I asked them whether the genetic information would change her treatment. Would we be able to forego insulin shots or prevent any other side effects? No, they said, maybe when she was older and could take an oral form of insulin, but it wouldn't change her treatment now when she was so young. And so, good patient as I had always been, I said no. This night, at least, I wouldn't be inviting the vampires in.

WE TOOK ALL of our things out of a hall closet—throwing out debris from single life that we had not touched since Willie was born: tennis rackets and picnic baskets and unused wrapping paper. We gave away Willie's baby things that she didn't need anymore: a rocking baby swing, a play mat, and clothes that no longer fit. My sister Jenny arrived with four bags from the Container Store full of multicolored storage bins and a label maker. We set to work labeling the new bins that would go in the cleared-out closet: "Needles," "Alcohol wipes," "Glucose testing," "OTC medications," "Emergency." Another bin went in the refrigerator: "Insulin." In the butter drawer of the refrigerator, we stuck a backup supply of Glucagon, a medication that triggers the liver to release stored glucose. We stuck a card to the refrigerator that said, "In case of diabetic coma, Glucagon is in the refrigerator." We scrawled a note in pencil on the other side: "Small child, use ½ dose."

While Willie napped, I sat at the kitchen table and filled out form after form for my Family Emergency Medical Leave. I answered the occasional email from work, always sent with a million apologies for disturbing me; the events that I had planned for the spring were marching forward without me and they needed to know what had and hadn't been done yet. Had catering been confirmed? Did the speakers know where they needed to go? Were the necessary forms signed? I forwarded emails, sent files, and knew, even while we were all pretending it was

a short-term leave, that I was forwarding myself into obsolescence. I was performing the rhythms of a job that was technically still mine, while everyone knew I was slowly unraveling the
threads that tied me to my work.

Dr. Stein asked us to keep logs of everything Willie ate. She
was still learning how Willie's body processed the insulin and we
would need to carefully track her food consumption to settle on
the right dosage. We would start out with 0.5 units of insulin per
10 grams of carbs. She gave us a schedule.

8 a.m.: Breakfast. Insulin.

10 a.m.: Snack. Low carb. Avoid giving more insulin.

Noon: Lunch. Insulin.

1 p.m.: Nap.

3 p.m.: Low-carb snack.

6 p.m.: Dinner. Insulin.

7 p.m.: Give daily long-acting insulin.

The logs were full of crossed-out entries where Willie ate a
few bites and then decided she didn't want more. Food that was
thrown on the floor. Our hesitations and second-guesses on how
much she ate and how many carbohydrates were in the meal.
Sometimes we were thorough and precise, other times rushed
and harried and incomplete in our note-taking. Some entries
were entirely in my hand, others were in Evan's, and, most often,
they were in a combination of his precise letters and my eccen-
tric scrawls. My mother's handwriting appeared on and off as
she came a week here and a week there to lend a hand. These
logs are a record of parenting a thirteen-month-old with diabetes. They remind me of the baby album that I made for Willie in

fits and starts. I began with high ambitions and was thorough in recording the first time she lifted her head or the first articulate "dada" and then, later, lapsed for months, forgetting to record the first time she sat up or her first step. But this was before. Now the logs had taken over any other baby albums.

I took medical leave. Because we had the same employer and Evan had taken parental leave within the year, we could not both take leave now. So, during much of the day, I was the one who fed her and bathed her and played with her and pricked her and pricked her and pricked her. She did not often protest, but I hated to be the one who was doing this to her. To see all the prick marks that were dotting her belly and her arms. Sometimes I would hit a blood vessel and the prick would bleed. Sometimes I hit a painful nerve and she would cry out. It was like being home with a newborn again—but now I was up every three hours to check her blood sugar instead of every three hours to breast-feed. And now, instead of three months of maternity leave before returning to work, I was looking at an indeterminate amount of time and uncertain prospects ahead. It would be two years before Willie was school-aged and eligible for a full-time nurse provided by the Department of Education. She could not stay at Mother Goose because day care staff were prohibited from giving medication and she was now considered a medical liability. I emailed the Office of Work-Life and asked if they had any ideas for childcare that would allow me to keep my job. They did not respond to me. Only when Evan followed up did we get a cursory response: they did not know of any options. It seemed that Work and Life were not so compatible after all. At least for me. Theoretically, Evan could give up his job, but where would that leave us? We were living in faculty housing. Without his job we'd be homeless on top of everything else. It was clear that I would need to leave my job. The job that was itself a backup plan when my first career fell apart. And then what? Would that make me a stay-at-home mom? And for how long?

My ANNUAL EXAM with Dr. Patel was coming up. I would be going back to the hospital for myself this time. A wellness visit. Evan would watch Willie on his own. He wasn't as comfortable watching her alone yet as I was. It still felt like a two-man job to him. I had set sail without him, becoming not only the default parent but the default nurse as well. He was still depending too much on me to help; I didn't always have him there like he had me.

I sat on the familiar crinkly white paper of the hospital bed and waited for Dr. Patel to arrive. As I sat, looking down at my socks with the holes in their heels that I ought to replace, I remembered all the other times I was here. Pregnant, not pregnant, pregnant again. I thought about all the dashed hopes and new hopes and the endless cycle of desire and disappointment. By the time Dr. Patel came in, I was swimming in a sea of memories. This was a routine visit for her and she was warm and congenial as she made small talk to distract me from the speculum's metallic pinch during the pelvic exam and checked on the location of my IUD. How is Willie doing? Did I have any pictures? With the exam finished and all clear, I showed her one of Willie where she didn't look too ill. I told her how Willie had been diagnosed with diabetes. My eyes filled up and my voice was thick with emotion. Dr. Patel looked at me with a flash of pity. She was kind, but busy and ready to get on to the next patient. She had done her part, had delivered a healthy baby. The rest was on me.

Coming out of the hospital, I took a deep breath and tried to collect myself. I found a coffee shop nearby and ordered a latte.

I hadn't sat and had a drink by myself since the diagnosis. I realized that Willie's diagnosis had become a marker in time. First subway ride since the diagnosis, first doctor's visit for me, first coffee, first time by myself with my thoughts. I asked the barista for a pen and took a napkin from the counter.

I started to write.

I wrote about Oedipus.

Since Willie's diagnosis (again, my fold in time), I had been thinking about Sophocles' *Oedipus the King*. I hadn't taught it in more than a year, but it was a play that kept coming back to me in moments like this.

Everyone remembers Freud's Oedipus, cemented in popular culture as shorthand for having the hots for one's mom. But reading Sophocles with my class last year, I was reminded how it is about so much more. It is about how we try to twist away from fate and how fate keeps twisting back at us with a vengeance. In the play, King Laius and Queen Jocasta do whatever they can to avoid a curse—that their newborn baby will one day kill his father and marry his mother. The parents bind his ankles and leave him on a hillside to die of exposure, where he is picked up by a shepherd and delivered to a childless king and queen in a different kingdom. When Oedipus later learns of the curse, he flees the people he believes to be his parents and inadvertently triggers his tragic fate. On his journey away, he meets a man in the crossroads who refuses to yield. He kills the man and retreats to a foreign town where he marries the widow of the man he killed, a woman who happens to be his mother. Oedipus is the tragic hero of the play and the class rightfully focused on his choices and how they paved the way for his destruction. But I started to think more about his mother, about how a child she thought was dead returns to her so grotesquely. Midway through the play, as Oedipus begins to piece together the details of his birth, Jocasta tries to stop him. She says to Oedipus: "Stop—in the name of god, if you love your own life, call off this search! My suffering is enough."[19] At this point, she understands what is about to unfold and is willing to be the only one who suffers. She sees clearly that in digging and digging, Oedipus will destroy everyone, including himself and their children.

On that napkin, I wrote about the twist-back of fate. Of wanting to avoid it. Of how the wanting itself becomes a kind of poison. I looked back to another diagnosis—the pregnancy that I terminated after testing positive for Pompe Disease—and I thought about how much I feared having a terminally ill child. And how my child was now chronically ill. It was an important distinction. Willie was going to live and she was going to flourish. We would make sure of it. But we would have to work every day to keep death at bay. And our dismal inheritance for her was that one day she would have to take over this labor herself. My rational mind tried to dismiss the idea that the seed for Willie's diabetes—a Greek word—had been planted long before her birth. It was in her genes. It was in the fates.

I covered every inch of the napkin with my thoughts about genes, fate, and tragedy. And then, I threw it away.

# 7

# Stay at Home

The key was under the mat when we arrived at the house on Franklin Street. We were back in my hometown in Michigan and not for a quick visit, but to live for a year. Sharon had told us the key would be there. She told us to use the side door rather than taking the uneven steps to the splintered front porch and trying the door with the antiquated twist doorbell. The side door was easier to open; it had been installed when Sharon had first moved into the house twenty-five years ago. Compared with the rest of the house, it was practically new. It was the door we would open and close regularly for the next year to let Willie out to draw snakes with chalk on the sidewalk or to rifle through the tools in the detached garage or to bundle her into the car (Sharon's car) to meet with her new doctors.

The house was massive compared to our New York City apartment, but it also felt smaller in some ways. The rooms were cramped—built on a nineteenth-century scale—and crowded with Sharon's life. She had inherited heirlooms from her Austrian relatives—heavy wooden furniture with ornate painted details; gold-framed paintings with regal scenes of military parades at the Schönbrunn Palace, rural scenes of farmers feeding their chickens outside of rustic chalets in the Alps, a portrait of a lady, gently smiling, in a fur stole; Tiffany-style lamps; a grandfather clock; silver tea sets; and pewter beer steins. Every cupboard was full. The coffee table in the living room contained drawers teeming with sparkling costume jewelry that once belonged to Sharon's aunt, chunky baubles that Willie would pull out and layer one on top of the other until the drawer was empty. Furniture only just fit the rooms that contained them. The living room was barely big enough for the overstuffed sofa and love seat and TV. The dining room nearly didn't contain the dining room table. There was a formal front room with a piano and two sofas vying for space. This room received the eastern morning light and yet still always seemed to be dark. A tight staircase led up to larger rooms that would become our bedroom and Willie's, and an office that would be my office—a luxury that I had thought about with anticipation in the months leading up to our move.

When I first imagined moving into this house, my first thought was of the gazebo. I had been to the house only once before, when I was nineteen years old. My friend Sadie was dating Sharon's stepson, Will, and we had gone over to hang out with him and his friends in the haphazard manner of college students home for their first summer break and not quite sure what to do with themselves. We sat in the gazebo as dusk turned into evening. We might have been playing euchre with a fresh deck of cards. I never forgot the screened-in gazebo, how we watched the fireflies light up the yard until it was time to go home.

And now we were going to be living here. For a year. Our family of three.

I looked over the gazebo again and saw that time had not been kind to it. There were small tears in the screen that let the flies and mice sneak in for the crumbs that fell from the table. A ceiling fan drooped down, its blades sagging toward the ground, exhausted by the force of gravity.

MOVING WAS HARDLY an idea; it was, rather, a compulsion. In March, Willie was diagnosed with diabetes. By May, I had formally resigned from my job. The spring and summer were a blur of administering insulin shots, calculating carbohydrates, placing medication orders, and calling insurance companies. We never left our neighborhood because I was still nervous that I would forget something and be too far from home. I might forget Willie's juice and find myself on the subway with a child crashing into hypoglycemia. I might forget her insulin and she would beg me for food and I would have to tell her no, we need to wait till you get home. I imagined all the disasters that could befall us if we were away from the only orbit I could comfortably navigate.

Spending the days alone with Willie was like living out an imitation of my old life. We went to the same parks, walked the same routes, and stopped for snacks at the same shops, but I felt like I was inhabiting a hollowed-out version of that self. My boss, Jeanne, asked me to come back to work one last time after my official resignation to help with the fellowship application process. I left Willie home with Evan and put on the work clothes and makeup that I hadn't touched in months. I sat in a room with faculty who were tasked with deciding which recent PhD students were the most promising. Who was going to go on to a stunning career? Who was worthy of joining the university-one-does-not-turn-down as a first step to their brilliant future? I didn't know any of the selection committee very well and so they weren't aware that I was leaving my job, that I was already out the door. I could sit in the room with a mask of professionalism and pretend to be someone different, someone who existed before. After the process wrapped up, a professor of African American studies, a man not much older than myself who always wore bow ties and had very kind eyes, asked me how my summer was going. I could have kept my mask on and told him that everything was just fine. Instead, I told him that my daughter was diagnosed with diabetes, that we had spent a week in the hospital, and now I was leaving my job. His eyes were kind, but it was not the answer he expected. He hoped that I would keep in touch and, with a nod of sympathy, slipped out the door.

I reminded myself that there were silver linings. I was getting to spend more time with Willie in her toddler years as her personality was beginning to blossom. She wasn't speaking yet, but she was asserting herself more. She was independent, wanting to do anything she could for herself; she was a comedian, repeating any action or noise that produced a laugh from Evan and me; and she was resilient, proving time and again that she was capable of so much more than I would have ever thought possible. And yet, despite these silver linings, while we remained in New York, I was stuck in a depressing loop of comparing my life before to my life now. I needed a new setting if I was going to create a different reality than the one I had planned for, a life that didn't feel like a defeat. We had no assets. We didn't own a home, didn't have any savings. But Evan had a sabbatical coming up—a year where he was meant to finish writing a book and several articles in order to qualify for tenure. He could write anywhere with access to a decent library. We were living in a rental apartment where we paid below market rate to the university-one-does-not-turn-down. We could sublease it easily and move somewhere cheaper and easier and closer to family. Evan got along well with my parents and liked the idea of moving to a place where we could get more help. He imagined that we might be able to have the occasional date night again or that he could stop at the gym after a few hours at the library instead of rushing back to relieve me. We might begin to feel like we were doing things together again rather than handing childcare duties back and forth.

Then, one day, a light bulb manifested over my head, cartoonlike. What about my friend's mother-in-law, Sharon? I had gotten to know her on and off over the years, at Sadie and Will's wedding, at family barbeques and holiday visits. I'd crossed her path, at several steps removed, as she and her husband, Greg, became grandparents, helping Sadie and Will with their two girls. Their extended family were close; the grandparents watched the girls on weekdays, they traveled together, had summer cookouts, walked back and forth to each other's houses. I knew Sharon to be an earnest listener and infrequent talker who spoke with a thick Midwestern accent. Her husband, Greg, was the bigger personality—an affable prankster with a love of mischief and mayhem. He had been a magazine photographer and an outdoorsman who rotated through new hobbies every five years or so—kayaking, wind surfing, and then, fatefully, flying small aircrafts. There was always something youthful about him and one felt that had he lived to 100, he would never have gotten old. But he had not. He had died three years earlier when his plane crashed while he took a flying lesson on a trip to France. And now, after the accident, Sharon was left alone in her house. I imagined she might be living her own sad loop—not the same as mine, but sharing some of its contours.

It was not a time when I saw much clearly. I was in a haze of learning new medications, new routines, and new fears. But I felt instinctively that here was someone who could understand the need to get away. I was becoming increasingly desperate to get out of the city and be closer to my parents for a while as we tried to sort out this new phase of our lives. There was something instinctual about wanting to run back to my past—to my hometown, to my mom. It was reassuring to think of being near my parents—my dad newly retired with a medical degree that we'd be happy to put to use, my mother anxious to help and eager to fix whatever was broken. I looked around our apartment and thought about Sharon. Wouldn't this apartment be just the kind of place that I would want to live if I were recently widowed? I might very well like to live in a modern high-rise facing the Hudson River, a short distance away from Riverside Park. I cataloged the features of our neighborhood like I was placing an ad. I remembered what it was like moving here for the first time four years ago, feeling the rush of potential and the sense that anything could happen on this pulsing island. When Sadie called back to say that her mother-in-law was interested, I couldn't quite believe that everything was clicking into place.

It was going to be a year to regroup and reassess. We would have dinners with my parents and Alex every Sunday. Willie would get a chance to know her uncle. We could take her to his bowling group and to potlucks with his community of intellectually disabled adults. I was looking forward to being a part of his life again as I hadn't in many years: knowing the names of his friends, bumping into him in town while he was out with his aides on a weekday, trimming his fingernails for him because he liked the way I did it better than anyone. My parents had agreed to watch Willie two days a week so that I could do a combination of freelance editing and some writing. What I was going to write, I didn't yet know, but I felt the pressing need to write something. Another academic book, maybe. Some articles. Perhaps something more personal. The idea of writing about myself was both terrifying and embarrassing. I hadn't done anything like that since I was a college student taking creative writing

classes and flirting with the idea of "becoming a writer." And to
do so now, at nearly forty years of age, when someone needed
me so completely, seemed like the most selfish thing I could
possibly do. It would be something for only myself: suspicious,
solipsistic, mine.

We packed up a large rental car with a year's worth of clothes,
toys, and medical supplies. It was not going to be forever. As we
made our round of goodbyes with our friends, we kept insisting
that we would be in Michigan for just one year. No one seemed
to believe us.


SHARON'S HOUSE LAY close beside its eastern neighbor, though
the two differed greatly in temperament. While Sharon's house
had the character of a respectable, if slightly ramshackle family home, her neighbor's house gave off a louche appearance.
Its bright blue paint was peeling off like damaged skin after a
bad sunburn. It was built on a shotgun model and all its open
windows faced Sharon's house in a wide-eyed stare. The house
was owned by Frank. His son had been a few grades ahead of
me in school and I remembered him as blandly handsome. The
father, Frank, had the look and manners of an elderly man who
had once been roguishly attractive—a certain winking charisma
matched by bad habits. He was a writer. I never knew exactly
what he wrote, but one day he told me to look out for a box of
freshly printed books that he expected to arrive while he was out
of town. I think he wanted me to know that he had published a
book. I should have thought to ask about it.

Frank was also diabetic. Type 1. Sadie had told me before we
arrived. I got the whole backstory on the relations between the
neighbors. Before Greg died, he and Frank had feuded for years
over the minutiae of living side by side—the loud skateboarding

of one kid, the late-night parties of another, barking dogs and un-kempt yards. Despite these hostilities, Sadie told me how, several times, they had needed to call 911 when Frank's blood sugar had spiked or crashed. He did not wear a continuous glucose moni-tor like Willie. He monitored his blood sugar the old-fashioned way by pricking his finger with a lancet and testing the blood on a glucometer. Sometimes he fell out of the habit or other habits interfered. Frank lived alone with occasional visits from an on-again, off-again girlfriend. He had two dogs—big, rough Labra-dors that fascinated and terrified Willie in equal measure. When we showed up at Sharon's house, Frank already knew that Willie was diabetic. It was obvious that he had no special affinity for children, but he seemed to be fascinated by her. He stood on the other side of the fence and asked us questions—how was her blood sugar, did she mind wearing her glucose monitor, did we think about getting her an insulin pump? He'd been diabetic for fifty years. The technology had changed so much in his lifetime. It would change so much in hers.

When Willie played in the driveway that ran alongside the two houses, I felt the eyes of the peeling house watch us with a kind of vague and sympathetic horror.

THIS YEAR, AT least, I was a stay-at-home mom. My mother had been a stay-at-home mom for most of my life, until she started working outside the home in a development position at a local nonprofit when I was in high school. My sister had been a stay-at-home mom. She had her three children fairly young and close together with the expectation that she'd go back to work some-time. And by the time the youngest was in kindergarten, she'd joined a friend in a florist business; she worked at this job part time so that she could still ferry the kids to their activities and be home when their school day ended. But most of the other mothers in my life worked outside the home. They worked full days in offices and classrooms and hospitals or, if they worked from home, they did so with children in their arms and underfoot. So was I, really, a stay-at-home mom now? I didn't have a salaried job, it was true. I had a whopping total of five hours a week of freelance editing to contribute to the household income. So why the hesitation about calling myself a stay-at-home mom? Many embraced the title. My mom and sister had. Perhaps it was that, with all the other parts of my old life gone—the teaching, the administrative work—I still felt the pull of my writing like an umbilical cord tethering me to some recognizable version of myself.

The term "stay-at-home mom" is relatively recent, replacing the now outdated term "housewife." I was interested in why the terminology had changed, so I read around, looking for some wider context. Jessica Clements and Kari Nixon argue that the change was part of a broader shift in how we think about motherhood from the nineteenth century to the present; over the last two hundred years, they argue, terms that suggest passivity, like "childbearing," have been replaced with more active terms like "childrearing" that emphasize mothering as a continual and strenuous activity aiming toward continual optimization.[1]

We no longer simply bear children, bringing them into the world, but we are more and more responsible for rearing them—raising them into adulthood with the right set of values, behaviors, attachments, sense of emotional well-being, marketable skill sets, and educational attainments. If the word "housewife" implied that a woman's primary duty is to the house itself, the phrase stay-at-home mom shifts the emphasis to the activity of mothering. The house becomes incidental—a site where the occupation of mothering takes place. Although we rarely use the word "housewife" anymore, it is the direct counterpart to the word that we still use, "husband." The etymology of the word dates back to thirteenth-century England: "husband" comes from the earlier spellings for "house," *hus,* and "bond," *bund.*[2] Marriage itself once implied bondedness to the home and the land on which it stood, which was tended, in their respective roles, by each member of the "household" (again, the word implies an emphasis on being held together or bound to the home). This version of householding was, of course, not for everyone. It emerged among a yeoman class. Small farmers. For them, marriage and children provided the labor necessary for a self-sufficient household. Houses teemed with parents and grandparents and children and unmarried relatives and other dependents. Unlike aristocrats, for whom marriage ensured political alliances and transfers of accumulated wealth, marriage for the yeoman class and emerging middle classes involved shared labor and survival. It was a privilege often denied the working poor, indentured servants, enslaved peoples, and the disabled. And for those who were able to be housewives in bygone years, their labor was understood as part of a larger group effort by multiple generations and all genders to keep the house going.

The housewife has been replaced by the stay-at-home mom at a time when the work of housekeeping has become more solitary, less visible, and more technologically mediated. In her formative book on the topic, feminist historian of science Ruth Schwartz Cowan discusses how technologies have created the illusion that housework has become easier when, in fact, technological developments have put more pressure on mothers to attain ever-increasing standards of cleanliness, culinary skill, and care work while reducing the role that men play in the household. Her book, *More Work for Mother,* shows how seemingly positive technological additions to the household have promised to make things easier for mothers while creating rising expectations and, because everyone agreed it was now easier, less support. In one example, she points to the cast-iron cooking stove, which replaced the open hearth, making cooking seemingly easier, more efficient, cleaner, and more precise in early America. Despite the obvious advantages of stove-top cooking, it also meant that cooking was no longer an all-gender affair as it had been when men would chop and haul the timber and manage the fire on the hearth. It also raised expectations around the American diet from simple one-pot stews to elaborate cakes that required extra shopping for specialized ingredients and then hours of whipping and layering and icing and presenting. Every time we bring a new technology into the house to make parenting and housekeeping easier, we seem to find new ways to raise the stakes. Cowan warns that as housewifery becomes increasingly technological, we need to look carefully at how those tools change women's lives. She writes, "Our tools are not always at our beck and call. The less we know about them, the more likely it is that they will command us, rather than the other way round."[3] What tools, I wondered, were shaping my new life as a stay-at-home mom in someone else's home?

Sharon was a working mom, now retired, and when I looked around her kitchen, I did not see the gendered sphere of the traditional housewife; instead, I saw a shared space where the various devices and technologies seemed every bit as much an expression of Greg's labor as Sharon's. Walking into their kitchen, you were met with an explosion of gadgets, and many of them had belonged to Greg—the coffee devices, in particular, bore his mark. There were three types of coffee makers in the kitchen, including an ornate Italian espresso machine that was hardwired into the water supply. He even had a bean roaster in the garage. Throughout our year in their house, Willie would find coffee beans in various stages of roasting, from green to deep black, in odd pockets of the garage like a trail of crumbs that he had left behind. In the kitchen, there was a gas oven and stove top, a microwave, a blender, a toaster, and a standing mixer. Drawers teemed with gadgets—a potato ricer, a lemon juicer, and a tortilla press. It was a kitchen that showed the marks of two people cooking side by side. It was the kitchen of two different personalities—one a pragmatist, collecting the things she needed to get dinner on the table, and the other a hobbyist, flitting between enthusiasms and experiments. They might not have cooked the same things or the same way, but they were doing it together. Or, at least, it looked that way to me, scanning the kitchen like an archaeologist studying a lost civilization.

Moving into someone else's house means finding room for your things alongside theirs and wondering what their things say about them and what yours say about you. We came with fewer kitchen tools. And it was a good thing too, since we would have had nowhere to put them. Instead, we arrived with a barrage of medical tools and supplies that we needed to accommodate. This year, if I was now going to bear a greater load of the housework and the parenting, I was also going to bear a greater load of the maintenance work that Willie's technologies required. We brought half a trunk of colorful containers of needles and hearing aid batteries and various chargers. We cleared out bathroom drawers and closets and found room for it all. Looking at all this stuff, I thought about whether Cowan's argument about women and technology and labor might apply to all the medical devices that we were stuffing into every available space in the house. These tools that were meant to make managing disease or disability easier but also made additional work: there was the bureaucratic work of managing insurance companies and doctor's appointments as well as the maintenance work of keeping all of these tools in working order. It also made all this work less visible, creating the illusion of seamlessness and ease. And it was increasingly gendered work. Receptionists called my number, not Evan's, to schedule appointments. It was a steady stream of appointments: annual checkups with the pediatrician and dentist, the audiologist every three months, the endocrinologist every three months, the speech therapist twice a week. Someone needed to make these appointments, drive to them, and pay for them. This last involved mountains of paperwork.

Since giving up my job, I was doing more of the ferrying to and from appointments, giving more shots, replacing more batteries, and sitting on the phone more often with a customer service representative or insurance provider. Willie's hearing aids needed new batteries at least once a week. In the summer her ears were often waxy and damp and the aids needed to be disassembled, cleaned out, and placed in a little jar with a desiccant to dry them out at night. The sensor on her continuous glucose monitor needed changing every ten days, which required pulling out the old sensor from her body and implanting a new one. The monitor itself needed charging at night. When the sensor failed, as it did with relative frequency, I would need to call the customer service representative and answer a barrage of questions: what was the precise date the sensor was installed, what is the inventory number on the box, the serial number on the sensor, where was it implanted on my child's body, etc. Then, inventory needed to be purchased: a rotating supply of insulin, test strips, hearing aid batteries, and alcohol wipes. Unlike the traditional housewife, I did not yet feel bonded to the house, perhaps because it was not really my house, after all. Instead, I saw myself fastened tight to all these devices that were wrapping me up in their steely tentacles.

The ideal of sharing a home and parenting with responsibilities divided evenly between Evan and me was feeling more

remote than ever. Sometimes I would look at the shut door of
Evan's home office and feel resentment like a dull weight on my
chest. In the early days after Willie's diagnosis, Evan and I had
worked hard to learn everything together and share the responsibilities as best we could, but now I was no longer employed
outside the home. Now I was a housewife, a stay-at-home mom,
living back in my hometown, which had been, after all, my idea.
I worried about the fragile equality that we had worked to hang
on to in our relationship since I had first stepped down from
my tenure-track job and how these new circumstances might
further erode it. Evan and I had tried our best to divide up these
tasks when it was a matter of juggling regular kid stuff with the
extra load of early intervention, audiology, hearing aids, and
speech therapy. If anything, Evan stepped up to help more with
Willie's audiological care because he felt an additional sense of
responsibility—they were his genes, as he would often point out.
But that was before Willie's diabetes diagnosis; now, the medical
and technological load was overwhelming. And now, I had left
my job and Evan needed to get tenure if he was going to keep
his. He was working uphill after the days at the hospital and the
pressing needs at home had cut into his meticulous timeline for
what he would need to publish. We had come to the point where
the labor was simply indivisible. When I stepped away from
my job, I knew that the lion's share was now going to fall to
me. This was temporary, we told each other, but how would the
balance ever reassert itself? The precedence of history was very
much against me. Sometimes it felt like I had signed on to run a
small medical practice out of the home without pay or recognition for my labor.

   As Willie sat at the kitchen table, smashing different colors
of Play-Doh together into a psychedelic blob, I looked around at
Sharon's things. There were photos of a family in various stages

of its metamorphosis—smooth-skinned babies held fast in the arms of new parents, teetering toddlers captured on two feet just seconds before a fall, gap-toothed school pics, formal wedding photos. The doorframe was covered with the ubiquitous markings of various heights. A small boy molting his smallness and roundness to become a gangly adolescent. None of these belonged to me and this could be both strange and comforting. In the hard moments—when Willie would knock over the plate of pasta after I had counted each noodle by hand to make sure I knew how much to dose her with insulin—I looked to the ghosts for reassurance. There were so many important milestones that I had yet to reach. I looked for these helpful markers along the way to guide me through the grueling day-to-day. It was comforting to slip into Sharon's life and remember that I was experiencing familiar frustrations and everyday difficulties, which others before me had encountered and, indeed, overcome.

My mom came by twice a week to pick up Willie and take her while I tried to do some writing. They had sold the house I grew up in and were living in a new condo about a mile away from Sharon's house. My mom never drove to see us, but walked back and forth for the exercise. Although it cut into my writing time, I would often walk halfway back with her. I would claim that I was also walking for the exercise, but it was really for the adult company. Walking through my hometown, I would see reminders of my past: I would walk by houses where I had been to sleepovers as a child and house parties as a teenager; an old boyfriend's derelict apartment building or the lit-up drawing room of a math tutor who tried valiantly to get me through algebra; neighborhoods where I had trick-or-treated; and a university quad where my friends and I implored college students to buy us beer. We would walk and talk about this and that—adjustments to life in a condo, Dad's ornery resistance to full retirement, the challenge of keeping Alex's aide workers from quitting. Alex was a frequent topic of conversation. We saw him every week for dinner on Sunday nights and sometimes he was in a good mood, kissing me on the cheek when he came in the door with a series of bird-like pecks and pushing off when he was done. Other times, he was withdrawn and more interested in watching YouTube videos of *Family Feud* on my mother's computer. He had two new aide workers who seemed like they were interested in sticking around but, as we discussed on our walks, there had been others before who seemed just as committed. As long as the pay that the state provided them remained so low, it was hard to keep anyone for more than a few years. Willie was easily lulled in the stroller and fell asleep along the way. After a half mile, I would peel off and either head to the university library to pick up a book that I needed or walk back to Sharon's house. For a little while, at least, I would be alone with my thoughts.

SOON AFTER WE had moved into her mother-in-law's house, Sadie asked if we'd like to go to the Renaissance festival with them. It was Evan's birthday and we hadn't made any plans. So we said, sure, why not?

We parked in a field outside of a town so small I'd never heard of it, despite it being thirty minutes from where I'd grown up. It had rained all night and into the morning, but the sky was clear and there was a slight post-rain chill in the air.

I put Willie in her stroller and we started down the forested path that connected the immense open-field parking lot to the festival. The path was full of visitors in various levels of commitment to cosplay—corsets, hoopskirts, feathered hats, flowered garlands, leather pouches, and fake daggers in holsters. The ground was soggy from all the rain, and the hundreds of feet clad in modern boots and sneakers had ground the earth to a muddy pulp. Willie's stroller wheels lurched and sunk as her head bobbed along, taking in the scene. Along the way, she soaked up the attention from Sadie's girls—six and eight years old—as our pant legs accumulated a layer of splattered mud.

Once we finally arrived at the festival, we unlatched Willie from the seat belt of her stroller and she wiggled her way out, bounding after Sadie's girls who were bursting with excitement to get their faces painted. We found the stall and each girl waited patiently in line to tell the face painter what she wanted. Willie couldn't yet say what she wanted, but she watched the other girls and waited her turn. Once it was her turn in the seat, she sat with unimaginable stillness. The quiet dignity of her upturned face and the solemn look in her eyes made a perfect canvas for the soft flicks of the painter's brush. The artist slowly transformed her face into a blue butterfly. Willie looked at the artist's work in the mirror and her eyes sparkled with delight.

As the day wrapped up—the jousts having been jousted, turkey legs consumed, and axes thrown at hay bales—Sadie and I turned to more serious topics. I told her about our recent appointment with the new audiologist that we'd be seeing for the year. It had not gone well. We had sat in a booth and watched as Willie did not react to a series of beeps—some so loud that we could hear them emitting from the headphones and piercing the soundproof room. The audiologist was concerned. She didn't like the test results. She threw out a few suggestions. Willie could have auditory neuropathy. I asked what that meant. She explained that it was like a faulty wire. Sometimes the wire worked, and sometimes it didn't. I asked if that was typically part of sensorineural hearing loss. No, she thought it might be an additional complication. Or, she went on, Willie's hearing loss could be progressive. Perhaps it had gotten worse since the diagnosis as an infant.

Recounting the scene to Sadie, I felt my anger flare up. The new audiologist was simply rattling off diagnoses with no consideration for how we might react or how plausible the diagnoses were. These were new diagnoses, not based on genetics, not based on Evan's family history. She was just throwing out ideas to see what would stick, like those axes flung at hay bale targets. And all of these ideas and theories were based on an hour-long behavioral examination of a not-yet-two-year-old.

She wanted us to do an MRI—Willie would need to be fully sedated—and consult about cochlear implants.

Sadie listened as I ranted on in the middle of a crowd of people dressed as thirteenth-century peasants. Pausing to look around me, I realized that, unlike many of the people here, I had no fantasies about living in a different time. I liked the present just fine. The Renaissance fantasy did nothing for me. In a different time, my child wouldn't have been alive, and so the past offered no magic for me anymore. And yet, there were things about the present moment that were nearly unbearable.

I thought back to rejecting the genetic testing after Willie's diabetes diagnosis and wondered whether I could keep saying no to medical interventions and what would be the stakes, for Willie, of that refusal. Was it possible to push back on some, or did each intervention inevitably lead to another? Did she really need cochlear implants, and did she need them now? Willie was on the cusp of language—I could see her listening and understanding more and more with her hearing aids. Or I believed she was. She responded to my words, at least sometimes. Why not wait until we had more reliable behavioral tests—until we had more information? Was it possible to make a decision like this with some input from Willie, or at least a better sense of what she wanted? Why not give her a chance to talk first? Why so much haste?

The faux medieval crowd seemed to follow a group instinct toward the exits. I felt people surge around us and realized that we'd been standing in a little island blocking the way out. I had never known Sadie to listen to me for so long without cracking a joke. She had no advice to give, but I was glad to have her there to capture and help dissipate some of my sour mood. Her girls understood enough to know we were having an "adult conversation" and they kept a respectful distance, entertaining Willie and goofing off for the dads. I smiled over at Willie and we broke up our island and joined the crowd, surging forward once again toward the twenty-first century.

I LOOKED FOR ways to get out of the house when I could and to keep my mind engaged. Jen was teaching a class on disability justice for adult learners at the Room Project in Detroit. Would I want to take the course with her? We could carpool together once a week. It would start after Willie's bedtime. Jen and I had gone to grad school together before she had ended up back in Michigan, where she'd been an undergraduate. I loved the idea of taking a class with her, of being a student again. Yes, I would love to take her course.

My fellow classmates came from all walks of life—there were two staff members from Detroit's Disability Network, one of whom was Deaf and accompanied by an ASL interpreter; there were three Ford employees working on self-powered cars and interested in discussing the implications of these developments for disabled people; there was one attorney who focused on disability rights and came for a few classes but quickly left when he realized he would not be allowed to teach the course; the rest of the class included a sprinkling of artists, teachers, therapists, and graduate students. When we went around to make introductions, I did not know how to classify myself. I told them that I was a writer.

During our classes Jen introduced us to the medical model versus the social model of disability. The former presents disability as a physical failure that can be overcome with effective cures, therapies, and technological devices. The social model, on the other hand, sees disability as a product of a disabling environment. My Deaf classmate, for instance, described how he does not consider himself disabled when he communicates through ASL with other signers—when he has access to this language, he does not experience a lack. It is only in hearing spaces that are not accessible to him that he feels disabled. Later in the semester, Jen discussed changing attitudes toward disability and a shift from a focus on disability rights (the fight for legal protections that includes the Americans with Disabilities Act) to disability justice (an intersectional approach to disability that pays attention to the overlapping injustices of ableism, racism, sexism, and transphobia, among others). It was heady stuff and our conversations would filter from the table at the Room Project into the empty weekday evening streets of downtown Detroit. On the ride home, Jen and I shared our carpool with a graduate student who was taking the course and lived nearby. Her name was Trina and she was writing a dissertation in linguistics specializing in American Sign Language. I asked her if she'd be willing to tutor me on the side. She said yes. And so, in addition to our weekly class, Trina came by twice a week at lunchtime to help me learn ASL.

Sitting at Sharon's dining room table, with Willie happily occupied at her grandma's house, Trina would show me the hand shapes of the ASL alphabet. For "A," a clenched hand with fingers pointing down; for "B," a flat palm with fingers pointing upward and a tucked-in thumb; for "C," about what you'd expect. I learned to spell my name and the sign for "name." Trina taught me to raise my eyebrows when asking a "yes/no" question like "Are you Deaf?" and to furrow my eyebrows when asking a "who/what/where/when" question like "How are you?"

I paid for Trina's lessons through Venmo and she sent me Google Docs with GIFs of signs to accompany our lessons. Early Intervention did not cover ASL classes. Nor had anyone ever put me in touch with resources for learning ASL, though I had asked everyone—Gary, my Early Intervention caseworker in NYC; audiologists; speech therapists. Nothing. Any ASL that I was going to learn would have to come out of pocket and in my own time. Since moving to Michigan, we had signed on for their state-level early intervention program, which was called Early On. We were assigned two caseworkers for Willie—a social worker and a speech and language specialist. They were slightly more accommodating of my desire to learn ASL. They gave us DVDs of Rachel Coleman's *Signing Time!*, which we had already been watching on YouTube, but I couldn't imagine ever becoming anything like fluent in a language through a boxed set of DVDs aimed at preschoolers.

I told Willie's new speech therapist that I was trying to learn ASL and teach it to Willie. She warned me that I ran the risk of delaying her language learning. She was concerned that Willie, who was now twenty months old, was already delayed. She asked me to draw up lists of words that Willie could understand and words that she could speak. I told her that Willie knew about fifty signs, but this was considered irrelevant. I insisted on including the words she signed whenever we discussed her language development—I didn't like the idea that this language didn't count and wanted to show, show off, perhaps, how much Willie knew. I filled out form after form after form to track her development. All of these documents seemed designed to remind me how much she couldn't do or didn't know and I wanted a record, at least for myself, of everything she was capable of doing.

Despite the lack of encouragement, I signed with Willie whatever I could muster. I found it especially helpful to sign with her while she was taking long baths. She could not wear her hearing aids in the bathtub—they couldn't get wet—so during her bath time, I'd sign everything I wanted to communicate with her. Yes (fist nodding like a head in assent) and no (thumb tapping against my pointer and middle finger). I'd manage simple little sentences. I didn't know the sign for "no splashing," so I'd say "water *in* bath." She would sign back "hot" or "cold" if the water was not to her liking. She did it with relish. Hot was a cupped hand at her chin, then the gesture of flinging the hand away. Cold was a full body sign for Willie. She'd put both hands in fists and shake her head and body as if shivering. Her cheeks would quiver as she signed "cold, cold, cold."

The two caseworkers from Early On came to visit once a month. I felt the need to spruce things up whenever they came, as if they were there to judge my parenting. They would stay through a meal and we would discuss the fact that Willie was becoming a pickier eater now that she felt able to exert more control over mealtimes. The list of foods that she would consistently eat was dwindling and, with her diabetes, I never felt in a position to play hardball with her. She needed to eat something to keep her blood sugar at an appropriate level and I'd always be the first to cave if she refused to eat what I served. The caseworkers asked me to make another list, this one of all the foods she would or wouldn't eat. I made up a list and each entry felt like a judgment—for every food that I didn't tick "has tried," I asked myself why I hadn't offered her that food. For every food that she wouldn't eat, I felt a pang of guilt.

Looking back over these long lists of words and foods—the ingress and egress on my daughter's lips—they strike me as love letters of a sort, a plaintive document of yearning filtered through the puny language of bureaucratic forms. Here are the gifts I have given you, my love—words on my tongue and on my fingers. Here are the foods that I have prepared for you. These I lay out before you. Taste, touch, speak. They will not all be for you, but they were all prepared with love. This is the best that I can do.

In March 2020, I boarded a plane for Atlanta. It would be a few days during which I could step away from this new life as a stay-at-home mom and back into my old life. I was invited by a friend who worked at the neighboring private university when I had been down the street in my first job at the public university. We had stayed in touch over the years and he had asked me to come back to give a talk on my research. Before Willie's diabetes diagnosis, I had started researching the life and work of Teresa Deevy, an Irish playwright who happened to have been deaf and whose work I had begun to take an interest in. I'd first encountered her plays when the Mint Theater Company in New York staged a production of five of her one-act plays. It was before Willie was born, in between pregnancies (I no longer remember which), and I sat, wearing my critic hat, parsing out which parts held up well and which felt dated or too far gone. Since Willie was born, my detached interest in Deevy had flared into something like an obsession. I wanted to know how she had built a career as a deaf playwright in the 1930s: How did she hone her sense of dialogue, how did she know when a performance was landing (or not), and—most miraculously—how did she adapt to writing for radio, a medium she had never heard? My approach to Deevy was fiercely maternal—I wanted to learn about her because I wanted to understand deafness better and, in some small measure, to understand Willie better. And I wanted to write about her because I wanted to share a story of a tenacious, accomplished deaf woman, a story my daughter might one day want to know.

I would be returning to my former university, the one that I had left for the university-one-does-not-turn-down, as well as speaking at the neighboring private university. As much as I was looking forward to being back in Atlanta and seeing old friends, the trip had me on edge. It felt like the return of a prodigal daughter—one who had taken a big risk in leaving and now was slinking back, tail between legs. Now that I didn't have a professional position of any sort, I felt like I was playing at being an academic. Who wanted this work? Why would they care? Why did I care? During my talk at the private university, I spoke about Deevy and her deafness: how she had lost her hearing to Meniere's disease when she was a college student; how she studied lip-reading at a time when oral instruction dominated education for the deaf; how she had two other sisters who were also deaf; how one hearing sister was her steadfast translator and confidante; and how she experienced deep sadness after the death of this beloved sister and translator. I found myself strangely moved as I spoke about Deevy and her family, of their large and small acts of consideration and mutual support.

During the question and answer session following my talk, a man asked me whether I had any personal investment in the topic of disability. Did I identify as disabled? I did not, I said, but then I hesitated. There was a fuller answer buried in me somewhere, but I didn't know how to articulate it. Growing up with Alex as my older brother, I wanted to say, I never knew a time when I wasn't thinking about disability. My sensibilities were formed by those moments of care and cruelty that came out of people when they encountered Alex. I went around all my life dividing people into categories based on how they might, hypothetically, respond to my brother. But this man didn't know Alex and I didn't know how to conjure him into this lecture hall. As for Willie, I had never spoken of her in a public setting like this and I was not prepared to do so. Disability rippled through my life, but it was also not mine to claim, I wanted to say. I was adjacent to disability, but this adjacency had shaped every contour of my personality and my sense of the world. My response, standing at the lecture podium, was halting and disjointed, but the man in the audience was kind enough not to point this out.

That night the faculty at the private university took me out for dinner. I hadn't heard of the restaurant when they suggested it, but when we arrived, I realized that I had been there before on a date with Evan when we had lived up the road, not a mile from there. At the time it had been a Persian restaurant, and now it was an upscale New American restaurant that served duck confit with hush puppies and things like that. I recognized the long, corridor-like dining room and the half-open kitchen tucked away at the back. We were seated at the same table where Evan and I had once spent a night eating kebabs and talking about the future. The conversation that night focused on departmental politics and the sorry state of academic hiring and the dwindling number of humanities majors. The usual thing. I tried to muster up an opinion about anything but was too haunted by the scene of a dinner past to be of much use in the conversation. Evan and I appeared in my mind's eye as different people then: brighter, more optimistic. And I thought about Evan's understanding of different selves and how a couple might also, together, take on different identities over time. We were duller now, more hard-pressed, juggling more, less successfully. And who might we be at some future dinner in some future iteration of this restaurant? It was impossible to say. I hoped desperately that we'd be at the same table, that we'd regain some of our lightness and buoyancy. But no one could tell whether this restaurant would still be here or if something else entirely would take its place.

The next day, I was back at my old public university. The one that I had left. In the time that I was away, the department had moved from the nondescript mid-century university build-ing where it had once been housed into a nondescript former bank building. The views of the city from the offices were in-credible, but it felt like I ought to be meeting with a mortgage lender rather than an expert in sixteenth-century drama. The whole downtown neighborhood had transformed. There were new, fancy buildings and a tramline running through the city center. The restaurants were nicer than the fast-food joints and mom-and-pop counter-service dives that had dominated the downtown area before; these were being pushed out by celebrity chef–owned gastropubs and high-end ramen restaurants.

Leslie took me out for lunch. Five years earlier, we had ar-rived at the public university as junior faculty together, but she was now tenured and settled in a nice house with her husband and two children. As we were talking and waiting for our food to arrive, she got a call from her son's day care. He had been sent home sick. They thought it was just a fever and bad cold, but everyone was on edge with this new virus that was all over the news. It had been a few months since the first U.S. cases had been reported in Washington and no one was sure what would happen next. We rushed the waiter for the check so she could get home. When I went back to the offices, I met up with my old department chair who had been planning to come to my talk later that day, but something had come up. They were canceling all study-abroad programs. He needed to start informing the students. Canceling, really? Yes, he'd gotten official word that the cases in Asia and Europe were spiraling out of control. It wasn't bad here yet, but studying abroad was now, suddenly, out of the question.

The private university put me up at a nice hotel, but I could barely sleep at night. I lay awake, staring at an endless stream of social media posts about the pandemic on my glowing phone, red-eyed and jumpy, thinking about getting back. I was shocked by my own loneliness and uselessness. After spending two years in intense proximity with a very young child—crawling on me, suckling from me, winding her fingers through my hair, touching any part of my body that she could reach—I'd thought that getting away for a few days would be a welcome antidote for this constant caretaking, this intense intimacy. And yet, here I was, feeling cut off. Staying awake when I didn't need to. Waiting for a call in the night that didn't come. I had been so excited to get away, if momentarily, from the house in Michigan, but I now realized that the thrill of independence was hopelessly compromised by the new fears that took their place. There was no slipping back to the comfort of a past life. Being away from Evan and Willie made me think about life without them. To think about this was to consider a deeply melancholy vision of independence, completely unlike freedom.

On the flight home, the girl sitting next to me wore a mask over her face. She was the only one. My thoughts were with Evan and Willie. I was anxious to get back to them. Now that I had been away, I felt the finality of coming home.

\* \* \*

ONCE A WEEK, we waited upstairs by the windows to watch the garbage collectors arrive. They were punctual, arriving at 10 a.m. every Monday morning. We watched from Willie's second-story bedroom—a room that once belonged to Sharon's son and bore the marks of his boyhood: a stuffed trout the size of Willie; SpongeBob SquarePants paraphernalia; a full-sized mattress that sat, unboxed, unbedded, on the floor. We sat on the bed and watched for the garbage collectors. When I heard the *beep, beep* of their reversals at the house next to ours, I signaled for Willie to come and see. We watched the metal arms clasp our bin and dump the contents into its gnashing mouth. That was the only thing on our schedule on Monday. The rest of our day stretched ahead of us. Willie was not particularly interested in the garbage collectors, but I asked her to notice them every week, if only to feel a sense of time.

I told my parents I didn't think we should see them or Alex until this pandemic thing blew over. We were going to quarantine as best we could, order as much insulin as the pharmacy would let us have, order our groceries online for curbside pickup. The news said that diabetics were at greater risk. Diabetics like Willie? I called Willie's endocrinologist who reassured us that a young, well-managed diabetic like Willie would not be especially vulnerable. But my parents were getting older. They didn't believe it themselves, but it was true. The people on the news told us that they were at the greatest risk. Over the phone, I teased my mom that this would be harder on her than on us. We were homebodies. We had a pile of books and a toddler to run after. She would lose her mind at home with Dad all day. I promised that we'd resume Grandma-and-Willie days as soon as they told us it was safe to do so. Now it was just us three again, like it was back in New York. We had moved across state lines to find ourselves back where we started. But now it was not just us.

Everywhere across the globe, families were shrinking inside the walls of the home. We were all bound. All alone together.

When Willie went down for a nap, I would hyperfocus, writing anything I could think of writing. Sometimes I would write about Teresa Deevy and sometimes I would write about Willie and sometimes I would write about myself. I joined a writing group that met over Zoom. We set our meetings for every other week and this, too, became a marker of time that I could orient my days around. Evan would take the post-nap childcare shift. When Willie woke up, they would sit side by side on the sofa, and he would put on Daniel Tiger. I would walk by to get a glass of water and see their two heads, the two heads I love most in the world, and be relieved to have a room, an office, that I could enter into and escape them, if only for a few more hours before I would start thinking about what to make for dinner.

Our freezer was full from our weekly venture into the world to pick up our preordered groceries. One week someone on my social media feed said that we needed to wipe down all the groceries with disinfectant before putting them away. Another week we thought we should leave them on the cold porch for twelve hours before bringing them in. No one credible was supplying us with this information, or misinformation. These were just the things that buzzed around online until they stuck in a head, like mine, that was hungry for someone to tell us what to do. In those days, I found myself more reliant on social media than I ever had been before. My phone was a lifeline and a tormentor—connecting me with others in a time that I desperately needed connection, but also laying out increasingly impossible standards. Here, on my phone, were other mothers to talk with, commiserate with, listen to, learn from. I followed friends and strangers who posted tips about managing small children through the long, uninterrupted days. I found myself following more and more strangers—moms who had advice for feeding children and playing with them. From these infinitely creative, highly involved moms, I learned how to make dinosaur claws out of paper plates and sensory bins with rice. I could peek into other people's lives, checking my progress against theirs. Was I doing okay? Would it be all right? The homes of these online moms were as different from Sharon's as could be. On my screen, I found kitchens that were sparkling clean and unrelentingly white. The messes, if they existed, were contained off camera. The more I scrolled through my feed, the more I came to resent these mothers with their glib cheerfulness and their endless supply of rice, which never seemed to find its way into the nooks and crannies of the kitchen floor, impervious to all attempts at sweeping and vacuuming. How realistic was this version of parenting? How long could anyone be expected to maintain it? Through the pandemic, through childhood? Still, I found my people—mostly friends and acquaintances who responded to these impossible expectations with skepticism and wit. I would have loved to be more like them, taking it all in stride. I wrote long posts about the tedium of these long days and these impossible, glossy images of motherhood, and then I deleted most of them before posting. I wanted to connect but I didn't want to be a complainer, a bore.

But I was not the only one with complaints. Mothers across the world were getting squeezed by the pandemic and many were very, very angry about it. My experiences from a year before—leaving my job to help a child through a medical emergency and losing access to childcare—were now happening on a vast scale. Sociologist Jessica McCrory Calarco and her colleagues, who would go on to study the impact of the pandemic on mothers, describe how "substantive, unanticipated increases in parenting time may negatively impact at least some mothers' well-being."[4]

Writing in the careful language of academic research, Calarco and her associates differentiate the kind of welcome choice of "more family time" from the emergency closures and sudden reversals of plans that characterized pandemic parenting and that can lead to stress, anxiety, and frustration. The study found that the women most likely to be adversely affected by pandemic parenting were those who lost access to childcare, were balancing working from home with parenting, were unemployed, or held themselves to high standards of "intensive parenting," the kind of child-centered parenting that radiated out at me from the various sensory rice bins of my social media feed.[5] This was my second unexpected interruption of childcare: first, we lost Mother Goose after Willie's diagnosis and now, we lost my parents' part-time help. As I watched other parents struggle with these changes, I felt a dull sense of repetition—as if I somehow knew this was coming and had gotten ahead of the shock of it. We were on our own again.

Some nights I fell asleep on Sharon's Laura Ashley bedding and slept, undisturbed, until morning. Other nights the unstructured days seemed to scramble my head and I could not sleep. I read books late into the night when insomnia struck me. I would read looking for some template for this moment. I stayed up through one night finishing Gabriel García Márquez's *Love in the Time of Cholera,* which I pulled down from Sharon's bookshelf. I entered the lush tropical squalor of Fermina Daza's decaying manor. I was drawn to books that feature Gothic houses—places closing in on their inhabitants. I read Carmen Maria Machado's *In the Dream House* in one feverish evening. Machado's memoir describes her descent into and out of an abusive relationship through vignettes of the house she and her partner shared. I picked up Edgar Allan Poe's "The Masque of the Red Death," which tells of Prince Prospero's escape from a plague into a walled-off abbey where he pursues a life of pleasure, only for the plague to find him at last. Disease, dysfunction, domesticity. I could not get enough of it. Gothic novels tell how it feels to be trapped in a house with a history. In these novels, the bones of the dispossessed stir beneath our feet, first wives rattle the locked door, letters and objects from long ago return to disturb our present. The static nature of the house belies the tumult of time; those past lives that once lived in this same place refuse to give it up. A Gothic novel knows that there is something sinister about staying at home. Each space was and wasn't like the one I found myself in. They described what it's like to feel stuck in a place while unseen threats pulsed outside and inside at once.

As I was up late one night, reading, I heard the dogs barking at Frank's house next door. It was 3 a.m. Evan and Willie were fast asleep. With their hearing aids out, neither was wakened in the night by sounds. The dogs barked and barked and barked. A light was turned on at Frank's house, but this was usual. He kept his lights on most nights. I didn't know whether he was unable to sleep, like me, or if he preferred to sleep in a lit house. But this night was different. The lights were on and the dogs were barking but I saw no fluttery movements of shadows next door. It was illuminated but still, like a doll's house. I thought about Frank's diabetes. Sadie had warned me that he did not keep his blood sugar in check. She had told me stories of his passing out and hospitalizations. What if his blood sugar crashed in the night and he did not know it? What if he had been running high for days and was now in a diabetic coma? I thought of all the things that I worried about for Willie and what would happen when she was on her own someday. The dogs continued to bark. I thought about going next door and pounding on the door. I thought about calling the police. Give it five more minutes, I told myself. Those five came and went. Another five, and I would call. But five minutes came and five minutes went and I was not pounding on the door and not calling the police. I started to wonder if I would let a man die this way, through inaction. A man who shared a chronic illness with my daughter. I looked at the clock: 4 a.m. I had spent an hour in indecision. Perhaps I was being paranoid and the last year of monitoring Willie's diabetes had forced me into a state of hypervigilance, in which imagined threats lingered everywhere. And was it the right thing to do, I asked myself, to knock on a neighbor's door in the middle of the night in the middle of a pandemic? Years of living in a big city probably didn't help; there, shouts and sirens in the night were routine, but everyday urban noise didn't have the horror of two barking dogs into the silence next door. I knew that these were just excuses and that, given what I knew about Frank and about Type 1 Diabetes, I was right to be concerned. The hesitation was the problem. Shut up in my own house and my own pain, I had bolted more than one door. I stayed glued to my bed, unable to walk the few feet to check on my neighbor, because I was worn down by the mental load of caring. This other person was more than I could handle. I was losing my ability to care for anyone outside the walls of this house. Constant caring was making me less compassionate or less able to act on my compassion. And yet, at any moment, I could have reversed course and done the right thing. I continued to weigh and consider what to do next and then I realized that my thoughts were pinging in silence. The dogs had stopped barking.

In a few hours, the morning would begin. Evan would wake up first and make a pot of coffee for us to refill our cups from throughout the morning. Willie would wake next and I would hear her high-pitched squeaks telling me to get her out of the crib. As we sat around the breakfast table, Willie in her high chair, eating yogurt and Cheerios, I saw a shadow pass across

Frank's living room. He was awake. It was a normal morning in an abnormal time. I felt more tired than I had ever felt in all my life.

WHEN IT BECAME clear that the pandemic wasn't going anywhere, we started seeing my parents and Alex again. We resumed our weekly Sunday suppers, trudging through the slurry of late-winter snow to be together. Willie went back to Grandma and Grandpa's twice a week. There were no more playdates or in-person music classes or indoor excursions, but we at least had the change of scene that involved visiting my parents and seeing my brother. Willie and Alex had formed a wary bond, ignoring each other when there were other things to occupy them, but coming together with fierce loyalty if it meant they could watch a movie together. They would sit side by side on the sofa watching *Pete's Dragon* and *The Little Mermaid*. If Alex had been watching on his own, he would have fast-forwarded and rewinded back and forth to his favorite parts but, with Willie, he was willing to sit and watch from beginning to end.

We had only three months left in Michigan before Evan would need to be back to teach his classes in the fall. Mom and I picked up our walks again. Now I would accompany her all the way to her door, stretching out the time we had together. We took different routes each time and I found myself refamiliarizing myself with the scenes of my youth. The placards in front of the houses were changing. Love Is Love. Black Lives Matter. Science Is Real. My mother's stories went deeper into her childhood, wrapping what was happening around us into the personal thread out of which her life had taken shape. She talked about memories of polio and Vietnam and mothering four children, largely on her own. We walked through the nice neighborhoods with the nice placards and remembered the time that Alex's neighbors, not too far from here, tried to keep him out. In the cold northern air, our talk took physical shape: condensation from our warm breath passed like tangible speech from each of our lips, floating above us as a single cloud.

THE MAGNOLIA TREE in front of Sharon's house bloomed too early. An unexpected warm spell in April stirred the first buds. Soft, downy pods appeared at the tips of the skeletal branches. Soon, furled white petals began to push upward through the buds like butterflies straining against the bonds of a chrysalis. Just before the buds started to open, there was another wave of cold weather. The morning frost froze them still. There they stood, suspended, not yet opened, waiting for the warmth to return. But it did not. One unrelenting week of subzero temperatures followed another. The white buds began to brown, and then their softness hardened and turned brittle. When the warmth finally returned in May, they were too far gone to recover. The magnolia tree stood this way through the summer, as the green grass spread a lush carpet around its roots and its neighboring trees sprouted thick green leaves; it stood in the midst of all the surrounding splendor, its buds frozen in perpetual fall. A dull, dark reminder of what remains.

Sharon put her house on the market in June while we were still there. She had bought herself a small place in town and would be selling her house. She apologized profusely for the interruption to our last days in Michigan. Her real estate agent assured us that all the agents and prospective buyers would wear masks as they trooped through. We tried to keep the house in good enough shape. I saw the house again through the buyer's eyes. It was going to sell for a bundle. As a historical home in a highly desirable part of town, it would make Sharon a good deal of money and the buyers would assuredly gut it and completely remodel. The kind of people who could afford a house like this in a neighborhood like this in 2020 would not put up with the unfinished basement, the uneven stairs, or the 1980s skylights.

As expected, the house sold quickly. Sharon stopped by every day to start the arduous process of packing a lifetime into cardboard boxes—residual children's toys, family heirlooms, sports equipment from long-lost hobbies, and boxes and boxes of Greg's photographs, which would head off to an archive in Florida. I watched as the various household tools made their way to piles marked "Trash," "Give away," and "Save." A family friend unhooked the espresso machine and carted it off. We tried to stay out of the way and began to pack up our more meager collection of things, which would fit into a small rental truck.

I had never spent as much time in a house as I did that year in Sharon's house, bound up by quarantine and parenting a toddler. I lived a version of my life intensely within those walls, staying at home. The word "stay" sounded different to me now. It seemed to be both a command—"stay put" or "stay where you are"—and also an endearment: "stay with me." Perhaps when we stay somewhere for long enough, something remains—a lingering presence or, as in my Gothic novels, a faintly haunting past that reverberates into the present. I looked around the house a final time, checking drawers and cabinets to make sure that we hadn't left anything behind. I surveyed the yard. We had planted mint and basil in the garden. Willie had squelched the dirt between her fingers and grabbed at the spade until I let her dig away. Would they remain after the new owners moved in and the potholed driveway had been torn up? What about the Styrofoam rocket that we had launched from the driveway that was now stuck on the rooftop? Styrofoam can last for five hundred years without decomposing. It could, potentially, sit on the roof for another half century unless a storm finally blew it away or the roof was replaced. And what else, in that storm or reroofing, would be dislodged? My memories, Sharon's memories, Evan's, Willie's? They all pile on top of each other, these memories, like sedimentary layers of different lives lived in the same place.

I climbed into the rental: Evan was in the driver's seat and Willie was strapped into her child seat in the back. We waved goodbye to the house on Franklin Street. I did not know what would come next for any of us, but we could not stay here in someone else's house any longer. It was time to go home.

8

## Motherboard

There were a few traces of Sharon left in the apartment when we returned to NYC. She left in a hurry as quarantine restrictions tightened up; she had been planning to return. We found a robe in the closet, a bar of soap, groceries in the pantry. We asked if we could send anything to her, but she was happy to part with such small things. We threw away the robe, used the soap, ate the groceries. The apartment was ours again, but things were different. There was still a pandemic going on. We had missed the worst of it. The days when, we were told, ambulance sirens rang endlessly and the streets were empty for all but those on the most desperate errands. It was still quiet, too quiet, but the edge of danger had blunted some.

After a year at Sharon's house, I realized that if we were going to stay in this apartment, we would need to make new memories; yet, still, the old ones had a powerful hold. I looked out over the same rooftops and treetops that I had gazed at, bleary-eyed, between pregnancies that were not to be. I watched the boats pull slowly up the Hudson, as I had watched them years ago while nursing Willie. I pushed the stroller—heavier now—to parks where I had spent listless days after Willie's diagnosis. But it no longer felt like I was living in a loop. Now things were different. Willie was different. I was different. The world, caught up in the haze of the ongoing pandemic, was different. We wore masks in the elevator and common spaces and, until we realized the threat had lessened, outdoors at the parks. The anxiety that I felt about Willie after her diabetes diagnosis—the need to be constantly vigilant against biological threats—had morphed into a general condition. The parents that I met on our daily visits to the playground were edgy and watchful. They worried about germs and long-term side effects; they worried about lost socialization and speech delays. Evan, Willie, and I continued to stay at home as much as possible. Groceries came in by delivery unless I needed to pop in somewhere quickly. And yet, despite all these differences, it still felt like a homecoming. I was ready to start the next chapter of our lives here, together, whatever was to come.

We enrolled Willie for two days a week at a day care nearby. It was a huge extravagance. The part-time editing that I had been doing was finished and I had plans to teach as an adjunct instructor at the university-one-does-not-turn-down, which would almost cover the expense of two days of childcare. We had worked out all the details so that we could manage her diabetes—checking her blood sugar and giving her shots of insulin—while she was in school those two days. Willie had started wearing a continuous glucose monitor (CGM) soon after she was diagnosed with diabetes. It was a miraculous device that tracked her blood sugar at all times and connected through Wi-Fi to our phones, allowing us to monitor her blood sugar from a distance. It was the only reason that we had been able to pull off sending Willie to day care. The center was close enough that I could run over when my phone alerted me that she was low or high. I would run over at mealtimes to give her insulin and at snack times. When a child's parents brought cupcakes for a birthday, it would mean another trip downstairs and out the door. But it was manageable. The school was willing to work with us—now that so many families were fleeing the city or keeping their kids home, they were desperate to keep our part-time tuition. But also, another side effect of the pandemic was that the school would allow only one parent entry. It would be me. Evan was teaching two classes online and was tied up on Zoom for two-hour stretches. It would not be safe or practical to make him the single parent on insulin watch. Another duty we had planned to share would now be mine alone.

In the fall, while still in Michigan, I got a call: due to the pandemic, all adjunct teaching contracts would be terminated through the coming year. I cried for two days over it. Such a small thing to lament so pitifully. But it was the tenuous straw I was holding on to—teaching again, going back to a small slice of my old life, introducing Willie to a wider world of day care teachers and schoolmates. When the teaching dried up, Evan and I discussed what we would do. Should we terminate the contract with the day care? Just swallow the lost deposit and walk away? We decided that we would stick with our original plan, minus the teaching income. The tuition was a significant amount of money and a big risk to take in a pandemic. It was a financial risk and a health risk. Write, Evan said. Just take the time and write.

SPENDING OUR DAYS together in such close quarters, under quarantine in a small apartment, five days of the week, I found myself wondering where Willie ended and I began. As close as Evan and I had always been, we could separate easily, moving into a different room from each other and retreating to our separate consciousnesses, our separate bodies. He would write and teach in the bedroom—he didn't have a desk, but a haphazard stand, much like a music stand, where he would prop up his computer and compose. When Willie was at day care, I would colonize the kitchen table, spreading out notes and books and concentrating, in intense bursts, on whatever was holding my attention until it was time to run over and give Willie her insulin. Sometimes our phones would alert us, letting us know that Willie's blood sugar was high or low. Both Evan and I had our phones connected to her continuous glucose monitor. When the alert would sound, we would hear it like an echo from across different rooms of the apartment. It felt like, even on those two days that she was away, a part of her body was still connected, umbilical-like, to my phone. Where were the borders of our bodies now, three years after I gave birth to her? I thought back to fetal microchimerism and the permeability of the borders between us that defined those first nine months of gestation and will linger on forever. And how did these technologies, like this phone, alter the discrete boundaries between parent and child; between inside and outside; between your insides and mine?

The messiness of this distinction first presented itself when I was pregnant with her. Seven months pregnant, I strolled across campus to teach a class with my belly preceding me. At a certain point, I was thinking about the novel I was about to teach—John McGahern's *Amongst Women*—and how I would address some of its difficult themes of violence and abuse with my students. As I was thinking, I stopped mid-step. What if these thoughts were bad for the baby? The campus, bustling with between-class foot traffic, swirled around me as I stopped. It seemed, for a moment, like it was a self-evident truth that the baby could think my thoughts with me: that she was a tiny eavesdropper on my unconscious. But she wasn't, was she? I laughed out loud at myself for such an idea and for literally stopping in my tracks to consider it.

I've continued to wonder whether this thought, which struck me with such force during pregnancy, was really so implausible. We know that at a late stage of its development, a fetus can hear in the womb, and that it can pick up on stress and other emotional changes. This body of research on how experiences in utero affect life outcomes is known as "fetal programming" and shares many of the contours of an older and discredited idea of "maternal impressionism," which argued that everything from mental attributes to physical features could be caused by the emotional state of the mother during pregnancy.[1] One study in "fetal programming" links maternal anxiety to asthma and another argues that changes in the emotional status of the mother between the time that the fetus is in utero and later, after birth, could lead to adverse health outcomes in the child.[2] Is the idea that a fetus processes, on some biological level, a mother's mental state so different from the idea of them thinking our thoughts? Although "fetal programming" continues to be a matter of ongoing debate, these studies have important implications for thinking about the long-term effects of trauma on health and how traumatic experiences may be passed on from parent to child. It is also easy to overstate the findings of studies like these and to use them as yet more evidence for maternal responsibility (and guilt). Nothing makes a person feel calm like being told repeatedly that one must remain calm, or face dire consequences.

Where does the barrier that separates us lie now, after Willie is out in the world? And has that barrier shifted now that I am not only responsible for basic caretaking, but as I have also become the custodian for devices that further trouble those barriers? I put her hearing aids in and take them out; we call them her ears. I say, "Willie, let's take out your ears," when she gets in the bath. I sign, "Hearing aids?" (index finger curved, tapping above my ear), when it's time to put them on. I am her ears. Or, at least, I manage the devices that allow her to hear. I am also her pancreas. I monitor her blood sugar with the CGM, tracking biodata at all times.

There are a few CGM manufacturers on the market, but the one we chose was Dexcom because it was small enough not to dwarf her tiny body and, from what little we knew, it seemed reliable. We call Willie's Dexcom "Dexxie." We took the nickname from Willie's new speech therapist, Selma, who also has diabetes. Selma meets with Willie over Zoom because in-person meetings are no longer allowed. It is not ideal for an easily distracted almost-three-year-old, but I am happier with Selma than I have ever been with a speech therapist. For the first time, we have someone in our lives who sees the full picture. She knows how hard diabetes can be to manage and the toll it takes on us all. She understands, from personal experience, the cognitive burden of diabetes management and, in her professional capacity, the "listening fatigue" that Willie experiences from the extra strain of listening with severe hearing loss. In other words, she knows that, in our conjoined lives in this small apartment, we're all exhausted all the time. She talks to Willie about the snacks she likes to eat—the ones that help stabilize her blood sugar—and they show each other their Dexxies. She goes through the Ling Sounds we have been practicing since Willie was three months old—"Ssss . . . Shhh . . . Ahhh . . . Ohhh . . ." Every time Willie hears a sound, she puts a peg in a pegboard. Selma pauses when she hears Dexxie beep. We laugh—whose beep was that one? Willie is low and I get her some juice and then we go back to listening for sounds: "Ssss . . . Shhh . . . Ahhh."

*  *  *

I HAVE TO remind myself that Willie's CGM is very new technology and that it, along with other technologies for diabetes management, will continue to change and evolve over her lifetime. Glucose testing shares a history with other at-home diagnostic tests, which have moved from the lab to the home and changed our understanding of home healthcare. Like pregnancy testing, glucose testing can be performed on blood or urine. But here the differences end. A pregnancy test is used at discrete periods of your life until you get the answer you are looking for. For someone with diabetes, glucose testing is a constant; knowing your blood sugar at any point in time can determine your sense of risk (is your blood sugar crashing?), what you eat and drink (do you need some juice?), and how much insulin to take. The first glucose tests for urine in the mid-1800s allowed for diabetic care as we know it, but the technology didn't take its current shape until 1908 when a copper reagent was first used to detect sugar in the urine followed by a blood test in 1965 for use by physicians. As the test became smaller and easier to use, making do with less blood at each permutation, self-monitoring of blood sugar became the standard of care.[3] The first CGM came on the market in 1999; these early tests collected three days' worth of information that was then downloaded to the endocrinologist's office. Only later did the CGM begin to offer "real-time" information to the diabetic—showing them their current (or slightly delayed) blood sugar information and allowing them to do away with the painful and irritating finger pricks to test blood. Studies show improved health outcomes for patients who wear CGMs, including better glucose control, fewer instances of hypoglycemia, and lower A1Cs.[4]

The CGM includes two pieces of equipment: a sensor that is implanted under Willie's skin that takes continual readings of her blood sugar and a monitor (or a Bluetooth-connected smartphone) that receives this data and shows us her current blood sugar and its movement across time. The monitor's visual interface includes an arrow that tells us that her blood sugar is going up or down and whether it is plummeting fast or dropping slowly. If her blood sugar is dangerously low, the monitor beeps, as does Evan's phone and my phone. We are all connected.

Every ten days, we need to implant a new CGM. We build a ritual around the implantation. Willie takes a bath and we pull the sensor off in the bathtub. It is like ripping off a Band-Aid but perhaps worse because of the small wire implanted under the skin. I do not know exactly how it feels. I think that removing it in the bathtub makes it less painful, but I don't know for sure. It is implanted on her body, not mine. On implantation night, Willie knows that she'll get to watch television after bath time—the only time we allow TV at night. While she's hypnotized by Peppa Pig jumping in muddy puddles, we take a plastic pod that looks like a hand-sized spaceship, clean Willie's skin with an alcohol wipe, and press an orange button. *Click*. The sound means that the pod has finished its purpose and that the small plastic wire is now under Willie's skin. We have implanted her. Next, we snap the sensor into place and, after a warm-up period, it is ready to start communicating to the monitor and telling us if Willie's blood sugar is high, low, or just right.

It is a miraculous piece of technology that has allowed us to do away with some of the pain and tedium of diabetes management. We no longer need to prick her fingers every three hours, including the night shift, which was particularly demoralizing in the days after her diagnosis. And yet, there's no such thing as an unmixed good. Willie's CGM often goes awry—waking us in the middle of the night to tell us she was dangerously low only for us to discover that it was incorrect. Errors can be caused by anything from Willie lying on top of it in her sleep to her taking Tylenol for a high fever; the Tylenol, for reasons I can never understand, causes faulty readings. Implanting it is not always straightforward—sometimes we have "bleeders" when the implantation hits a blood vessel and Willie's blood drenches the mechanism and renders it unusable.

My relationship with the machine is vexed—I'm dependent on it in myriad ways and I resent this dependence. I look at it often, checking and rechecking her blood sugar when I am with her and when she is at day care, when she is awake and when she is asleep. It is another screen that I forget how to do without. It's changed the way that I mother my child. Sometimes, I find myself looking at her CGM to decide whether she might be hungry rather than asking Willie herself. I defer to the machine. When it goes offline, I feel adrift.

When we came back from Michigan, Willie was still in her crib. It was a convertible crib so, at any point, we could lower and remove one side of the high bars that kept her in. I asked my sister Jenny her advice. Should we convert the crib to a toddler bed yet? She told us to wait—it's a hard transition once they can get out of bed all night. Unless Willie was trying to climb out, we might as well keep her in. It was the kind of advice Evan and I wanted to hear; we were in no hurry to have a free-range toddler protesting bedtime every night.

And then, one night, we put Willie to bed in her crib as usual. She was having a harder time going down, wanting one more story and then one more story; wanting snuggles from me, then Evan, then insisting that I had not actually snuggled with her yet; wanting a parade of stuffed animals to be put in her crib one after the other, never satisfied that we had found the right one for optimal sleep. Finally, we tried to play tough guys. No more, Willie, that is enough. It's bedtime. She cried and protested, but we shut the door and turned on *The Great British Bake Off*, sinking with exhaustion into the sofa. After about fifteen minutes, it was quiet. Good, we thought, it worked. We continued to watch as contestants mixed batters and frosted cakes. Kitchen timers beeped on the television. Cakes were tested for doneness. And then, another beep, this time from inside the house. The CGM has different kinds of beeps—low, slow ones for a mild high blood sugar and urgent, staccato-like beeps for an urgent low. I know them all without looking. This beep that we were hearing now included a series of trills like a 1990s computer modem straining for a connection. It was the error alert. I peeked my head into Willie's room. She was asleep, curled up with her stuffed dragon. Next to her head, crumpled and ill-used, was the sensor that she had ripped off of her arm in protest.

The next day, we converted her crib to a toddler bed. She never ripped a sensor off again.


WILLIE'S BELLY IS a canvas of purple bruises. They look like tiny fingers have pressed blueberries, *squish,* all around her belly button. She will no longer let us give shots anywhere but the center of her belly. We used to give her shots on the back of her arm and on her thighs. Never on her bottom, which would always make her shake her head and squirm away. But now that she is vocal and very much her own person, she tells us, No, belly. All the brochures we received at the hospital said that we would need to move the shots around to prevent lipohypertrophy, in which lumps of fat build up around a site of frequent injection and slow down the rate of insulin absorption. But Willie wants to be able to see the shot piercing her skin. She does not want a shot on her bottom or the back of her arm where she can't see it. She does not want to be surprised. She wants to pinch her own fat and watch, attentively, as the needle enters. There is so little that she can control, but she has this and so we give her the shots where she wants them. The little purple bruises circle her belly button like darts forever missing the bull's-eye.

Willie and I go back and forth struggling between safety and autonomy. I want to keep her healthy and well. She wants to do things for herself, to be a big girl. I want this too, but sometimes those two sets of needs clash. There are some nonnegotiables: insulin when she eats, seat belts in the car. And then there is an enormous expanse of gray zone where I might need to give a little or she might need to give a little. I try to give her choices: you can have another snack, but that means another shot. So what will it be, snack and a shot or no snack and no shot? She chooses the snack and I give her another shot. She doesn't want me to take her hearing aids out for her to go to sleep or go to the pool. We negotiate and negotiate. You can nap with your hearing aids on but you must take them out when you get in the water. You can take them out yourself, but you cannot pull on the tubing—not like that, like this. She loves to negotiate. Five more minutes till bedtime. Ten more? No, five. Ten? Fine, eight. It is exhausting but it is also thrilling to see that flash of willfulness, which has been there since she was a baby, materialize into independence and self-possession. She is her own person, through and through. She is her own person and her person requires assistance—me, Evan, CGM, hearing aids. It is a group effort.

Every time we meet with Willie's endocrinologist—every three months—we talk about adding another piece of technology into the mix; we consider getting Willie an insulin pump. The insulin pump is another piece of hardware injected under the skin. You fill the pump with a three-day supply of insulin and inject a small catheter into the skin to dispense the insulin. Whereas the CGM is a surveillance technology—allowing us to see what is going on in the body—the pump actually administers insulin, regulating the blood sugar. For the most part, these two systems have worked independently. These systems eliminated finger sticks and needles, but they did not take away the mental labor of counting carbohydrates and calculating dosages. Nor did they take away the human error of miscalculations. Although some aspects of diabetes management would remain, with the insulin pump, we could dispense with shots and use an app on our phone to communicate with the insulin pump and tell the device how much insulin she needs.

The goal for many diabetics is to fully sync these two systems so that the monitor can communicate directly with the pump, anticipate behaviors and patterns, and provide proper dosages without human intervention. What was available now was far from a fully automated system. Every three days, we would change the pump site. The pumps are becoming smaller and sleeker, unlike the first prototype pump designed by Dr. Arnold Kadish in 1963, which was an enormous device carried like a backpack that overwhelmed the frame of the adult man who carried it.[5] It looked like a space-age jet pack. Modern insulin pumps can hide easily under a shirtsleeve. Some have tubes and need to be worn in a fanny pack, but others are cordless and not much bigger than the Dexcom Willie is already wearing. Getting a pump would allow us to give smaller dosages of insulin—fractions of units as opposed to the blunt 0.5-unit measurements of the pen needles we use. And yet, we have not done it.

Despite all of these advantages, we were not ready for a pump quite yet. I often asked myself why I was reluctant to get a piece of technology with such obvious benefits. Part of it was a fear of rocking the boat. We had finally fallen into a good routine—her A1C, the number that the doctors use to gauge the overall health of a person with diabetes, was very low, meaning very good. Why change things up now? But this wasn't the real reason. I looked at Willie's small body as I dressed her in her pajamas for bed. The green lights of her hearing aids blinked back at me, not yet completely covered by the blond hair that was only slowly starting to grow. Her Dexcom, which looks so small and discreet peeking out of a short-sleeve shirt in the promotional pictures on an adult's proportions, takes up a considerable part of her forearm or half of her belly. Where would a pump go? There is so little real estate on her body and so much of it is already occupied. The only insulin pump that, at her age, would be covered by insurance involved cords. I didn't worry so much about her pulling them out herself, but I worried about her snagging them on the playground or another child pulling at them. The needles were awful, but they were better than they used to be—instead of syringes, we used an insulin pen that required only two quick twists—one to put a new disposable needle on the top and another to twist the base to the correct dosage.[6]

We have a picture book for Willie that features Supreme Court Justice Sonia Sotomayor, who is also diabetic. In the book, she is pictured as a little girl reading a book while, beside her, a long needle and insulin vial lie waiting for her use. Willie asks why the needle is so big. I try to explain that when Sotomayor was diagnosed, when she was seven years old, it was before the use of disposable needles. I look up her story online and read how she had to wake up early to boil water and sterilize the needles she would need for the day and, before the use of small lancets to prick a finger, how she had to use a razor to get blood samples.[7] For Willie, we order the smallest needle available and if we need to give her a shot while she sleeps, she will often sleep through it. When we're out in public, we do not hide the needles or the process of giving her a shot—I treat it the same as asking a kid to blow their nose into a tissue at the playground. I do not want Willie to think there is anything shameful about needing a shot. But the greatest advantage of the pen needle and the reason that I was not ready to get her a pump yet was that the needle is something that *I* can carry. It does not need to live on Willie's body. She is carrying enough already.

THE TECHNOLOGY OF diabetes management is changing rapidly. Researchers continue to explore other treatments, such as stem cell therapy and pancreas transplants, but for an increasing number of diabetics, treatment involves the daily embrace of technology. The historian Chris Feudtner attributes the American approach to diabetes management to our "propensity to embrace more technology as the best solution to our problems" and argues that "[p]erhaps no story of medical progress . . . has been more influenced by this technology ethos than the history of diabetes."[8] With the CGM, we've waded tentatively into that "technology ethos"—a world of devices, algorithms, and cloud-based networks that are inching closer to automating the process of diabetes management. Extending beyond Elliott P. Joslin's doctrine of self-control, we now have a host of technologies that allow for tighter control than Joslin, treating diabetics in the first half of the twentieth century, could have ever conceived. The goal for many is to create a technological system that can function like an artificial pancreas—that can, through self-regulating technological systems, simulate the endocrine system: monitoring blood sugar, registering changes such as food intake and exercise, and dispensing the appropriate amount of insulin. Many diabetics are already using a "closed loop" system, which relies on an algorithm to "close the loop" between the CGM and the insulin pump—previously separate devices that did not communicate— allowing the pump to respond to changes in blood sugar noted by the CGM and dispense insulin without human intervention.[9]

Before the major biotech companies got in on the action, it was individual diabetics who created these algorithms to close the loops between the two systems—the CGM and the insulin pump. These do-it-yourself "loopers," as they call themselves, discuss their techniques over message boards and community forums and freely share their data with each other to improve the algorithms. They use the hashtag #WeAreNotWaiting to share information on social media; the name registers their impatience with the rate of change from biotech companies and approval bodies like the FDA.[10] Only now, the biotech companies are catching up with them, creating devices that communicate better with each other and that require less and less user oversight.

The closed-loop system is an example of a smart technology that uses the data it collects to learn and improve. It is artificial intelligence and, as such, raises the specter of machines that become smarter than their inventors and users. The philosopher Mark Taylor describes his own experience with a closed-loop CGM and insulin pump system as follows:

> When I began to use the closed-loop system, my pump and I had to get to know each other. It had to learn my patterns of eating, sleeping, exercising, and glucose levels throughout the day and night, and I had to learn to trust the pump and let it do what it wants to do. More challenging, I had to learn to be willing to do what the pump wants when it wants me to do it. My pump really does have a mind of its own—it can be a harsh taskmaster that allows no disagreement.[11]

Taylor goes on to discuss the dangers of smart machines, which includes the unregulated data that they generate for the corporations that control them. CGMs and insulin pumps are "smart things" that learn about our bodies, share that information, and adapt to provide more accurate care. There are many potential misuses of this data; corporations can use this data for profit or bad actors can hack into systems with mortal consequences. Despite Taylor's sense of caution and regard for the big-picture stakes of biodata gathering, he also speaks lovingly about the complex interplay between himself and the machine that he relies on to live. In gaining excellent diabetic management—what diabetics refer to as "tight control"—he, paradoxically, cedes more control to the machines that take on an intimate role in his life. He writes that this reliance on biotechnology taught him to reconsider the relationship between the human body, machines, and networks: "Diabetes has taught me that I am never only myself, but am always also other than myself."[12] And yet, Taylor sees the good results—the improved health and lower burden on his everyday life—and remains hopeful about the medical consequences of what he describes as "intervolution," or the further enmeshing of bodies, things, and networks.

The CGM and insulin pump become part of the body—literally implanted under the skin, producing biodata, and substituting for some of its natural functions—but they are also connected to broader cloud-based networks that circulate the information and "learn" from it. I wonder how my experience as the parent of a child with diabetes differs from Taylor's description of the collapsing of the self/other distinction. Motherhood, at least how I have experienced it, is itself an experience that troubles the distinction between self and other. Pregnancy taught me what chronic illness taught Taylor—that the boundaries between the self and the other are never firm; that they are, in fact, shockingly permeable. Willie is outside me—is very much herself apart from me—and yet, I hold her biodata in my hand, rely on medical technologies, and the companies that create them, to perform the functions that would otherwise happen internally, automatically. I care for her and I care for her devices. I am part mother, part machine.


I HAVE ONLY recently come around to science fiction. It is not a genre that used to speak to me—as a child, in particular, I gravitated toward old-timey historical novels like *Anne of Green Gables* and *Little House on the Prairie.* My other worlds were set in the past, not distant galaxies. Looking back, this aversion to science fiction fell neatly into the gender codes of a 1980s childhood. Even years later, as a college student, when I might have outgrown that bias, sci-fi still felt like an aggressively masculine domain and the examples that I knew best, *Star Trek* and *Star Wars,* ping-ponged between ascetic futurism and Wild West survivalism, neither of which appealed to my love of history and realism. But I've recently started to take an interest in the genre. I've started to realize that sci-fi is able to tell us something important about our moment and, particularly, about our increasing dependence on intelligent machines.

Science fiction, after all, gave us the figure of the cyborg. Donna Haraway's formative essay, "A Cyborg Manifesto: Science, Technology, and Socialist-Feminism in the Late Twentieth Century" draws upon her extensive reading of science fiction. In this essay, Haraway describes a feminist future arising from out of the interface of human and machine. She describes cyborgs as "creatures simultaneously animal and machine, who populate worlds ambiguously natural and crafted."[13] Whereas women, in Western culture at least, have long been associated with "the natural"—defined by our bodies and their functions, including childbirth—Haraway argues that by the late twentieth century, this distinction between the natural and the crafted (the body and the machine) no longer holds up. Haraway, in her provocative argument, breaks down these binaries, arguing that we are all "chimeras" or "hybrids of machine and organism."[14] Our technologies have become intimately connected to our bodies and have expanded their capabilities: phones augment our voice, allowing us to speak across distances; computers augment our mind, expanding our ability to access information; and cars and other vehicles expand our speed and geographical range. Voices, brains, and legs are not what they once were. Haraway's language recalls the idea of microchimerism, that we cannot get away from the blending of parts that defines motherhood and, perhaps, that defines twenty-first-century life in general. You don't have to look far in the current discourse on parenting to see a divide between ideas of the natural and the technological. On social media, we have natural moms, "crunchy" moms, breast-is-best moms, and vegan moms on one side, and "trust science" moms, statistics moms, fed-is-best moms, and let-them-have-their-screens moms on the other.

If you have ever lost your phone and realized your profound reliance on the device for managing your schedule, knowing directions, or communicating with others, you have some sense of how certain machines not only become tools, but feel like they are a part of our mental and emotional composition. My hand will curl involuntarily in moments of rest or repose as if it is holding a phantom phone. It is easy to lament this state of affairs, but Haraway, critically, does not. She celebrates our enmeshment with technology, which allows us to extend and exceed the boundedness of our bodies. She ends her essay with the memorable line: "I would rather be a cyborg than a goddess."[15] When women's lives are so often reduced to the biological body, especially their reproductive role, Haraway's feminist vision involves a technological release from these restraints. Reading Haraway's essay in the wake of parenthood, I wonder about the role of caretaking in this cyborg future (or present). An earlier generation of scientifically minded feminists, like Shulamith Firestone, imagined a feminist future as the final eradication of biological motherhood. Firestone argued for artificial reproduction as a way of freeing the human race from the bonds of maternity and creating the conditions for equality.[16] Only by breaking out of the biological bonds of pregnancy and the social bonds of the family could women be truly free.

I lack the imagination to go this far. Perhaps I am, as an eminent writer once called me at a cocktail party, "a bourgeois girl from Michigan." I'd be in good company. Science fiction writer Ursula Le Guin described herself as a "Portland housewife."[17] She could imagine other planets, other galaxies, and other genders, but she could not imagine for herself a more solid basis for reality than the four walls she shared with her husband and children. But there's something else that's missing from the accounts that I have read of cyborgs. The fact remains that someone needs to take care of all those machines. Their batteries run out and their equipment wears down. They take relentless, often tedious amounts of maintenance. And what is maintenance if not care? In her article "Maintenance and Care," Shannon Mattern argues for the importance of "care work," broadly conceived, as essential to repairing our world. She includes digital preservation and data management as care work alongside domestic labor and reproductive labor.[18] Who will be caring for these machines in our future worlds? Will we continue the cycle of treating care work as unskilled labor, either not paying or underpaying the people who carry it out? Will the cyborg maintenance workers be mostly women, especially women of color and immigrant women? Although I cannot imagine a future that dispenses with the human activity of care work, I would like to imagine a future that spreads it out more evenly and that treats it as the highest form of labor that we, as a species, can perform.

Caregiving is complicated in science fiction. It can be, as in works like Kazuo Ishiguro's *Never Let Me Go,* something one is compelled to do as an act of personal sacrifice. In Ishiguro's dystopian world, "carers" are removed from their parents and raised in boarding schools where they learn to give up their autonomy and their future to ensure the well-being of others. In one of the cyborg novels that Haraway cites, Anne McCaffrey's *The Ship Who Sang,* parents must decide whether to allow the state to euthanize their disabled child or give her up to be re-created into a part-woman, part-spaceship named Helva. The parents choose to revoke their care duties to allow the state to care for, and profit from, the highly efficient woman-ship. In the book, the parents and their decision occupy no more than a few paragraphs, after which Helva's adventures begin. Ceding caretaking responsibilities in both these works is closely associated with an overarching state that benefits from the labor and sacrifice of the child whose care they provide for and whose future they proscribe. This is a dominant trope when thinking about care in science fiction (especially dystopian) novels, which can make it difficult to imagine what a more equitable distribution of care would look like in the real world.[19]

And yet, there are other writers, activists, and political thinkers who are doing just that, imagining how we might base social change around the just distribution of care. Indigenous Water Protectors who position themselves as caretakers for our threatened waterways, advocates for parents and children separated at the U.S. border, disabled individuals creating forms of mutual aid to support each other in the face of unreliable governmental or family-based assistance, and trans individuals and their families fighting for gender-affirming care are all examples of political activists who foreground the importance of care work. For radical thinkers, like scholars Hiʻilei Julia Kawehipuaakahaopulani Hobart and Tamara Kneese, care must be collective in order to open up new possibilities for the future; they write, "As the traditionally undervalued labor of caring becomes recognized as a key element of individual and community resilience, radical care provides a roadmap for envisioning an otherwise."[20] But care discourse also offers a large umbrella for individuals on the other side of the political divide; conservatives and liberals alike have a long history of invoking care work to support their political views. Among conservative movements today, parental rights have become a significant platform for asserting the primacy of family care over various forms of educational, governmental, or medical authority. Just as there are conservative, liberal, and radical approaches to science fiction, no political orientation has a monopoly on considering the societal implications of care work.

I find myself thinking more and more about science fiction because, among all the literary genres, it is most concerned with what kind of future path our actions in the present guide us toward. In that sense, it shares a future-orientation with activists who likewise call us to account for how our actions today will impact tomorrow. The future of care work might, as we see in Ishiguro's and McCaffrey's novels, lead to a subclass of dehumanized care workers conscripted by the state; or, perhaps more likely, we might see the acceleration of our current trends of hyper-individualized approaches to care work that rest largely on unpaid or underpaid labor; or, as radical scholars and activists imagine, we might yet change our direction and create new collective possibilities of shared caretaking.

And where, I wonder, does technology fit into all this? In

much science fiction, technology is both the solution and the problem, getting us out of one mess only to mire us in another. As H. G. Wells, the father of science fiction, put it, "All these new things, these new inventions, these new powers come crowding along. Every one of them is fraught with consequences, and yet, it is only after something has hit us hard that we set about dealing with it."[21] In the world of parenting too, we are constantly caught unprepared. Technological solutions come along, championed as replacements for the extensive demands of care work without a sense of the consequences. As our devices become smaller and smaller, the labor and maintenance work of the technology becomes less and less visible; we see the progress and sweep away the mess. Some of the things that we don't see are the resource-extraction, manufacturing, and production of the technology or the work required to keep it working. This human dimension fades away into the invisible labor of caretaking. I wish that I had more solutions clearly in my mind, but it seems to me that the first step to creating more equitable care work must be the simple act of bringing this invisible labor to light and thinking through the tangled consequences of our technological solutions.

WILLIE IS AT day care, watched over by teachers who are loving and kind, but who are not paid nearly what they deserve. I stop by at lunchtime to give her the insulin she needs with her apple and bagel and goldfish crackers. As I wait for Willie to finish her lunch, I chat with the teachers about how the day is going: it is one of those wild days when the kids are full of antic energy. The teachers talk with me about their kids—a daughter finishing college, a son in the marines. I've come to enjoy this little ritual. In the two months since she started, Willie has attained a queenly status in the classroom. Coming in only two days a week, her appearances have the bearing of a television guest spot. She is also the only girl in a room full of boys and the only one whose mother comes to visit every day for lunch. The other kids either don't notice or don't care about the shots. It has already become mere background.

I take the elevator back up to our apartment. I will have three more hours until pickup. Evan is in the other room and I hear the soft clicking of his laptop. Our phones will alert us if I need to go back down—if I've given Willie too much insulin or too little. Now the teachers will be getting them ready for their naps, lining the children up on blue cots and dimming the lights to prepare them to sleep.

I flip open my laptop and resume the YouTube video that I was watching before I left to give Willie her insulin. It is a dry, educational video explaining the different parts of a computer. There is so much I don't know about the technology I use every day: the technology that I increasingly do not know how to live without. On the video, low-budget animation and still images swipe across my screen, each showing a square of plastic hooked up to various knobs, sockets, slots, and wires. This is the motherboard, I am told. A man narrates. He tells me that the central processing unit (CPU) is the brain of the computer, but that the motherboard is the heart. He labels all the parts that are attached to the motherboard—all the bits and pieces that allow the computer to run, to store and access information, to connect to other devices and networks, to play sound and video. The motherboard holds all of these parts and enables all of these activities. But what is she, really? A rectangular piece of plastic? She is neither the heart of the computer in the anatomical sense, pumping blood to the other parts, nor is she a heart in the metaphorical sense, an emotional lodestar for the rest of the parts. Computer parts do not have emotional lodestars.

I look at the image of the computer motherboard in front of me and I imagine taking off all the pieces like I'm plucking the feathers off a hen. *Pluck,* there goes the CPU. *Pluck,* there goes the RAM. *Pluck, pluck, pluck.* I'm left with an image of pock-marked plastic that tells me nothing.

I'm typing these words on a computer. The motherboard sits millimeters below my fingers, translating the letters I type into binary code. But no, I must remind myself, *she* does not do this. The motherboard holds together the myriad processes that turn these keys into code. It is a receptacle or container at best.

This is surely making too much of a metaphor. A motherboard is not a mother. But watching these videos, I'm drawn to the motherboard as if it might tell me something that I haven't yet been able to understand about what motherhood means to me. I might, writing these words that are being processed by a computer, learn something about how we got here.

I feel increasingly like a mothering machine. My daughter is linked to me by a complicated set of devices and networks. As she sleeps, her biodata lives on my phone. I watch her blood sugar rise and fall. When she comes home from school, after I put her to bed, I'll watch her sleeping body, snoring softly, as her chest rises and falls. Once she falls deeply asleep, I will take her hearing aids out and all will be silent. But I will continue to listen for cries in the night, for the beep of her monitor, for threats internal or external. The mothering machine does not sleep; it keeps its steady vigil, waiting for the light of dawn and for a new day to begin.

# 9

# In Your Electronic Arms

It was the fortieth anniversary of Laurie Anderson's debut album, *Big Science* (1982), and her unlikely hit song "O Superman (for Massenet)" was playing on the radio. The song begins with an eerily mechanized chant, "Ha, ha, ha, ha." The sound of the voice is synthetic, like a robot from a '70s sci-fi flick. Her voice is synthesized using a machine called a vocoder. Then, in comes Anderson's strangely distorted voice, speaking the song's lyrics. "Hi, Mom!" she says—we recognize the phrase, have heard it a thousand times before. It should sound chirpy, spoken in high notes. But it does not. The vocoder flattens even this.

When I heard Anderson's song, the mechanical sound of her voice was familiar to me from watching internet videos of cochlear implant simulations. Ever since the audiologist in Michigan suggested that Willie might need cochlear implants, I had reluctantly pushed myself to learn more about them. It was a step that I did not want to take. Another device. Another biotechnology company that Willie would be tied to for the rest of her life. More invisible labor keeping the machines running. But I needed to read more and to watch more to make an informed decision. I learned how a cochlear implant would differ from

Willie's hearing aids. Instead of amplifying sound, as her hearing aids did, the cochlear implant would bypass the damaged hairs of her inner ear and send electrical signals directly to her brain stem. There would be two main components: an external processor and an internal processor. The external processor would sit on the outside of her head and would include a battery and a microphone to capture sound, which it would then pass on as electronic signals to the internal processor. This internal processor would be surgically implanted inside her head and would include a series of up to twenty-two electrodes that would send the electrical signals directly to her cochlea. Each of these electrodes would be placed on a different location of the cochlea to approximate different pitches. For all the information that I was able to find about what cochlear implants do, there was far less information about what it was like to hear with a cochlear implant. I wanted to know what cochlear implants sounded like—what would sound *sound* like for Willie if she had cochlear implants? How would Willie hear differently from the way that I could hear or from how she currently experienced sound through her hearing aids? How would hearing electronically differ from hearing acoustically? And would that difference matter to Willie?

In a video simulation that I found online, a vocoder is used to approximate the experience of listening to speech for a cochlear implant user. The video comes from the Cochlear Implant Research Lab at Arizona State University, directed by Michael Dorman, and features a blond audiologist in a short sleeveless dress—just right for the Arizona heat—questioning a preteen girl with a cochlear implant on one ear. They sit together behind a computer, which the audiologist uses to play different voice simulations. The girl's cochlear implant faces the camera and her hair is pulled back in a long French braid. They are interviewing this girl because she has hearing in her non-implanted ear, so she has a comparison point for explaining the differences between her two sides. The audiologist first plays a simple sentence into the girl's implanted ear: "The sun is finally shining." Then, she manipulates the sound using the vocoder and plays it into the headphones in the girl's non-implanted ear. The audiologist asks the girl whether this is what the voice sounds like when she is wearing her cochlear implant. The girl listens to a few different voices and says that none of them are quite right. The vocoder voice, she tells the audiologist, sounds more like a demented robot.[1] The audiologist resets the computer, moving away from the rudimentary sounds of the vocoder to more sophisticated synthesizers, and tries again. She wants to understand what the girl is hearing. The girl can't quite explain it to her, but no, she repeats, that's not quite it either. It needs more white noise, more static. I watch her grasp for words, her fingertips delicately pinching the air in front of her trying to nip the right expression to describe a sound that only she can hear. Imagine a wall, she says, and someone is talking to you from behind the wall. No, more, she tells the audiologist, when she plays the phrase again. Like someone is holding their hand over their mouth while they talk. She demonstrates, cupping her hand over her mouth. The audiologist plays another setting. "The sun is finally shining." The girl claps her hands. That's it. They both laugh in relief. I listen again. It is as she describes—muffled speech, slightly high-pitched, heard through an unseen obstacle. "The sun is finally shining."

ALEXA, PLAY LAURIE Anderson's "O Superman."

We're sitting at the dinner table—Evan, Willie, and I—eating pasta. Evan and I have pesto on ours and Willie's noodles are plain with a big scoop of butter melting on top. We calculate the carbs in our head—40 grams, most likely. She may need an extra shot of insulin later. Willie likes to salt and pepper the noodles herself, wielding the plastic grinders like a waiter at an Italian restaurant. I'm telling Evan about hearing the song on the radio and the strangeness with which it struck me. Would that be what listening with cochlear implants sounds like? The song begins to play on the Alexa device.

"Ha ha ha" and in comes the vocoder-synthesized lyrics.

Willie's face scrunches up in distaste. No music!

She often tells us to turn off music, especially at dinnertime. I'm not sure what music sounds like to her, amplified by her hearing aids, but she doesn't seem to enjoy it. Even children's music—"Baby Shark," "Baby Beluga"—seems less pleasurable to her than to other children. She would listen to a few bars of "Let It Go" then tell us she'd had enough. We'd let it go. Sometimes at bedtime, I'd try to sing "Twinkle Twinkle Little Star" to her and she'd cover my mouth with her tiny hands with a soft No. I'd try to muffle a few more lyrics, my cheeks comically puffed. She had a point—I have a terrible singing voice. But I also realized that music, even at a low volume, seemed aggressive to Willie. At dinnertime, it was intrusive noise that masked the voices she was already straining too much to hear. Would that still be true with implants?

Just a little more, I protest.

No music!

Okay, okay, I sign and say, Alexa, turn off music. The voice recognition recognizes my voice and Anderson's cuts out. I think about the voice of the Alexa device—that strange, not-quite-human cadence. Like many other voice assistant devices (Siri, Google, GPS), it is a feminine voice, relatively high-pitched but not shrill; mature and nonthreatening; ready to serve your needs.[2] It is vaguely maternal. In Ray Bradbury's sci-fi story "I

Sing the Body Electric!," the AI servant named "Grandmother" comes to fulfill the maternal function after the death of the children's mother. In one scene, the salesman programs the voice of "Grandmother" by splicing together the voices of the family, "until at last a final switch was pushed and a voice spoke free of a far electronic deep . . . And she was indeed there. And by her voice, she was beautiful."[3] In Bradbury's story, it is the grandmother's voice that is electric and that promises to bring the family together, and yet, her presence is resisted by the only daughter in the family, who resents this uncanny substitute for her mother.

Willie looks from Evan to me and defiantly slurps a long strand of spaghetti. A spray of butter showers the table. We listen to the quiet of the room. The song's lyrics play as an aftereffect echoing in the chambers of my brain.

Unnervingly robotic.

"There's always Mom. Hi, Mom!"

THE VOCODER WAS developed in the Bell Labs in the 1930s: a decade after Alexander Graham Bell's death. His childhood quest to create a speaking machine continued. As a research center fueling the innovation of AT&T, the labs continued Bell's early research into voice technologies and the dual tracks that defined his life and career—telecommunications and the eradication of deafness. Disability studies scholar Mara Mills describes the Bell Labs as contributing to our current approach to testing hearing as a form of quality control—phones and ears alike are subject to rigorous standards of measurement and assessment.[4] It was in Bell Labs where the audiogram was first developed to give a visual representation of sound. The audiogram became the central image for representing hearing loss: visits to the audiologist involve looking at images of the "speech banana"—the banana-shaped area between the axes of frequency and levels (decibels) where human speech falls. The degree to which one's hearing differs from the normative banana corresponds to the categories of "mild," "moderate," "severe," and "profound" hearing loss. In addition to the audiogram, Bell Labs gave us the decibel—named after Bell—which was invented by Bell engineers as a unit of measurement for sound and which did not previously exist. These labs were the home of significant innovations in sound technologies and, later, cybernetics, before they were broken up in antitrust legislation.

An early prototype of the vocoder, called a Voder, was part of the AT&T exhibition at the 1939 World's Fair in New York City. On the newly sculpted grounds of Flushing Meadows, Queens, audiences encountered exciting new communications systems that would define the world of tomorrow. The Communications Zone at the fair, with exhibits ranging from traditional publishing to cutting-edge telecommunication systems, was central to the "World of Tomorrow" theme and the Hall of Communications, housing the AT&T exhibition, was its most imposing structure.[5]

To demonstrate the vocoder, Bell Lab engineers would show audiences how the machine could speak in different humanlike voices. The vocoder was played by a young woman seated in front of a keyboard shaped like her hands. On each of these keys was a phonetic transcription of the consonants and vowels of speech, while tone and pitch were simulated through foot pedals.[6] In a somewhat misguided effort to give the voice a human presence, an enormous open-mouthed metallic frieze of an androgynous human head loomed above the girl, "speaking" the words she played out of its O-shaped speaker-mouth. The vocoder demonstrations changed for their audiences, but in one

account published in *Nature,* the writer describes listening to the voice of a father reprimanding his daughter, then the machine's pitch was increased and the voice transformed from the low, gruff fatherly voice to the feminine, high-pitched voice of a young girl; then the pitch was lowered much further, and the voice became lower and weaker like that of a grandfather interceding on behalf of the girl.[7] When Alexander Graham Bell first synthesized the voice of a child calling "Mama" in his adolescent experiments, he could not have conceived of a machine capable of mimicking the voices of three generations playing out a scene of familial strife.

Like Bell's speaking machine, Laurie Anderson uses the vocoder to address an imaginary mother. One can draw a clear line from Bell's early experiments with a mechanical voice—a voice that called out "Mama"—to the vocoder's mechanical voice—"Hi, Mom!" Even as machines create life or the semblance of life, they cannot ever seem to dispense with a primal call to a phantom mother. In her lyrics, she imagines a sequence of loss (the loss of love, of justice, of force) and at the end of all this loss, we're left with mom.

After listening to the vocoder, visitors to the AT&T building at the fair could go to the next room to try out Bell's newest auditory tests, checking to see whether their hearing fell within a normal range. Attempts to create an artificial speaking voice remained closely linked to the development of hearing tests.[8] One of the central lessons of the vocoder was that speech could remain intelligible even if it was reduced to a small number of frequency bands. It was an early example of information compression and showed how speech sounds could be transmitted, manipulated, and shared with minimal bandwidth. In its early development, engineers at Bell Labs thought it might be useful as an encryption device for making phone calls private or to reduce the range required to transmit intelligible speech.

Invented at a time when battle lines were being drawn on the European continent, it was quickly conscripted into the American war effort. In a special room in the Pentagon, engineers used vocoders as part of a massive computer system, taking up 2,000 square feet, to allow Harry S. Truman to talk with Winston Churchill without enemies intercepting the call and listening in.[9]

Using a range of code names, including the Green Hornet, the Special Customer, X-Ray, Project X-61753, and SIGSALY—the latter meant to convey a children's nonsense phrase—engineers coded and decoded confidential conversations across international lines.[10] The voices came through stilted and robotic, but the goal was not to make them sound good—it was to make sure that the military leaders could understand each other without anyone else understanding them.

From World War II to electronic music, the vocoder ran a strange parallel path—it became the noise of war and the noise of funk. In Dave Tompkins's study of the vocoder, *How to Wreck a Nice Beach,* he describes the instrument's military reach: "During World War II, the vocoder reduced the voice to something cold and tactical, tinny and dry like soup cans in a sandbox, dehumanizing the larynx, so to speak, for some of man's more dehumanizing moments: Hiroshima, the Cuban Missile Crisis, Soviet gulags, Vietnam."[11] From these inauspicious origins, the instrument caught the attention of postwar musicians looking for a new sound. The vocoder went on to fuel the rise of electronic music, allowing artists to experiment with a huge range of vocal sounds on a small number of frequency bands. The technology behind the vocoder would lead directly to Auto-Tune, responsible for the uncannily smooth vocals of twenty-first-century pop music. The vocoder began as an amusement at the World's Fair and then turned into a military tool, before becoming avant-garde art in Laurie Anderson's hands.

But the influence of the vocoder doesn't stop here; it also extends into medicine where it played a role in the development of cochlear implants. It served as an early model that illustrated the basic fact that speech could run through a small number of channels—ten frequency bands, in the case of the vocoder—and still be understood by a listener as intelligible speech. When

IN YOUR ELECTRONIC ARMS

scientists began to consider the idea of bypassing a damaged middle ear and delivering sound directly to the cochlea using electrical signals, they thought that it might work somewhat like a vocoder. Biomedical engineer Robert V. Shannon ran a number of studies that used vocoding to show how cochlear implants, like the vocoder, needed only a handful of frequency bands for the user to understand speech with high intelligibility.[12] Instead of relying on those thousands of hairs in our middle ear that each transmit acoustical sound into electrical signals, they would use twenty-two electrodes to deliver sound directly to the cochlea. Twenty-two electrodes was a far smaller number of channels than thousands of individual hairs but, as the vocoder demonstrated, speech transmitted on a reduced number of bands could still be intelligible. It would sound worse, most likely, but it would still be perceived as speech. The deaf could hear. But what, exactly, were they hearing? It might be intelligible, but it wouldn't be the same. It would be a different kind of sound. But how different? I wanted to know what we would be getting into. If Willie got cochlear implants, how would she hear, and how would it differ from what I understood as hearing?

SHIP . . . ship . . . ship.

Willie and I were sitting in a sound booth with the resident-in-training. The audiologist, Jesse, was on the other side of the glass, covering her mouth with a piece of paper.

Ship . . . ship . . . ship.

Willie looked down at the pictures in front of her. She pointed to a picture of a white button-down shirt.

But wait, I interrupted, I don't think she knows the word "ship." We usually say "boat." Jesse looked at me and blinked. She didn't say anything, but she must have wondered why I thought "boat" was a more reassuring answer than "shirt" for "ship." At least Willie got the first syllable right. It wasn't the first time she got the last syllable wrong. She was getting at least half of the answers wrong. The audiology tests had started to change as Willie got older. She was able to do more complicated behavioral tests now that she was leaving her toddler years. Instead of simply tracking her eye movements when they played a beep, the audiologists could now speak a word through the headphones at various volumes and ask Willie to point to a corresponding picture. Whenever she got an answer wrong, the resident did not correct her or reprimand her. "Good! Shirt!" They were trying to encourage her and keep her engaged. I sat on my hands and closed my mouth. I wanted to intercede. She's getting tired. She doesn't know that word. Why is "gun" part of the test? I wanted to ask, looking at a picture of a boy holding a toy rifle, as Willie pointed to a picture of a piece of "gum" instead of the "gun." She gave wrong answer after wrong answer. But wait, I wanted to say, Willie doesn't know anything about guns. I wanted them to know that I was the kind of mother who doesn't give my child toy guns—I was one of those nice moms who is against violence or, at least, keeps violence at bay in the toy department. I also wanted my daughter—so smart, so capable—to pass her test. As those impulses rose to the surface, I had to push them back down. This was not that kind of test. No one needed to prove themselves, Willie least of all.

We were still getting used to our NYC audiologist, Jesse, since our return home. We liked her better than our audiologist in Michigan; she was less given to grand pronouncements and seemed more experienced, but we still had our reservations. She lacked the warmth and reassurance that I badly needed. She would talk in technical detail to her assistant—numbers and thresholds and frequencies—and not translate the information to Evan and me. The new behavioral tests caught us backfooted. I had failed to notice the degree to which Willie was struggling. Before this test, I could look at Willie and see a child who was speaking so well, talking up a storm at home, and understanding so much. Evan and I felt reassured by her speech, which seemed very intelligible to us who spent our days talking with her. Others had a harder time, but wasn't that typical for this age? Willie had a good vocabulary, often choosing words that surprised adults, calling a piece of fruit "tart" or a shade of blue "turquoise" or inserting the word "actually" into her sentences like a tweedy professor contesting some obscure point. Her language seemed to validate our sense that Willie's hearing was just like Evan's and that she would one day sound like him. After she started speaking, I continued to sign with her, but she stopped signing back. Spoken English was the dominant language in our household and in her school and on the playground. My limited vocabulary of signs was not going to be able to compete. Willie loved for us to read to her and, when I asked her questions about the books, she would answer me with thoughtful responses. She was understanding and speaking, so how could she not be hearing? In her speech therapy, she was hitting all the speech milestones that were expected of a preschooler. At school, her teachers told me that she was keeping up with her peers. And yet, she couldn't hear the difference between "ship" and "shirt."

I asked Jesse how that was possible. How could she be doing so well with her speech and understanding while hearing so little? Jesse shrugged. She's a smart kid and she's working hard. She gets a lot from context and pieces things together. If you ask her to hand you a shirt in the morning as you're dressing, she knows you're talking about clothing, not asking for a boat. Had we noticed that she's very tired, especially when she comes home from school? We had. The other night she had fallen asleep at the dinner table, her eyes blinking slowly as she chewed, her head bobbing up and down as she fought off a wave of exhaustion. At school, she would nap for two hours and the teachers would have a hard time waking her up. But there was also the diabetes to consider. Her body and her mind were both working overtime and it was hard to know which causes went along with which effects.

Jesse told us that we needed to do more tests to know for sure, but that we might be reaching the limit of what hearing aids could do for Willie. We had already replaced her first pair of hearing aids with a high-powered pair. We were able to do so in the final months that Willie qualified for Early Intervention and the City of New York would cover the costs. After this pair, we were on our own. The volume of these high-powered aids was set as high as they could go before speech started to morph into noise. Willie loved her hearing aids—she would go to sleep with them in and refused to have us take them out. We would wait until she had fallen firmly asleep to gently ease them out of her ears to turn them off overnight so that they didn't churn through even more batteries than we were already using. Willie's "ears" were part of her; she was used to them and we were used to them. Jesse knew we were reluctant to switch from hearing aids to cochlear implants. It had come up before. She hesitated before she told us that Willie's hearing was never going to be perfect in hearing aids.

Was that the goal, I asked, for her hearing to be perfect? Evan's hearing was not perfect. I had never tested mine, but I doubted that mine was perfect either. Was perfection an appropriate goal?

Jesse tried to clarify, but we were already on a bad track. The thing we needed to think about was school. She might do well at home where it was quiet and just the three of us, but her results showed that any background noise brought her comprehension way down. Her teachers could wear a special microphone called an FM, which helped, but it was going to be harder and harder for Willie to keep up as more was expected of her academically. Since the teachers were wearing masks due to the pandemic, she was losing even more visual information—she could no longer rely on lipreading. It might get so frustrating for her that she won't want to engage anymore. Those words stung me in a soft place. I knew that cochlear implants had entered the conversation, but I wasn't ready yet and I didn't want to start that process with Jesse as our audiologist. We didn't know how to talk to each other without defensiveness on both of our parts. I didn't fully trust her. It was looking increasingly likely that we would pursue cochlear implants, but I would find a new audiologist first.

COCHLEAR IMPLANTS REMAIN controversial in the Deaf community. When they first entered the picture, Deaf men and women were immediately concerned that Alexander Graham Bell's long-deferred dream of eradicating deafness might actually be realized through technological means and that they were facing the loss of their language, their community, and their way of life. With deafness cured, as some advocates of the new devices claimed, what would happen to schools for the Deaf, those central hubs for fostering Deaf pride and community identification; what would happen to ASL? Would financially strapped state agencies continue to provide funding for interpreters, and would young cochlear implant wearers want to learn a language that signaled their otherness? What would happen to aging Deaf men and women who grew up in this community and now found themselves isolated and alone?

On top of these social concerns, the devices themselves were not very effective. Early cochlear implant users, especially Deaf adults, found only small increases in their ability to understand speech. It was never as simple as flipping a switch. For modest gains, cochlear implant users had to endure surgery and a long road of adjustments and retraining a brain that had, in many cases, not shaped itself around speech. Their brains would need to form new pathways to hear and, even more challenging, to hear along the crude electronic channels of those early devices. For older Deaf adults, cochlear implants often don't work. When a brain has not heard sound before, the neural pathways have never formed and may never form. The brain stem might be receiving sound for the first time, but the brain does not know what to do with the sound or how to organize it into linguistic understanding. The first attempts to market cochlear implants to adults were often met with indifference. Deaf adults had learned to value ASL and Deaf communities; they knew that the odds were stacked against them being able to talk and listen like hearing people at this stage in their lives. Many simply had no interest. With Deaf adults indifferent or hostile to the new devices, cochlear implant manufacturers realized that they would need to market their devices to children. Which meant they would need to market to parents.[13] The focus on implanting children coincided with more research on brain plasticity, the widespread implementation of early hearing tests such as those that Willie had at birth, and the lowering of the age that cochlear implantation was approved by governing bodies.

Cochlear implants are now one of the most commonly used neuroprosthetic devices: a prosthesis—like eyeglasses or a cane—but one that we implant in our bodies to replace a function that our body cannot perform on its own.[14] Neuroprosthetics are currently being developed to treat a range of nervous system disorders from epilepsy to paralysis, but cochlear implants have had early success, in part because, compared to these more complex and deeply embedded nervous system disorders, the cochlea's functions are more straightforward to replace. And yet, contemplating the idea of implanting a child with a piece of technology feels like standing on the border of a new scientific frontier. It is a procedure that changes the way the brain functions. In her study of ten families undergoing the process of implantation, sociologist Laura Mauldin discusses the pressures placed on mothers, in particular, to commit themselves to medical intervention in order to help their children overcome deafness. Mauldin argues that the "good mother" of a deaf child, in this medicalized context, becomes defined by her willingness to pursue technological solutions and to perform the long-term care work required after implantation.[15] These pressures intersect with class and race in America. The procedure itself is expensive and the road to hearing with cochlear implants is labor intensive. It requires either a nonworking parent or the kind of job flexibility that is most often found in white-collar employment. Audiologists and other primary care providers decide who is a good candidate for implantation, and more often than not, those who are referred for cochlear implants are from white, middle-class families.[16] Time must be taken off for surgery, making follow-up appointments, sorting insurance, maintaining devices. For two weeks after the surgery, the child needs to heal—they cannot wear their cochlear implants yet and may have no access to sound. If they were previously wearing hearing aids and especially if they were not taught ASL, as many cochlear implant candidates are not—a parent's constant attention becomes critical in that time. Even after this two-week period, once the device is activated, a child must be coached to listen through their new device even if they don't like what they hear. This is a period of adjustment that a child may well resist and it is the parent's job to coax and cajole and reassure their child that it will be better soon, even if they do not know when or if hearing with the implant will ever sound normal.


I CAN'T HEAR! I can't hear!

I woke up from bed with a whole-body start. It was as nearly dark in our bedroom as it ever got; no moon was out and only the distant streetlight spread dim illumination before my eyes. My child was crying in the other room, but it took a while for my brain to match up her cries with the words that were coming out of her mouth.

I can't hear! she wailed.

I ran into her room. She was sitting bolt upright looking around her in despair. Was it a dream? A sudden realization? Why was she suddenly upset that we had taken her hearing aids out as we had done every night of her life?

I cradled her in my arms and stroked her soft blond hair, which was only now starting to reach her chin. It's okay, I said to no one. My arms were too busy holding her to sign, nor could she see my lips in the dark of the bedroom. It's okay, my love.

Reaching me in the cold, dark night, those words rung of prophecy and despair: I can't hear.

Evan and I were rattled into wakefulness by the incident. Willie has never been so distressed about not hearing. We lay awake that night, side by side, and discussed what it meant. We knew that she preferred to wear her hearing aids, that she kept them in as long as she possibly could and was frustrated when we removed them. We turned to look at each other, faces dimly perceptible in the dark. We also knew that hearing aids are imperfect tools and that she was working overtime to fill in the many ellipses and gaps that they left behind. And what about cochlear implants? Another imperfect tool but, perhaps, a better one. As the sun started to break, releasing a warm orange light over the rooftops, Evan and I had made a decision—a tentative one, but a decision nonetheless. We would find a new audiologist. We would get a second opinion. And, if cochlear implants were the next best step, we would take it.

We met with a new audiologist, Melissa. She was across town on the East Side. Willie's beloved speech therapist, Selma, had recommended her and that alone was reason to try her out. It took only the first five minutes of our first meeting to realize that she was the right one. She ran the same behavioral tests that our previous audiologists ran, but already there was a difference. Willie was given a plastic ice cream cone and colorful scoops of plastic ice cream to attach to the top. Every time she heard a beep, she put another scoop on the cone. As soon as her interest flagged, Melissa's assistant set her up with a new toy: a monkey-shaped bucket that Willie fed with plastic bananas each time she heard the beep. As soon as her interest in this too started to wane, Melissa said we could stop. She had all the information she needed.

Melissa was interested in Evan's family history, asking engaged questions about his experiences. She had a family history of her own. Her uncle and aunt were Deaf and their daughter, her cousin, was a sign language interpreter. They were against her becoming an audiologist at first, especially one whose job increasingly involves cochlear implants. It caused something of a rift. But since then, when they saw the good that she could do, they had come around. And what about Willie? What did Melissa recommend? She was reassuring—she's a smart kid, she's speaking well and advocating for herself, she reassured us. We'll do more tests, but there's no rush. It was the first time I didn't feel pressured in an audiology appointment. I asked if she was concerned about brain plasticity—that the window for her brain to adjust to cochlear implants was closing or had closed. She told us she was not worried. The fact that Willie was listening and speaking meant that her brain was already creating the pathways it needed for speech. We could take our time and decide if and when the moment was right.

In 1983, one year after Laurie Anderson released "O Superman" on her album *Big Science,* Neil Young made the surprising decision to release an album titled *Trans* with six songs that replaced his distinctive voice—the sensitive, tremulous voice of "Heart of Gold"—with the mechanized voice of a vocoder. Fans hated it. Record executives sued for breach of contract.[17] His motivation, as he later described it to his biographer, was to find a language for his son. Young's son Ben was born with cerebral palsy; he was quadriplegic and non-speaking and Young and his wife Pegi spent the early years of his life in speech therapy and physical therapy, trying to find the tools to communicate with him. When he set out to write an album about this experience, he deliberately avoided the sentimental or the mawkish. He wanted to transform his approach to his voice—no longer would the Neil Young voice represent authenticity and connection, but rather, it would trouble our basic assumptions about the voice as a marker of selfhood. The vocoder was uniquely able to facilitate this self-transformation. Young described his decision as follows: "I was looking for a way to change my voice. To sing through a voice that no one could recognize and it wouldn't be judged as me. [It's] my search for a way for a severely handicapped non-oral person to find some sort of interface for communication."[18] In response to his frustrated fans, Young replied: "You gotta realize you can't understand the words . . . and I can't understand my son's words. So feel that."[19] Instead of approaching technology as a tool to fix his son, he reimagined it as a way to confront his audiences with a radical shift in perception. Rather than make his son intelligible for them, he would make himself—his golden voice—stranger.

After watching and rewatching the video of cochlear implant voice simulations, I decided to email Dr. Michael Dorman, the lead scientist on the project. Would he be willing to talk with me? To my immense surprise and gratification, he was. We scheduled a phone call. He had recently retired and was in a reflective mood, interested in taking into consideration not only his own research, but the long arc of cochlear implant development and what it taught us about the human brain and our capacity for understanding speech. He told me that when he thinks about the brain, he realizes his own limitations as a scientist— the brain does what it wants, exercising a kind of free will. This is what allows cochlear implants to work, but also what makes an individual's response to implantation so unpredictable. One person might immediately recognize the signals from their new implant as intelligible speech. It might sound normal to them with just a short adjustment period. Another brain might struggle for months and years to adjust, while still others may never really accept the noise as intelligible sound. On the other hand, cochlear implants work because we, as a species, accept a wide range of sounds as speech. Dr. Dorman told me, "We're adapted to deal with all kinds of variations of sound from all kinds of vocal tracts, from a baby babbling to a seven-foot-tall basketball player." Early cochlear implants put this flexibility to the test and, as he went on to explain, researchers used intelligibility as their basis for success, not sound quality. This is where his research came in. Dorman was interested in moving past this focus on intelligibility to consider the quality of the sound—this meant better understanding what cochlear implants sound like to their users and finding ways to improve them. Intelligibility was a low bar for speech and focusing on it exclusively put limits on how the technology developed.

His research focused on understanding how cochlear implant sound quality differed from unaided hearing. Some of his research subjects described a muffled sensation in the implanted ear. Voices came to them as if spoken by a Stormtrooper from *Star Wars*—as if a helmet were interceding between them and the speaker. Others described "munchkin voice," an unusually high pitch, as if Mickey Mouse were speaking to them. He explained that the first quality issue, muffling, was caused by the relatively poor frequency resolution of cochlear implants and the second issue, "munchkin voice," was caused by the short length of the electrodes, which didn't go deep enough into the cochlea where lower frequencies are registered. And yet, even these distortions often disappear with time as the brain accepts these sounds as normal speech.

In Dr. Dorman's telling, both the limitations of cochlear implants and their amazing potential existed in equal measure. I started to feel excited—electric even—about what these devices might do and how they might change and develop over time. But, like a heavy anchor preventing me from flying too high, other worries came—worries that were more maternal than scientific. Cost, care, failure. It would depend not so much on the perfection of the device, but on whether Willie would accept the change. Whether her brain would make the necessary pathways. Whether she would actually hear better. Whether, years and years from now, it would, in retrospect, have been the right decision that we made for her.

* * *

I WAS TEACHING again, though teaching itself had changed. The university-one-does-not-turn-down had offered to let me teach a summer course in exchange for the year I had lost. The class met online and I had to quickly learn the basic rudiments of online teaching. Teaching to a gallery of square-framed faces was new for me, but the class soon fell into the classroom rhythms that I was so familiar with. The topic was literary modernism; we would spend six weeks with those twentieth-century trickster-writers who plumbed new psychological depths and sought ever-changing forms to reflect a changing reality. As I read the books that I had carefully selected, I found myself reflecting on the difficulty of knowing another person, even (perhaps especially) someone you gave birth to. I thought about how the modernists searched for a way of expressing the intractable particularity of consciousness—the way that each person sees the world differently and how these differences give human life its infinite beauty and also create some of our most awful divisions. The psychologist William James, brother of novelist Henry James, coined the term "stream of consciousness" to describe the way that individual perception functions. In his essay on the topic, he writes:

> The only states of consciousness that we naturally deal with are found in personal consciousness, minds, selves, concrete particular I's and you's.
>
> Each of these minds keeps its own thoughts to itself. There is no giving or bartering between them. No thought even comes into direct *sight* of a thought in another personal consciousness than its own. Absolute insulation, irreducible pluralism, is the law. It seems as if the elementary psychic fact were not *thought* or *this thought* or *that thought,* but *my thought,* every thought being *owned.* Neither contemporaneity, nor proximity

in space, nor similarity of quality and content are able to fuse thoughts together which are sundered by this barrier of belonging to different personal minds. The breaches between such thoughts are the most absolute breaches in nature.[20]

Stream of consciousness made its way from psychology to literature and was developed by James Joyce and Virginia Woolf in the English-speaking canon; with this and other modernist techniques came a devotion to the particular sensory landscape as a means for charting the universal. Only by embracing our differences, our idiosyncrasies, our strange private minds, can we understand anything like human experience. They explored the outer limits of representing this personal consciousness in complex, difficult novels like *Ulysses* and *Mrs Dalloway* that bore deeply into the different thoughts and sensory experiences of their protagonists. I thought about Dr. Dorman's description of the incredible plasticity of our brains—all those rivulets and channels, streams almost, that change with time and experience. I thought about how we are built to recognize diversity—to understand a broad range of expression as speech—and yet, we cannot evade the difficulty of understanding how another person hears, sees, and feels.

And so, if I accept that I cannot hear what Willie hears and, as close as I might feel to her, I cannot share her consciousness, then how, in the days before her ability to communicate is fully developed, can I act according to any understanding of what she wants or needs? I cannot. And yet, at a certain point I must act on that uncertainty. Choosing cochlear implants is an action; choosing not to get them is also, in the face of the information and options available to us, a form of action. Or it is inaction as action. Now that Willie is three years old, she is starting to advocate for herself. This is something that her teachers and speech therapists work on with her. When she cannot hear me, she now tells me: Say it again! Louder! She reminds me to look at her when we're speaking when I accidentally turn my head away. When a group conversation runs away from her, she raises her hand and shouts, My turn! There is hardly a conversation that passes when we don't hear her say, I can't hear you. Evan and I discuss this at night, once Willie has gone to bed. We open a bottle of wine and have a variation of the same conversation that we keep replaying. Evan and I agree on all the particulars—there is no single point where we are at odds, no observation that one of us contests, no conclusion that either of us resists. But even with all this concordance, we hesitate. It is a big decision and we have come to accept that we are both slow, deliberate decision-makers. But the signs are getting clearer. She wants to hear; she isn't hearing as much as she wants. I am grateful that we waited this long so that we could see something of her own wants and needs emerge. I watch her closely. I ask her questions. With my limited means, I try to understand her as best as I can.

We sign up for sign language classes once a week online with a woman in Texas named Lucia. She is Deaf and her daughter, who makes occasional guest appearances on-screen, to Willie's great delight, is also Deaf. My signing is getting better and worse in that two-steps-forward, one-step-back, halting manner of midlife language learning. I learn some new vocabulary words and promptly forget some others that I learned just last week.

We have a hard time keeping Willie engaged online. She wants to show Lucia all her toys and runs back and forth getting a procession of stuffed frogs, bunnies, and bears; some slime we picked up at the gift shop at the Museum of Natural History; a unicorn necklace that Evan's sister sent for her birthday. Lucia engages with her each time she comes back: fingers bouncing on her chin to ask, What color? Willie responds by speaking the word: "pink." I remind her to sign the word, not say it. I spread two fingers out and stroke my chin with the upper finger: pink. Willie begrudgingly mimics me. Pink.

I think about my French sister-in-law, my brother Sam's wife, who is trying to raise her daughter to speak French as well as the English she is surrounded by in their Washington, DC community. She speaks only French to her daughter, who responds in English. It is hard not to take it as a rebuke. Quelle couleur? she asks. Pink, her daughter responds. The mother tongue is drowned out by the wider social cues that my niece receives. English is the language of friends and teachers and television and understanding outside the home.

In our case, my paltry attempts to sign consistently are seen for what they are—a vague simulacrum of a community to which Willie does not have consistent access. I wish we knew more Deaf children or that she could enroll in a class or program with others rather than online, but we're still in a pandemic and there are no options that I know of until she turns four and can begin attending a school for the Deaf located on the Lower East Side of Manhattan. If we choose to do so. Our class with Lucia is the best I can manage at this age.

Could I have tried harder? Certainly. Here's what I did: I sought resources for ASL through Early Intervention, audiologists, and speech therapists and the best they could offer was online classes, often "baby sign" classes taught by hearing instructors. I reached out to Deaf colleagues whom I vaguely knew and whom I sent somewhat embarrassed emails asking for help; they were generous with their time and I had pleasant conversations in my halting ASL and their much-more-adept lipreading and note-writing, but they were better positioned to point me to resources for adults rather than children. I learned so much from these conversations about signing and Deaf culture; and yet, I still hadn't integrated our lives into a wider Deaf community that Willie could see and in which she could find validation and acceptance. There was still time, I hoped. But the question was, what to do now? Was I willing to continue the present inadequate arrangement—hearing aids that were offering only incomplete sound and ASL instruction that was ad hoc and cut off from the larger stream of Willie's day-to-day life? Was it enough to hold out for a deferred future when I might be able to give Willie full access to a Deaf education and community? Proponents of ASL were themselves ringing the alarm that cochlear implants and the continued emphasis on speech and auditory education might further minoritize ASL and Deaf culture. Would the ASL-speaking community be as vibrant in ten, twenty, thirty, forty, fifty years as it was today?

Time passes. Time passed. Willie went from 3-K to pre-K. After graduating from Early Intervention in the New York City system, we were given a new caseworker from the Committee for Preschool Special Education named Linda. Willie would need to be evaluated for special services, despite the fact that her deafness and diabetes were resolute facts. We met with three educational specialists online—an hour each. They each observed Willie playing through their computer screens and asked her questions. They were checking her behavior, expressive language, receptive language, fine motor skills, gross motor skills, etc. . . . and after hours of testing, told us what we already knew—she was a deaf child with diabetes who had no additional intellectual or developmental delays.

From here, Linda took the reports (a small volume in and of themselves) and made a recommendation. She told us that Willie would need special services, including a speech therapist and a hearing education specialist to work with Willie and her teachers. The hearing education specialist was a new one to me and I asked Linda many questions about what they would do. The hearing education specialist would work with Willie and the teachers to improve her self-advocacy skills, to make sure the classroom environment was conducive to her learning, and to teach the teachers how to use an FM device—a microphone that the city would provide, which the teachers would wear around their neck to send their words directly into Willie's hearing aids. But Linda's recommendations did not end here. She also submitted that Willie would need a full-time nurse to accompany her to school. Someone to do everything that I was currently doing—monitoring her blood sugar, treating lows, and giving her insulin with her meals. It would be the first time in two years that someone other than a family member would perform these tasks. It meant that Willie could go to school full time next year. It meant that I could go back to work. What that work would be, I still needed to discover.

We'd been regularly meeting with our new audiologist, Melissa, going back and forth to her audiology office on the Upper East Side, over the course of six months. The mood had started to shift as the accumulated evidence began to paint a clearer picture. I knew that this would be the meeting when she recommended cochlear implants. Evan and I had decided that once we received an official recommendation, we would move forward with cochlear implants. The last time we were in the booth, we were back to the dreaded picture tests. Ship . . . ship. Willie was old enough now that she knew what a ship was. No excuses. She pointed to the shirt. I was getting better at staying out of the way. Encouraging Willie when she needed a little boost, but otherwise stepping back.

After wrapping up the session, Melissa came over to our side of the glass partition. It was time to have the conversation.

In a flurry of words, I told her about my concerns. Although we had already decided that we would say yes, I wanted to give my reservations full vent. I was afraid that Willie would not like the way they sounded—that the muffled, robotic voice would be as alien and strange to her as it was to me. Melissa assured me that the brain adjusts. The sound may be foreign at first, but it simply becomes the way that a cochlear-implant user hears—no better or worse than anything else. She reminded me that Willie's hearing was already profoundly different from mine. I should not think of whether cochlear implants would sound different from my hearing, but whether they would be better than Willie's current situation of partial, aided hearing. We talked more about the implants. Any surgery is dangerous for a person with diabetes, whose blood sugar needs to stay stable through a period of fasting and sedation. Aside from my fears about the surgery, I could not make peace with the idea of implanting proprietary hardware into my daughter's head. She would always be beholden to a biotech company. What if it went out of business or the product was recalled? Unlike a continuous glucose monitor or insulin pump, this was not a temporary implantation, but a permanent one. What kind of financial obligations was I saddling her with—she, a child who would already shoulder the enormous cost of insulin and diabetes-related biotech? My eyes started to well up. Melissa subtly gestured for her assistant to watch Willie so we could go outside.

Not for the first time, I realized I was more angry than sad. Angry that anything I was suffering was something my daughter might one day feel. It magnified the sadness and frustration I felt—it stung me twice over because I knew this feeling could one day be hers. Had we done enough to introduce her to sign language? Should we pull her from her current school, the one that I could still look down on from my apartment to watch her play, and send her to the bilingual ASL/English school on the

Lower East Side? What would it mean to raise a child in a second language—one that I still knew only on a rudimentary level? Would she get everything that she needed? Plenty of Deaf people would say yes. Plenty of cochlear implant users would say no. And then, I kept coming back to the hardest question of all to answer: Who was I to make a decision that would affect Willie for the rest of her life? Just her mom. It meant everything and it meant nothing.

IN THE MUSIC video of "O Superman (for Massenet)," Laurie Anderson appears against a black backdrop, wearing a white jacket with white gloves and white sunglasses. About halfway through, a spotlight highlights her hands and she begins to sign the song's lyrics in ASL. She sings about longing to be held in her mother's arms but, as the song progresses, those maternal arms morph into "automatic arms," "electronic arms," "petrochemical arms," and "military arms." The mother's long arms represent comfort and love but, in the troubling permutations of Anderson's lyrics, they become weapons. In an interview, Anderson describes the song as about the "failure of technology" in the wake of the Iranian hostage crisis of 1979 and the ways in which militaristic appeals often take the form of calls to a motherland.[21] Like the instrument she speaks through, Anderson's lyrics remind us of the way that something as intimate as a mother's care is imbricated with the social world that she reproduces in raising a child. Her loving arms are also petrochemical arms and military arms; the maternal embrace morphs into the picking up of weapons in the ongoing oil wars. Most resonant of all, for me, are those electronic arms, a phrase that she repeats twice. Can one, as Neil Young tried to do, demonstrate love through a machine? Can I wrap Willie up in my electronic voice and provide her some kind of comfort? Anderson chose the vocoder because of its association with surveillance technologies. [22] The mother is a watcher; she looks over the child but also, in our age of surveillance technologies, relies on devices to monitor the child from infancy (baby monitors) to adolescence (geolocation tracking on cell phones).[23]

I not only watch, but I listen and, on a deep level, I want my child to be able to listen as well. I want my child to hear me. I want to whisper, It's okay, my love, in the pitch-black of night's despair, and for her to understand me. On the one hand, I can point to these desires and feel certain that they are pure—I want my daughter to be happy. On the other hand, my desires are compromised by my own experience. My conception of happiness revolves around the abilities that I possess and would be sad to lose. I am blinkered when it comes to understanding the world as my daughter experiences it—her particular stream of consciousness. I cannot see through her eyes or hear through her ears. This was true the moment she was born with the vision of a newborn—seeing the world as a kaleidoscopic blur that I could not know, communicating in cries that I tried to interpret as best I could. And the limitations of my ability to know my daughter will only grow with time as she passes through the stages of life with senses and experiences that differ from my own. This gulf is as true now as it will be when she gets cochlear implants.

Willie will get cochlear implants. She will probably have them by the time you read this book. Much can happen in the time between. I cannot know how the procedure will go. How she will feel in those long two weeks after she heals from the surgery and before the new device is activated. I don't know how long it will take her to adjust to her new implants.

We have met with the surgeon, who said we would first need an MRI of her head. Willie loves the idea of X-rays. They are overrepresented in every alphabet book we own—"X is for X-ray." Willie was excited when we went to the office on the Upper West Side to get an MRI. The technician told her to lie still and she looked at him with big, serious eyes. It was a great responsibility. She lay down as still as a plank on the mobilized bed as it was drawn into a giant O-shaped scanner. "O is for Owl." This is what she looks like to me now—a wide-eyed owl taking in everything she sees. Watching her go through the scanner, I think about how she entered the world, at a different hospital, just uptown. I stand with the technician on the other side of a glass partition. I want to stretch out through the glass and hold her, but I stay on my side and look at the scan of her skull on the computer in front of me. When she is done with the scan, the first thing she'll ask is whether she can see the X-ray. The technician will show her. This is your skull; this is the inside of your ear. Once we are all done—just minutes, really—we meet Evan in the waiting room so that the three of us can go get some ice cream.

Like so many decisions before it, I don't know if this one will ever feel like the right decision. When I speak to other parents of children with cochlear implants, they are very positive about the choice. It is a miracle device and they would do it again in a heartbeat. I speak to adults who say the same. I arrange for a phone call with a Deaf physician, a friend of my father's. He tells me that he got the cochlear implant too late in his life. His brain never really accepted the sounds he was hearing as speech. He knew that would be a likely possibility going in, but he wanted to give it a try nonetheless. I asked if he would do it again if he was faced with the same decision. He told me that he knows for certain that he would. There are so many corridors of chance. I have learned this many times before.

Willie sits on my lap eating vanilla ice cream with sprinkles. She wants a bite of mine (mango sorbet) and a bite of Evan's (butter pecan). This is part of her ritual. She will coo over each. Delicious! A difficult, three-syllable word. Her therapists and caseworkers and teachers and doctors would be proud. It is a sunny day and the light catches her hair. She reflects light, this girl. I hold her tightly in my arms so she can feel my heartbeat. This too is language. This is also what it means to communicate. And so we speak silently, us three, sharing ice cream on a noisy street in Manhattan. Wordlessly, we pass back and forth our hopes and our fears, and they travel through the air, quiet and invisible, like electronic signals.

# 10

# Spinning Webs

Every night Willie asks me to tell her a story about Spider-Man. At first she insists on absolute fidelity. I must repeat every scene from the animated series that she is currently watching. In this series, updated for the under-five crowd, three charismatic spider kids fight bad guys who are just bad enough for preschoolers to handle. The villainous plots generally involve a foiled attempt to "spoil everyone's fun." I repeat the storylines, curled up as small as I can make myself in order to fit with Willie in her toddler bed. I must be careful not to forget any essential part of the story or Willie will exclaim, No, Mommy, not that way. Sometimes I start to drift asleep as I talk and inject nonsense phrases into the narration—bits of my dreams that overlap a story oft told. The blue night-light illuminates Willie's face waiting for the expected twists and turns. When I refer to the three characters as the "spider crew," she corrects me: the spider *team*. But as one night follows another, she starts to loosen up and gain confidence, adding her own little flourishes. When I tell the story of the Green Goblin spraying the city with laughing gas, she now wants Doc Ock and Rhino and the villainous Vulture to be there too. The bad guys multiply and the stakes get higher.

Tonight she introduces a new character: a girl Spider-Man who wears a hood and is covered with rainbows. Her name is Willie. She tells me how the new spider-girl Willie was bit by a rainbow spider and her hands turned into rainbows. She can fly and her wrists shoot rainbow webs.

Night after night she will flesh out the story of the rainbow spider-girl, giving her more adventures and characteristics. She is folding herself into the stories she hears, making them her own. Night after night my part of the storytelling recedes. I am ready for it. I will fade into the background and let the rainbow spider-girl take over.

THE DEPARTMENT OF Education approved us for a full-time nurse to spend the day one-on-one with Willie at school. This means that she can now go to preschool full time and I can start to step away from full-time caregiving. Theoretically, at least. The approval goes through but there are no nurses. They are all tied up in the pandemic or taking more lucrative jobs as traveling nurses. We wait and wait. We've moved from two days a week to full-time preschool and so Evan and I take turns running the lunch shift and the snack shift, giving insulin in quick visits. At least now that pandemic restrictions have lightened up, more than one parent is allowed in the school and Evan and I can share the labor at last.

We get a call. They've found a nurse. I am elated. It is time to start cutting some of these threads.

I ready Willie in the morning with everything she needs for the day. I pack her lunch, labeling each plastic bag with the number of carbohydrates in her sandwich, goldfish crackers, and apple. I write out detailed instructions for the nurse: here's what to do if her Dexcom alerts that she is high; how much juice to give her if she is low; what to do if (when) the Dexcom goes offline; the amount of Glucagon to inject if she loses consciousness. It is a hard-won list of instructions—coming out of two years of labor and experience. As I'm trying to coax Willie into her shoes, I hear a knock on the door. I look through the peephole and see an elderly woman, hunched over in a coat that is too heavy for the warm morning. She reminds me of my grandmother toward the end of her life, only somewhat sturdier and not confined in a nursing home. My mind flips through ideas of who she could be when I realize that this aging figure is the nurse. She has come to our home address rather than the school.

I open the door and she tells me who she is and that the instructions were unclear and that she doesn't know this neighborhood, but her cousin dropped her off. She didn't know where to get breakfast. Could I order her an egg on toast? Send it to the school. Only then does she notice Willie hanging on to my skirt, eyes wide. I introduce them. The nurse gives Willie a cursory look and goes back to her instructions for the egg and cheese. She doesn't have a smartphone and doesn't know the neighborhood. Make sure it has bacon, she reminds me, as I scroll through the options.

I walk Willie and the nurse to the front door of the school. I ask if she has ever taken care of a diabetic child before. No, she says flatly. When she sees my expression drop, she tells me she had been a school nurse. She graduated top of her class from high school when she was sixteen years old, got a nursing degree, and was a school nurse. She is proud of her accomplishments. There are steep stairs going down to the bottom of the school, stairs that the kids go up and down several times a day to go out to the play-deck. No one mentioned stairs, she complains. I take her arm and feel the thick, coarse fabric of her wool coat. It's the kind of fabric that has gone out of favor for lighter, synthetic, breathable materials. It is an unseasonably warm day and the coat looks stifling. The school director greets us at the door. This is Willie's new nurse, I say. Her face looks at me in alarm. She opens the door, though her expression suggests that she does so reluctantly. I show the nurse the needles. She's never seen pen needles before; has only used syringes. I show her how to dial the needle to the correct dosage. She squints and squints. Her hands, tangled in an arthritic twist, have trouble dialing the unseen numbers.

Her egg and cheese arrives. I pull the director aside as she eats. I promise that I'll be back for morning snack and lunchtime and afternoon snack. Do not, I repeat, do not let the nurse give Willie a shot.

It took three days for me to convince the agency of the severity of the mismatch. Each day I went down and the nurse was sitting in a corner watching the children with mild malevolence—no real harm unless she got it in her head to try to do good and give Willie some medicine. She couldn't make heads or tails of the monitor. When it beeped, she showed it to the teachers who knew what to do by now—they would scuttle off to get Willie her juice and the nurse would sit on. I bought her an egg and cheese each day.

Although I knew that we couldn't sustain this situation, I thought about the loss of pride the nurse would feel if she knew how little I trusted her. She had graduated top of her class. She had helped generations of children. But time had moved on; the technology had advanced beyond her and so too had her body— eyes and hands that couldn't keep up with the smaller, more ac- curate devices and legs and arms that couldn't keep up with a quick preschooler. As I moved to get a new nurse behind the scenes, I also found myself troubled and moved by this woman, Willie's first nurse. I thought about what aging would look like for Willie. Would she one day find herself in a similar position, bound to devices that were increasingly difficult for her to see, hear, or understand?

I'VE ALWAYS HAD a soft spot for Victorian novels—those triple-decker tomes with leather covers gilded with gold lettering. In my awkward adolescence, I took William Thackeray's *Vanity Fair* with me to a California beach for spring break. One of the things that always drew me to them was the way they depict the interconnectedness of human lives. They show how a life can radiate outward and urge us to consider the responsibilities we owe to each other. For this reason, I often come back to George Eliot's *Middlemarch* with its masterful representations of the individual in relation to their community. In *Middlemarch,* Eliot describes this interconnection as a web. It is the supremely important job of the narrator, omniscient and all-knowing, to render these connections visible. In one passage, Eliot's narrator speaks directly to the reader: "I at least have so much to do in unraveling certain human lots, and seeing how they were woven and interwoven, that all the light I can command must be concentrated on this particular web, and not dispersed over that tempting range of relevancies called the universe."[1]

Her novel, a very long one, is not about the universe, but about the lives of small-town people in an insignificant but representative nineteenth-century British town—Middlemarch. No fame, no great feats, but attempts to live good, meaningful lives in the face of enormous, but rather ordinary, obstacles. As a storyteller, Eliot aims to weave a "particular web" and, in so doing, to say something about all of our rather ordinary lives. With the web metaphor, Eliot's ideal narrator acts like a spider, of sorts, weaving and unweaving our destinies together. Pull on this thread and we see all the connecting threads quiver.

I APPLIED FOR a job. Just one job. It was all I could talk myself into. I applied on the speculative future that we would be approved for a full-time nurse and that she would be competent and kind; that Willie would adore her and feel just as safe with her as she did with Evan and me. This hypothetical nurse was someone I thought about a lot; I imagined how it would feel to share some of the responsibilities that had defined our last three years.

The job I applied for was a three-year fellowship. It was unusual enough to catch my attention. I would spend half of my time teaching college students in a liberal arts setting and half of my time running lifelong learning programs for elders in an adult care community. I would be paid two-thirds of my previous salary and it was technically a demotion—short-term and provisional. It was really meant for someone right out of graduate school. Hundreds of people applied. And yet, despite the insane odds in a job market that had no reason to take my candidacy seriously—two years unemployed with a stale PhD—I felt very strongly that this was my job to lose. It would be a return to teaching with a difference. I was animated by the idea of teaching outside of the traditional university seminar and rethinking the way that I approached higher education. I would get to know a new demographic of students—senior lifelong learners—and learn how literature speaks to them.

I sent the job materials that the school requested. A cover letter, writing sample, sample syllabi, letters of recommendation. I decided to be painfully honest. I explained why I'd stepped away from my last job. It was embarrassing to talk about parenting in a job letter, even more so to say that I had left a job to stay at home with my child, but I leaned in to it. I acknowledged that I was an unconventional candidate for this job, but fervently believed that this would make me better at it. My experiences made me want to break out of the academic bubble that had been too comfortable for too long. I wanted to teach nineteen-year-olds and ninety-year-olds. There was so much that I still wanted to learn and so much more that I had in me to teach than when I was a thirty-year-old with a freshly minted PhD. But I also knew that I couldn't go back to the track I was on. It had moved on without me. Or, maybe I had moved on.

A few days later, as I was reviewing the materials, I realized that I had written the wrong college's name on the cover letter. Blood rushed to my face. Was I self-sabotaging? Not yet ready to leave Willie? To start a career all over again?

I emailed the woman who was running the search. I noticed a typo on my cover letter, I said. (A typo, I called it!) Would she mind if I resubmitted the attached file? It hadn't gone out to the search committee yet, she replied. She was willing to swap the old cover letter for the new.

Bless the hearts of kind strangers.

I got the job.

I would be working full time again. It was a position that gave me room to make of it whatever I wanted. I could teach and research, but I also had the opportunity to redefine what teaching meant to me, inside and outside of the academy. It wasn't necessarily a path back toward the tenure-track job that I had left. It might be a path somewhere else entirely. Teaching outside the academy, speaking to new audiences, expanding what research meant to me. After three years, I might be further away from an academic job than I had been before, but I no longer regretted that path as bitterly as I had done. I couldn't tell where I'd be when the fellowship ended. And, for once, that was just fine with me.

ARACHNE, IN GREEK mythology, was an artist. In the telling of the myth from *Metamorphoses,* the Roman poet Ovid writes: "Arachne's distinction lay not in her birth or the place that she hailed from but solely her art."[2] Arachne was a weaver who created beautiful tapestries. She boasted that these elaborate designs, meticulously crafted, were hers alone to claim; when her fellow villagers exclaimed that the goddess Minerva (the Roman Athena) must have blessed her with her skills, she scornfully renounced any divine influence. She had patiently and proudly honed a skill that put her on the level of the gods and was not willing to share the credit with any greedy immortals. When Minerva heard her boasts, she challenged the mortal woman to a weaving competition. In that competition, Minerva created a tapestry depicting the gods punishing humans for their pride. Arachne, in response, spooled colorful threads into a stunning design depicting the abuse of humans by unjust gods. As Ovid writes, Arachne and Minerva "each spun out an old tale in the weft of their separate looms."[3] Although no champion was declared, Minerva was enraged by Arachne's beautiful style and her accusatory message. Flashing in anger, Minerva touched Arachne with a magical potion. Ovid describes the scene as follows:

> As soon as the poison had touched Arachne,
> Her hair fell away, and so did the ears and the nose.
> The head now changed to a tiny ball and her whole frame shrunk
>    in proportion.
> Instead of her legs there are spindly fingers attached to her sides.

The rest is merely abdomen, from which she continues to spin
Her thread and practise her former art in the web of a spider.[4]

Arachne morphed into a spider destined to weave her threads
through all of eternity. But, reading Ovid's account now, I wonder whether Arachne would feel herself punished. Arachne, the
master weaver, weaves on. She used her art to portray injustice
as she saw it. Minerva confirmed her point. What might we still
find in the gossamer strands of her spider's web? What worlds
does she weave on and on? She has a story to tell and, damned as
she is to a spider's form, has the means to tell it yet.

ALEX IS NOT doing well. I try to check in as often as I can, knowing I am getting only kaleidoscopic pieces of the full picture—like
the stained glass windows my mother once made, laid out in bits
on a worktable. I see only the darkest parts of the story emerge
when my parents are uncharacteristically confiding, often when I
catch them in a moment of panic or frustration. When they have
their wits about them, their instinct is to keep things from us,
their other children.

Willie is home from school and I think we might talk on a
video call with my parents and Alex, who are visiting my grandmother in Iowa.

The screen pops up and my mom and Alex are in a parked
car. They've been running errands and Grandma and Dad are in
the store. Immediately, I see that my mother is tense. Her mouth
is drawn tighter than usual in a clenched smile. She tries on a
happy voice with Willie. Alex is on-screen in the backseat, im-
mobile. His face is so vacant that I don't see him in his eyes. We
talk superficially for a few minutes. How the trip is going, where
Grandma and Dad have gone.

Willie looks up at me: What's wrong with Uncle Alex?

He's having a bad day, she's told. Then a slight shift in voice to a lower, grown-up register. We can talk about it later.

We sign off the call.

They're all back from Iowa and we have a phone conversation, just my mom and me. The trip was a disaster. Alex was on new medication to treat some behavioral issues. What behavioral issues? My mom is vague at first, then fills me in. He hasn't been sleeping. At night, he wakes up and rages, pulling his blinds down, throwing his beloved stereo against the wall. In the morning, he is ashamed but claims not to remember what happened. During the day, he's having more and more outbursts. Attacking aide workers who then quit, which leads to a revolving door of staff, which further agitates him. He's biting his hands till they bleed. Some of this behavior we've seen before, but it was rarer. Now it's regular. And then, there are new symptoms. Hallucinations. He sees a man at night who frightens him. In Iowa, he wouldn't sleep alone in his bed; my mother spent every night in a twin bed with him as he clasped her hands like a frightened child. Alex is fifty. My mother is seventy-three and my father is seventy-nine.

I just don't know how much longer we can do this, my mother tells me. I know how hard those words are for her to utter. I feel useless, miles away. I listen. I call more often. My voice is a feeble lifeline, but I unspool it in her direction.

FOR LOUISE BOURGEOIS, spiders were intimately linked to the figure of her mother, the matriarch of their family tapestry business. Bourgeois, who went on to succeed as a woman artist in the high-octane, highly masculine environment of the mid-twentieth-century New York City art world, would often think back to her mother's quiet, overlooked artistry. In a series of enormous, overpowering sculptures, she depicted her mother as a towering thirty-foot-tall spider with knobby legs supporting a bulbous head that reaches up into the sky. She is a godlike spider, reaching toward the heavens and rendering us, the viewer, ant-like below. It is as if Bourgeois bundled up all of her childlike awe for her mother and her middle-aged fury over the indignities leveled at women's work, and physically manifested these feelings into bronze.

Looking up at one impressive specimen of a Bourgeois spider at the Museum of Modern Art, I wondered: What kind of mothers are spiders, really? If the spider, in mythology, is a portrait of the woman as artist—skilled, proud, righteous, and punished—then what is she in the natural world?

As mothers, spiders are a varied lot. One species that can be found in the Middle East, the desert spider (*Stegodyphus lineatus*), creates thick, funnel-shaped webs in bushes to catch insects. Like other spiders, this one weaves her web by secreting a liquid from her inner glands that she then spins with her spinnerets into strong, lustrous silk.[5] For the desert spider, this life of weaving will be short-lived. Shortly after building her web and gorging on the insects she catches, she will use the same silk to create an egg sac to carry a brood of young. When these infant spiders exit the egg sac, they will be utterly helpless—unable to feed themselves or fend off predators, including hungry male spiders who prey on the young. In order to care for her baby spiders, the mother will regurgitate the food—that cache of insects she stored up—until she herself wastes away. Then, the young will begin to eat her body. She will wait patiently, not fleeing, as they consume her legs, her eyes, her organs. They will leave the ovaries and the heart for last. Female relatives—her sisters—may join in as well, sacrificing their bodies to ensure that the next generation can survive in the harsh desert. This gruesome process is called matriphagy.[6]

But this is not the only version of motherhood among arachnids. The black widow spider of North America is named for her cannibalistic tendencies. Although she does so rarely, the black widow is known to eat her mates and sometimes her young. She lays an enormous brood of as many as 300 eggs. If she is unable to source other food, she will eat the spiderlings, just as the young will eat each other. If attacked by a predator, she will save herself first, leaving the young on the outside of her web to draw the attacker. If we understand a creature's evolutionary drive for procreation, then the black widow has a different set of priorities than the desert spider. Living in a more forgiving climate, the black widow prioritizes herself and the possibility of laying several broods of offspring over her lifetime rather than protecting her young at all costs.

In both cases—the good, self-abnegating mothers and the bad, predatory mothers—the silk for which they are so well known is used in creating webs and egg sacs alike. For these species, the art of weaving is closely connected to the biology of reproduction. The spiderweb is beautiful, deadly, generative. The mother weaves life into and out of the world. Like the Greek Fates, those three goddesses presiding over the looms of destiny, the spider's weaving is an art of creation and destruction at once. It is merely a matter of what will be created and who will be destroyed.

WE SWITCH AGENCIES to try to find a nurse. I've started my new job and Evan and I are managing a precarious juggling act so that one of us can be on hand to give Willie her insulin each day. I'm lucky that no one expects too much from me right out of the gate. I'm teaching a class that combines undergraduates and elders—nineteen-year-olds and ninety-year-olds—as I was hoping. The class is called Objects and Memory. We talk about memory and the way that it slips through our fingers. How an event that seems so vivid might not have happened the way we remember it. How history differs from memory and how each informs the other. We read Marcel Proust and Alice Walker and Samuel Beckett and Oliver Sacks and Natasha Trethewey and Maria Stepanova.

I get a call from the new agency. They have found a nurse. She can start the next day.

I am not ready to believe that this is real. I get ready to take Willie to school in the morning and expect a knock on our door and, as I walk into the classroom with Willie, I wait for someone to call and tell me that the new nurse has canceled on us.

Instead, Farah enters. She smiles a warm smile at Willie that lights up the room. Willie is entranced. She is a student—studying to be a nurse in a children's hospital. She lives in Brooklyn where she grew up. It is a long commute, but she had seen the description of Willie's case that the agency had posted and wanted to work with her. She chose us. In a rush of nerves and suppressed hope, I show her Willie's devices: her Dexcom, her insulin pens, my seven-page list of instructions. Like the previous nurse, she has never worked with a child with Type 1 Diabetes, but she asks good questions. When I ask if she's ever used a pen needle, she laughs. Of course she has.

I stick around the apartment in case Farah needs anything. I get a few text messages with questions and then a few more with pictures of Willie playing and enjoying herself. The next day, I go to work.

I used to think that going back to work was a matter of cutting cords, but now I start to see that, instead, it is as if the silken thread that ties us together has stretched a little further and a new thread is woven into our web. After two years in which Evan, my parents, and I were the only ones who could care for Willie, here is Farah. A stranger. A carer. Another silken thread.

And now it is Alex who is unraveling. I watch helplessly from afar. Now that I am spending more time with seniors with dementia in the adult care community, the symptoms seem more familiar to me. He is sundowning at night—losing his sense of self and his sense of reality. He is aging rapidly. What hair he has left is now completely gray and his body is unsure of itself. I look back at the paperwork from the genetic testing that we did several years ago now. I scour the paperwork for an indication of whether Alex's life span is expected to be shorter than mine. It was exactly this information that I did not want to see several years ago when I received the PDF from the genetic testing service. And now, when I want to know, I cannot find the information. I know that the life span for someone with Down syndrome is statistically shorter, but I also know that this life span expectation has changed over time with deinstitutionalization, quality-of-life improvements, and better awareness and treatment for comorbidities like heart defects. But about Alex's microdeletion syndrome, I still don't know.

I talk to my mother on the phone. We are speaking from opposite points of motherhood. I'm building up Willie's support system and learning to step away. After half a century of creating a support system for Alex, my mother is watching her work swept away by new realities. There are no more aides left to take care of Alex. He refuses to go to work or join the social activities that he once enjoyed—going bowling or potlucks with his community. He now spends most nights with my parents in their condo because he is afraid to be in his apartment alone and they are afraid he will hurt himself. One night, when he is raging, they try to check him in to inpatient psychiatric care for observation, but they are turned away because the facility does not accept individuals with intellectual disabilities. Hesitantly, my mother tells me that they are looking into a group home. Like the Benedictine School, it is run by the Catholic Church. In place of the older model of large institutions, group homes like these have emerged that offer some collective care but on a smaller scale, with more attention paid to individual needs and self-determination. At least that is the hope. She doesn't know what else to do at this point.

WE SPEND THANKSGIVING together near my younger brother Sam's home in Maryland. When Alex arrives, he is agitated. He recognizes the drive over from his years at Benedictine and wants to go see the school. My mother promises him that she will take him on their way home, but he doesn't want to wait. He paces up and down the living room, mumbling to himself. He won't respond to any of our attempts to distract him. When he's upset and preoccupied by something, his lips twitch. When I was a child, the twitch reminded me of a bunny, but a dangerous one; I knew to steer clear of him when he was in this mood. "We'd better take him today," my mother relents. She and Dad drive him to the town outside of Annapolis that had been his school-year home from the ages of ten to seventeen.

When they get back from Benedictine, Alex is in a jubilant mood. I see a glimmer of his old self. He tells us about seeing Sister Mary and his old classroom and the vacuum cleaner that he used to clean the hallways and the record player that he listened to. He holds my hand and strokes my arm as he talks. He looks me in the eyes. I realize that it has been a long time since he's looked in my eyes or held my hand. I peer into the unfathomable celestial blue of his eyes. I feel a pang of loss upon realizing how rare these moments have become.

When they return home from Thanksgiving, my mother starts the process of moving him into the group home. She says it is like undoing thirty years' worth of labor. Giving him an independent life had become her life's work since he came back from the Benedictine School. She learned everything there was to know about supportive services, found employers who were open to hiring Alex, fostered relationships that had flowered into strong friendships, and made a home for him to live in. And now she would start the process of undoing it all. He is aging and his needs are changing. The world that she helped build for him can no longer sustain him.

*Snip, snip,* go the silken threads.

WHEN I ASK Willie what she wants to be when she grows up she tells me that she is going to be an artist and a doctor and an astronaut. I do not tell her that diabetics are not allowed to be astronauts. I do not tell her that in this country she'll need a job with good insurance, the kind that is increasingly rare, in order to afford the insulin that she needs to live. Better stick with the doctor path, kid. Instead, I tell her, yes, you can be all those things. No, Mommy, she says, I *am* an artist, a doctor, and an astronaut. Now. Even better, I say. Why wait?

Her drawing starts to evolve. The color splotches of a two-year-old give way to the vaguely animalistic and anthropomorphic shapes of a three-year-old. A distinct style emerges. She calls them her "creatures." What did you draw, Willie? It's a creature. Each one has a round circle for a head, a single eye, a curved line for a smile, and straight lines emanating outward for legs. They look like cyclops spiders with big smiles. Every day she comes home from school with a stack of colorful construction paper, each with a series of arachnid creatures. I can flip through them and see a story emerge. One day there are three creatures on a page. Mommy, Daddy, and Willie, she declares. She is writing our story, just as I am.

I feel a twinge of guilt when I realize that Willie is in pre-school so that I can have the time away from her to write about her. I look at pictures and videos of her that I have saved on my computer and imaginatively reconstruct the last three years. It is amazing how much I have already forgotten. In one video, she is two months old and I am talking to her. She doesn't have her hearing aids yet and I see now what I didn't fully understand then—that she wasn't hearing my voice, but we were still communicating. She could feel me as she sat in my lap and see, with her limited infant's vision, the mom-like blur in front of her. Most important, she knew me already. She knew me before she was born. My body communicated directly to her: consoling, soothing, feeding, lulling. And how does that communication compare to what I am doing now, in writing her story? Writing about the experience of motherhood is a compromised endeavor. It is, in many ways, a betrayal of that intense privacy, that just-the-two-of-us language that held us together from the start. And yet, I keep writing. I have a web that I feel the compulsion to weave in order to feel less alone. This is my web. It is made of the same stuff that I used to make a life for my child. It is silk: the mother stuff. I don't know if this makes me a good or a bad mother, but I expect that I am a little of each.

And meanwhile, Willie draws her creatures, one of whom is meant to be me. I can't help but wonder what kind of creature I am in her eyes.

\* \* \*

WILLIE'S SCHOOL YEAR comes to an end and we spend a week at a rented lake house in Northern Michigan with my parents and Alex. After a morning of swimming and playing in the sand, Alex and Willie watch *The Little Mermaid* together. Willie watches with big eyes but doesn't want to talk about it when it is over. I ask if she is scared of the Sea Witch and she denies it. Willie knows herself to be brave and will not admit she is scared of anything. The next day, she watches it again. She and Alex both stare at the screen with shared intensity. I wish I knew what either was thinking.

That night, we walk out on the dock to watch the sunset. The sky blazes in ultraviolet hues and the still lake repeats the same in reverse. Alex stands more rigid than usual. He starts to laugh, a strange, stilted laugh. Ha ha ha ha ha ha ha. We ask what he is laughing at. He points at the lake. The Sea Witch, he says. He resumes laughing and I hear it—the cackle. Ha ha ha ha ha ha ha ha ha ha ha . . .

At night he takes his medication and my parents argue about whether it's working, whether they need to call the psychiatrist and adjust the dosage. They're wearing each other out—maybe as much as or more than Alex is wearing them out. They talk in circles about what to do next. Do they need to find a new psychiatrist? They waited months to get an appointment with this one. Is he on too many meds or not enough? And, the eternal question: What is coming next?

I wake in the night and hear Alex moving in his room, pacing the floor, muttering to himself in angry, aggressive tones. He is not damaging anything or hurting himself, so I stay out of his space, letting whatever is overtaking his mind run its course. But I stay awake, on the night watch, keeping an eye on Willie sleeping in a race car–themed bed in our room, keeping an ear alert to any changes next door.

In the morning, Alex is in a placid mood, as if whatever possessed him in the night let go of its hold. We sit down and look at photos on the computer of past vacations in Northern Michigan. There are pictures of Alex tubing from the back of a boat; roasting marshmallows beside a bonfire; holding on to my mother's shoulder on a hike out to the dunes of Lake Michigan. I realize, looking back at summer vacations past, that the flash of personality in his eyes in these photos is now only rarely glimpsed. I look at photos of my brother while he sits next to me and feel that I have lost him.

Within six months of our vacation, Alex will move from his condo, where he lived independently for almost thirty years, into a group home with four other older men with intellectual disabilities. The house itself is nice—newly built with quaint daisies out front that are maintained by church members, family, and volunteers. During the day, some of the residents go to their jobs, while Alex and the other hard cases are watched over in the adult day care center. The room where they stay is no better than a collection of worn-down La-Z-Boy chairs assembled around a shared television. Alex is occasionally allowed to leave to vacuum the chapel—the only job left to him, but one that he cherishes. My parents are frustrated that he's not allowed to do it every day. Only weekly with special permission from the priest. It is a sacred ritual for him, this vacuuming. The vibrations soothe him. The rhythmic pattern of the vacuuming (back, forth, back, forth) puts him into a meditative trance. He feels useful. I wish it were more. I hope it is enough.

My mother is trying to let go. She sees him twice a week, but she is no longer responsible for staffing his aides or for planning the day-to-day activities that kept him busy and active as she had over the decades since his return from Benedictine. The staff at the home dress him in mismatched sweatpants. He has gained thirty pounds since he arrived. She winces. She is watching her mothering—the nice clothes she dressed him in, the healthy food she prepared—come undone. When I talk to her about Alex's life in the group home, I can hear in her voice how defeated she feels. It is not what she wanted for him. It feels like failure.

Perhaps a parent's job is to create the conditions that render their parenting unnecessary, but it is not the same story for us all. Not all of us can rejoice over what it means to pass the baton on to our children. I think of the medical burden that Willie will inherit from me. All the things that I am holding for her—the devices, the medical appointments, the forms, the bills, the dosage calculations—will be hers one day. It is a burdensome inheritance, but one I cannot and should not shield her from. She is beginning to take an interest in parts of the job that will be hers someday. She asks how many sugars are in her food. She lets me know that she needs juice when she hears her CGM beep. She wants to help clean her hearing aids. Someday she will do this all herself. That, I remind myself, is the goal that we are working toward. That is what independence will look like for Willie.

I know all this, and yet, another impulse reigns. I want to hold on to them both—Alex and Willie—as long as I can. I want to preserve the image of them watching *The Little Mermaid* in my head forever. I cannot separate Willie's maturation from Alex's decline. I wish I could stop time—for them, but also to hold on to my mother and our newfound closeness. The curves of our motherhood met at a single point and will curve apart again. But for a brief time, we were held in the same moment and were able, for once, to really see each other.

WE GO TO Denver for my college friend Eleanor's wedding. The last time we saw each other, she was still living in NYC and frustrated with the dating scene. Since then, she made a plan to change her life: she left the city, got a job in Denver, joined all manner of recreational clubs, and met someone on a ski mountain. They are now getting married. Since most of their friends have children and it would have quadrupled the guest list, no kids are allowed at the wedding. My parents come to NYC to watch Willie for the weekend. I'm reminded that they're able to do this only because Alex is now in a group home. For the last year, they've been unable to leave him alone. Once again, I can't separate my gains from his losses. I'd like to stop thinking about his entering the home as a loss—he is gaining a new community, I tell myself, he's learning new routines—but every time I see him he looks diminished. It does not feel like a triumph to know that my parents are now free to help us out.

Willie is thrilled to have her grandparents here. We brace ourselves for her to be upset with our departure, but there is far more to be excited about.

Denver was a place we might have lived. For a brief window of time, before we moved to NYC, Evan got a job in Colorado and I was offered a one-year visiting position. It might have been Colorado instead of New York. On the flight over, we find ourselves talking about that unlived life. Would I have found a job more easily? Would we have started trying to get pregnant earlier? Would Pompe Disease have reared its head; would it have been detected? Would Willie even exist in this alternative universe? I am forty now. Perhaps this is what midlife looks like. The snaking paths of the unlived pasts start to outnumber the unrealized futures. We hold each other's hands—the first time, I realize, that we have engaged in this simple act of intimacy in a long time—and we decide that neither of us regrets our choices. But we are now at an age where choices leave their mark.

In Denver we stay in a down-at-the-heels nineteenth-century

hotel. My grandparents on my mother's side used to stay here in the 1950s when they visited for skiing trips from Iowa. My aunt on my father's side had once worked on the maintenance staff here, in her hippie years, developing a bad case of asthma from polishing the banisters. It is the kind of place where debutantes may have once been presented. All faded glory.

We meet Rebecca and her husband at the hotel. She was my college roommate—this is a reunion of sorts. We haven't seen each other in ten years. She is an ob-gyn in California with three kids, all of whom have just been taken to summer camps or stowed away in the grandparental home so they could come to this wedding. I want to ask her what she thinks of the recent Supreme Court decision on abortion, but I decide to wait till we've had a chance to settle in and talk about gentler topics. We are joined by another college friend and I don't have to wait too long. She asks the question right away. How would her patients be affected? Her practice? I'd always loved Rebecca for how she balanced a certain blunt matter-of-factness with deep empathy. It had sustained us through long late-night talks over bad beer in worse apartments throughout four years of college. I thought about her often and didn't reach out enough.

Rebecca pauses before she answers. She tells us that she is heartbroken about the decision and the impact on physicians and patients in other states, but she is hopeful that the decision will not affect her practice—she is in California and they have strong laws in place to protect reproductive care. One of the reasons she was drawn to her practice was that it is a whole-health practice, meaning that she provides care no matter the outcome of the pregnancy. She routinely delivers healthy babies and routinely performs abortions. Her focus is on caring for a patient through a pregnancy, no matter the outcome. I think back to the experience of being passed to a different doctor for a termination and wish I had been able to stay with my initial ob-gyn through the process. It would have felt less like a handoff from a successful to a failed pregnancy. As we talk, I wonder how I might have felt differently about the last six years if I had known where the political winds were blowing, if I had any sense that the rights that had sometimes seemed like burdens would come tumbling down. I wonder what it would have been like if Evan and I had stayed in Texas, where we met and spent our graduate school years; what would it have meant, psychologically, to live in a place where we would now be forced to carry to term a child who wouldn't survive childhood?

That night, we go to the rehearsal dinner at the faded-glory hotel and watch, from inside, as protesters gather at the state capitol. They are a colorful swirl of people in summer dresses and jeans. They are young and angry. We go through the motions of toasting the bride and groom. We are on the wrong side of the glass.

TELL ME THE story of the rainbow ghost spider, Willie implores. She no longer spins my hair in her fingers at bedtime, but she still likes to press her face close to mine so that I can feel the warmth of her breath between us. No, you tell me, I say. You first, she insists.

Once upon a time Rainbow Ghost Spider was at school. No, Willie interjects, the playground. Okay, the playground. She was there with Spider-Man. And Hulk and Black Panther and Ms. Marvel, Willie adds. That's right. They were all there.

The story continues with each of us adding a sentence or two into the thickening darkness. I nod off to sleep as Willie goes on, adding layer upon layer.

I start to lose consciousness, drifting between the world she is building and some vague dreamworld that I can only dimly perceive. My mind slows down and my body sinks into the mattress of her new big-girl bed: the one that she picked out at the store herself and that Evan spent two days assembling. With her voice in my ear, I start to let go, surrendering myself to sleep.

It is her story now.

# ACKNOWLEDGMENTS

Most parents do not have the support to write or publish a book about their experiences. I have been unreasonably fortunate to have people in my life who encouraged me to write and who made space for me to do so. Firstly, I want to thank my agent, Laura Usselman, and my editor, Anna deVries, for their eagle-eyed wisdom, their experiential knowledge as parents, and their continual encouragement. When this book was just a kernel of an idea, Lauren Arrington and Keri Walsh invited me to join them in a writing group and, over biweekly transatlantic Zoom meetings lasting three years, they became an indispensable writing community. Stephanie Rosen was another steadfast writing partner, as well as a very talented website builder. Critical early support from Jaime deBlanc-Knowles and Jessica Goudeau allowed this manuscript to become a book. Members of Columbia's Motherhood and Technology Working Group, led by Rishi Goyal and Arden Hegele, helped me expand and refine my thinking on these topics. Writing this story took me well out of my disciplinary comfort zone and I was lucky to be able to lean on those with real subject expertise to answer my highly specific questions, including Michael Dorman, Joseph Howley, and

David Adamcyk. A roster of saintly humans provided us with free babysitting and necessary changes of scenery, most notably Susan Topol, Julie Crawford, Aubrey and Tom Gabel, Anna and Sebastian Langdell, Barb and Skip Campbell, Kirsten (and Gary and Jaci) Sasaki, Courtney Mills and Natalie Kahanek, and the Fowle, Stewart, and Bloom families. Thank you to the staff of the Ann Arbor YMCA, the Red Balloon, Bank Street, and early childhood teachers everywhere for your tireless work on behalf of children. This book owes a special debt to the doctors, nurses, and therapists who saved us and remade us many times; if I give vent to certain negative experiences, it is because I was taught to hold the profession of medicine to such a high standard. Along the way, many friends and family shared their stories with me and helped me to put my own story in perspective, and I hope I did them justice. To my parents and my siblings, thank you for trusting me to tell my version of our story, and to my mother and Alex most of all, for beginning a journey that I am still on.

E and D, with my whole heart, you are the reason for any lines of beauty in this book.

# NOTES

**EPIGRAPH**

1. Euripides, *Medea: A New Translation,* trans. Charles Martin (Berkeley: University of California Press, 2019), 91–92.

**INTRODUCTION**

1. Mara Mills, "Technology," *Keywords for Disability Studies,* ed. Rachel Adams (New York: New York University Press, 2015), 176.
2. Susanna Davidson (writer) and Simona Bursi (illustrator), "Bellerophon and Pegusus," *Illustrated Stories from the Greek Myths* (London: Usborne Publishing, 2011), 135.
3. Amy M. Boddy, Angelo Fortunato, Melissa Wilson Sayres, and Athena Aktipis, "Fetal Microchimerism and Maternal Health: A Review and Evolutionary Analysis of Cooperation and Conflict Beyond the Womb," *BioEssays* 37, no. 10 (2015): 1106–18.
4. D. W. Winnicott, *The Child, the Family, and the Outside World* (Boston: Perseus Books, 1987), 17.
5. Adrienne Rich, *Of Woman Born: Motherhood as Experience and Institution* (New York: W. W. Norton, 2021), 1.
6. Dani McClain, "Reading *Of Woman Born* in 2020," *Of Woman Born: Motherhood as Experience and Institution* (New York: W. W. Norton, 2021), xxiv–xxv.
7. Cynthia Dewi Oka, "Mothering as Revolutionary Praxis," *Revolutionary Mothering: Love on the Front Lines,* eds. Alexis Pauline Gumbs, China Martens, and Mai'a Williams (Oakland, CA: PM Press, 2016), 52.

8. Rima D. Apple, *Perfect Motherhood: Science and Childrearing in America* (New Brunswick, NJ: Rutgers University Press, 2006), 9.
9. Melissa Febos, *Body Work: The Radical Power of Personal Narrative* (New York: Catapult, 2022), 18.

## 1. ON BEING AND NOT BEING PREGNANT

1. The advertisement was produced by a creative team that included Jason Gaboriau, Doug Cameron, Laura Potsic, and Jon Yasgur for Clearblue Easy and can be found at < https://adland.tv/adnews/clearblue-easy-pee -ship-cable-version-2007–30-usa?fbclid=IwAR0wwDMUEkwITE8d v5xvzZzqK_lmlKdNKFWJq0xSOlXoxwHRjL9-klqbQ-U>.
2. Selmar Aschheim and Bernhard Zondek believed that the hormone responsible for pregnancy detection was produced by the pituitary gland. It was not until 1945 that Georgeanna Seegar Jones presented her discovery that the placenta secretes hCG. Randi Epstein, *Aroused: The History of Hormones and How They Control Just About Everything* (New York: W. W. Norton & Company, 2019), 94–98.
3. Lara Freidenfelds describes each mouse as a "martyr to the cause of pregnancy diagnosis" in *The Myth of the Perfect Pregnancy: A History of Miscarriage in America* (Oxford: Oxford University Press, 2020), 171.
4. Qtd in Sarah A. Leavitt, "'A Private Little Revolution': The Home Pregnancy Test in American Culture," *Bulletin of the History of Medicine* 80, no. 2 (2006): 317.
5. Ibid., 325.
6. Ibid., 326.
7. J. Burstein and G. D. Braunstein, "Urine Pregnancy Tests from Antiquity to the Present," *Biology and Medicine* 1 (1995): 288.
8. Ibid., 289.
9. Ibid.
10. Ibid., 290–91.
11. Roberto Romero, "Giants in Obstetrics and Gynecology Series: A Profile of Judith Vaitukaitis, MD, Who Made Possible the Early Detection of Pregnancy," *American Journal of Obstetrics and Gynecology* 220, no. 1 (2019): 40–44.
12. Leavitt, "'A Private Little Revolution,'" 324.
13. J. L. Vaitukaitis, G. D. Braunstein, and G. T. Ross, "A Radioimmunoassay Which Specifically Measures Human Chorionic Gonadotropin in the Presence of Human Luteinizing Hormone," *American Journal of Obstetrics and Gynecology* 113, no. 6 (1972): 751–58.

14. Lara Freidenfelds, *The Myth of the Perfect Pregnancy,* 5.
15. Ibid., 137.
16. James Joyce, *Ulysses* (New York: Vintage Books, 1986), 31.
17. Adrian M. K. Thomas and Arpan K. Banerjee, *The History of Radiology* (Oxford: Oxford University Press, 2013).
18. Lauren Goode, "I Called Off My Wedding. The Internet Will Never Forget," *Wired,* 6 April 2021. <https://www.wired.com/story/weddings -social-media-apps-photos-memories-miscarriage-problem/>.
19. Ibid.

## 2. GENETIC TESTING AND ME

1. Franklin's work photographing DNA rested on two prior discoveries: first, Oswald Avery's identification of DNA as the biological molecule that carries genes, and second, Maurice Wilkins's development of the X-ray diffraction technique to photograph DNA. Franklin's important insight was that Wilkins's photographs were blurry because the DNA molecules were drying out and changing form from their humid to dry state, which caused the images to blur. She created a device that kept the chamber humid enough to take a clear photograph that made the molecules visible, thereby paving the way for the mapping of the human genome. Siddhartha Mukherjee, *The Gene: An Intimate History* (New York: Scribner, 2016), 145.
2. Mukherjee, *The Gene,* 142–43.
3. Ibid., 149–50.
4. For more on Rosalind Franklin's photographs and her fraught interactions with Maurice Wilkins, Francis Crick, and James Watson, see Carl Zimmer, *She Has Her Mother's Laugh: The Powers, Perversions, and Potential of Heredity* (New York: Dutton, 2018), 124–25, and Siddhartha Mukherjee's *The Gene: An Intimate History,* 142–59.
5. Rayna Rapp, *Testing Women, Testing the Fetus: The Social Impact of Amniocentesis in America* (New York: Routledge, 1999), 1.
6. George Estreich, *Fables and Futures: Biotechnology, Disability, and the Stories We Tell Ourselves* (Cambridge, MA: The MIT Press, 2019), 55.
7. National Council on Disability, "Genetic Testing and the Rush to Perfection: Part of the Bioethics and Disability Series," 23 October 2019, 43. <https://ncd.gov/sites/default/files/NCD_Genetic_Testing_Report_508. pdf>.
8. Abbott Pathology, "Does Medicare Cover the Cost of Generation(R) Prenatal Test?" The U.S. is one of seven countries out of twenty-eight surveyed in 2015 that did not offer full or partial funding for prenatal

screening. The other countries included Argentina, Ireland, India, the Netherlands, Mexico, and Qatar. Mollie A. Minear, Celine Lewis, Subarna Pradhan et al., "Global Perspectives on Clinical Adoption of NIPT," *Prenatal Diagnosis* 35, no. 10 (2015): 959–67.

9. Medical professionals in countries with universal healthcare have debated whether co-pays ought to be required or whether they create a barrier to access. The rationale for these co-pays is to reduce the number of tests requested or to avoid the implication that patients are being coerced to submit to testing. Eline M. Bunnik, Adriana Kater-Kuipers, Robert-Jan H. Galjaard, and Inez D. de Beaufort, "Should Pregnant Women Be Charged for Non-invasive Prenatal Screening? Implications for Reproductive Autonomy and Equal Access," *Journal of Medical Ethics* 46, no. 3 (2019): 194–98.

10. In her memoir of parenting a son with Down syndrome, Rachel Adams describes the way that genetic screening frames an expectation that well-educated parents should not end up with a child with Down syndrome. She writes, "health care professionals often saw him as a failure of medical science" and colleagues and acquaintances questioned whether she had done enough to avoid having a child with Down syndrome. Rachel Adams, *Raising Henry: A Memoir of Motherhood, Disability, and Discovery* (New Haven, CT: Yale University Press, 2013), 106–7.

11. Dorothy Nelkin and M. Susan Lindee, *The DNA Mystique: The Gene as Cultural Icon* (Ann Arbor: University of Michigan Press, 2004), 2.

12. Alondra Nelson, *The Social Life of DNA: Race, Reparations, and Reconciliation After the Genome* (Boston: Beacon Press, 2016), 4.

13. See Rani Molla, "Genetic Testing Is an Inexact Science with Real Consequences," *Vox*, 13 December 2019. <https://www.vox.com/recode/2019/12/13/20978024/genetic-testing-dna-consequences-23andme-ancestry>.

14. Shelley Zipora Reuter, *Testing Fate: Tay-Sachs Disease and the Right to be Responsible* (Minneapolis: University of Minnesota Press, 2016), 3.

15. Ibid., 6.

16. While it is difficult to generalize about the diverse traditions and interpretations around religion and medical ethics, some patterns do emerge. Rhami Khorfan and Aasim I. Padela summarize the approaches of three major monotheistic religions—Judaism, Catholicism, and Islam—and find prohibitions against abortion in each and exceptions relating to the life of the mother in each as well. In Orthodox Judaism, the only

branch of Judaism that Khorfan and Padela examine, the fetus is not considered a full life on equal footing with the mother's and abortion is not considered murder. Rhami Khorfan and Aasim I. Padela, "The Bioethical Concept of Life for Life in Judaism, Catholicism, and Islam: Abortion When the Mother's Life Is in Danger," *The Journal of the Islamic Medical Association of North America* 42, no. 3 (2010): 99–105. For a summary of American religious groups' stances on abortion, see David Masci, "Where Major Religious Groups Stand on Abortion," Pew Research Center, 21 June 2016.
17. Alexandra Minna Stern, *Telling Genes: The Story of Genetic Counseling in America* (Baltimore: Johns Hopkins University Press, 2012), 1.
18. Rapp, *Testing Women, Testing the Fetus*, 2.
19. Sophocles, *Antigone,* in *The Three Theban Plays,* trans. Robert Fagles (New York: Penguin Books, 1984), 91.
20. Gwendolyn Brooks, "The Mother," Selected Poems (New York: Harper and Row, 1963), 4.

## 3. DESIGNING FUTURES

1. Arthur Kornberg, "The Biologic Synthesis of Deoxyribonucleic Acid," Nobel Lecture, 11 December 1959.
2. Pearl S. Buck, *The Child Who Never Grew* (New York: The John Day Company, 1950), 19.
3. Ibid., 34.
4. Ibid., 35.
5. Henry Herbert Goddard, "The Elimination of Feeble-Mindedness," *American Academy of Political and Social Science* 37, no. 2 (1911): 509.
6. Zimmer, *She Has Her Mother's Laugh*, 94.
7. Katharine Hepburn, *Me: Stories of My Life* (New York: Random House, 1991), 405.
8. Buck, *The Child Who Never Grew,* 25.
9. Ibid., 27.
10. Ibid., 50.
11. The aspartame in diet sodas is an unlikely source of phenylalanine and manufacturers are now required to include a warning on their labels.
12. Somatic cells include blood cells, stem cells, and neuron cells, among others. Changes made to a somatic cell can alter the individual but are not inheritable and cannot be passed down to the next generation. Belen Hurle, "Somatic Cells," National Human Genome Research Institute. <https://www.genome.gov/genetics-glossary/Somatic-Cells>.

13. Rachel Adams, "Gene-edited Babies Don't Grow in Test Tubes—Mother's Roles Shouldn't Be Erased," *The Conversation,* 29 May 2019. <https://theconversation.com/gene-edited-babies-dont-grow-in-test-tubes-mothers-roles-shouldnt-be-erased-117070>.

14. Ibid.

15. Sui-Lee Wee, "Chinese Scientist Who Genetically Edited Babies Gets 3 Years in Prison," *The New York Times,* 30 December 2019. <https://www.nytimes.com/2019/12/30/business/china-scientist-genetic-baby-prison.html>.

16. Adams, "Gene-edited Babies Don't Grow in Test Tubes."

17. Robert Sparrow, "Yesterday's Child: How Gene Editing for Enhancement Will Produce Obsolescence—and Why It Matters," *The American Journal of Bioethics* 19, no. 7 (2019): 6.

18. Buck, *The Child Who Never Grew,* 50–51.

## 4. THE NIGHT WATCH

1. Mark P. Connolly, Stijn Hoorens, and Georgina M. Chambers, "The Costs and Consequences of Assisted Reproductive Technology: An Economic Perspective," *Human Reproduction Update* 16, no. 6 (2010): 607.

2. Ibid.

3. Tarun Jain, "Socioeconomic and Racial Disparities Among Infertility Patients Seeking Care," *Fertility and Sterility* 85, no. 4 (2006): 876–81.

4. Much has been written on the landmark first IVF baby, Louise Brown, whose birth was credited to a team of researchers in the UK led by Patrick Steptoe and Robert Edwards for their work. The central role of Jean Purdy, the lead nurse on the project, has more recently been acknowledged as central to the success of this first IVF procedure. Louise Brown has written a first-person account, as has her mother: Louise Brown, *Louise Brown: My Life as the World's First Test-Tube Baby* (Bristol: Bristol Books, 2015) and Lesley Brown, *Our Miracle Called Louise: A Parents' Story* (Magnum Books, 1980). For the Indian procedure performed by Subhash Mukherjee mere months later, see Sahar Ferber, Nicola J. Marks, and Vera Mackie, *IVF and Assisted Reproduction: A Global History* (Singapore: Palgrave Macmillan, 2020). Dr. Mukherjee committed suicide in 1981 after three years of trying to convince medical authorities that he had, in fact, performed a successful IVF procedure concurrently with the UK team. John Leeton's *Test Tube Revolution: The Early History of IVF* (Monash, Australia: Monash University Publishing, 2013) describes the development of IVF and related procedures

in Australia. Robin Marantz Henig's *Pandora's Baby: How the First Test Tube Babies Sparked the Reproductive Revolution* (Boston: Houghton Mifflin, 2004) describes the events leading up to the birth of Elizabeth Jordan Carr in the U.S. as well as other IVF firsts that did not come to pass.

5. Robin Marantz Henig, *Pandora's Baby: How the First Test Tube Babies Sparked the Reproductive Revolution* (Boston: Houghton Mifflin, 2004), 26–27.

6. Ibid., 6.

7. Gretchen Livingston, "A Third of U.S. Adults Say They Have Used Fertility Treatments or Know Someone Who Has," Pew Research Center, 17 July 2018. <https://www.pewresearch.org/fact-tank/2018/07/17/a-third-of-u-s-adults-say-they-have-used-fertility-treatments-or-know-someone-who-has/>.

8. The wave of state-level abortion bans in Arkansas, Kentucky, Missouri, South Dakota, and Texas, followed by the overruling of *Roe v. Wade* in 2022 with the *Dobbs* decision, have opened the question of the legality of IVF under anti-abortion laws. Aria Bendix, "States Say Abortion Bans Don't Affect IVF. Providers and Lawyers Are Worried Anyway," *NBC News,* 29 June 2022.

9. Sarah Franklin and Celia Roberts, *Born and Made: An Ethnography of Preimplantation Genetic Diagnosis* (Princeton, NJ: Princeton University Press, 2006), 22.

10. Barbara Katz Rothman, *The Tentative Pregnancy: Prenatal Diagnosis and the Future of Motherhood* (New York: Viking, 1986).

11. In 2021, Chidiebere Ibe's medical illustrations of a Black mother carrying a fetus made headlines for breaking from representational practices that position white motherhood as the norm. A. Rochaun Meadows-Fernandez writes that the image "loudly communicates that Black people deserve to see themselves reflected in medical settings." A. Rochaun Meadows-Fernandez, "Med School Student's Illustration Shows a Black Fetus in Utero—Here's Why It Went Viral," *Parents,* 8 December 2021.

## 5. TINY EARMOLDS

1. Katie Booth describes this scene in her biography, *The Invention of Miracles: Language, Power, and Alexander Graham Bell's Quest to End Deafness* (New York: Simon & Schuster, 2021), 19–30. See also Alexander Graham Bell, "Making a Talking Machine" (Undated), Library of Congress, Alexander Graham Bell Family Papers (1834–1974). <https://memory.loc.gov/mss/magbell/376/37600301/37600301.pdf>.

2. The character of Henry Higgins in George Bernard Shaw's *Pygmalion* was based on Alexander Melville Bell.

3. For more on Visible Speech, see Booth, *The Invention of Miracles*.

4. Alexander Melville Bell, "The Tongue: A Poem" (London: Cleaver, 1846), 2.

5. Ibid.

6. Booth, *The Invention of Miracles*, 26.

7. Bell, "Making a Talking Machine."

8. Ibid.

9. Richard Ellman, "Yeats's Second Puberty," *New York Book Review*, 9 May 1985.

10. W. B. Yeats, "Sweet Dancer," *The Collected Works of W. B. Yeats* (New York: Simon & Schuster, 1996), 296.

11. William Wordsworth, "I Wandered Lonely as a Cloud," *Selected Poems and Prefaces* (Boston: Houghton Mifflin Company, 1965): 191.

12. Booth, *The Invention of Miracles*, 89.

13. Gerald Shea, *The Language of Light: A History of Silent Voices* (New Haven: Yale University Press, 2017), xiii.

14. Ibid.

15. Ibid.

16. Alexander Graham Bell, "The Poet," Library of Congress, Alexander Graham Bell Family Papers (1834–1974). <https://www.loc.gov/resource/magbell.39100208/?sp=5>.

17. Booth, *The Invention of Miracles*, 327.

## 6. SWEETNESS

1. Chris Feudtner, *Bittersweet: Diabetes, Insulin, and the Transformation of Illness* (Chapel Hill: University of North Carolina Press, 2003), 4.

2. Ibid., 24.

3. Michael Bliss, *The Discovery of Insulin* (Chicago: The University of Chicago Press, 1982), 24.

4. The "starvation diet" limited caloric intake for an adult to 800 calories a day. See *The Journey and the Dream: A History of the American Diabetes Association* (American Diabetes Association, 1990), 2.

5. These experiments were conducted by Oskar Minkowski and Joseph von Mering at the University of Strasbourg in 1889.

6. The medical student was named Paul Langerhans.

7. The stated reason for the exclusive nature of this contract was that Lilly had the production capabilities that smaller labs did not, and the University of Toronto did not want the added administrative burden

of consulting with multiple laboratories. The awarding of the exclusive deal to Lilly was largely the result of the concerted efforts of Lilly's director of research, George Clowes, who established close relationships with members of Best and Banting's research department. See Bliss, *The Discovery of Insulin,* 137–38.

8. Grace Fernandez, "Why Eli Lilly's Insulin Price Cap Announcement Matters," Johns Hopkins Bloomberg School of Public Health, 13 March 2023. <https://publichealth.jhu.edu/2023/eli-lilly-lowers-insulin-prices>.

9. Baylee F. Bakkila, Sanjay Basu, and Kasia J. Lipska, "Catastrophic Spending on Insulin in the United States, 2017–18," *Pharmaceuticals and Medical Technology* 41, no. 7 (2022): 1053–60.

10. Feudtner, *Bittersweet,* xv.

11. Joslin's method had its detractors at the time. Chris Feudtner writes that the at-home use of multiple daily shots was seen by some physicians as an inappropriate expectation for lay people without medical training. Others, such as Rollin Turner Woodyatt, argued for only two shots a day and testing urine for acid rather than regularly testing blood for sugar. According to Woodyatt, the goal was not strict control, but rather "to keep the patient as well and strong as a normal individual with the least effort and the lowest economic outlay possible" (qtd in Feudtner, *Bittersweet,* 136). The problem with this approach is that it runs a very high risk of overdosing and hypoglycemia, especially during the nighttime. Medical studies continue to support Joslin's approach, and careful diabetic control is most often maintained through multiple daily injections, monitoring of blood sugar levels, and the calibration of insulin dosages according to the number of carbohydrates consumed and the current blood sugar level. However, even as late as 1999, scientists continued to warn of "the added burden placed on the child and family by such an intensive approach at such a young age." Denis Daveman et al., "The Infant and Toddler with Diabetes: Challenges of Diagnosis and Management," *Pediatric Child Health* 4, no. 1 [1999]: 57–63.

12. Feudtner, *Bittersweet,* 65.

13. Ibid.

14. Scott Gottlieb, "Early Exposure to Cows' Milk Raises Risk of Diabetes in High Risk Children," *BMJ* 321, no. 7268 (2000): 1040.

15. Jean-François Bach and Lucienne Chatenoud, "The Hygiene Hypothesis: An Explanation for the Increased Frequency of Insulin-Dependent Diabetes," *Cold Spring Harbor Perspectives in Medicine* 2, no. 2 (2012).

16. There is no scientific consensus that either cow's milk or excessive

hygiene are the causes of Type 1 Diabetes in infants and toddlers. Other theories include the idea that a specific virus triggers diabetes; that environmental or chemical exposures may cause the disease; and that vitamin D deficiency may play a role. See Bach and Chatenoud, "The Hygiene Hypothesis."

17. Arleen Marcia Tuchman, *Diabetes: A History of Race and Disease* (New Haven: Yale University Press, 2020), 14.

18. Ibid., xii.

19. Sophocles, "Oedipus the King," *The Three Theban Plays,* trans. Robert Fagles, (New York: Penguin, 1984), 222.

## 7. STAY AT HOME

1. Jessica Clements and Kari Nixon, *Optimal Motherhood and Other Lies Facebook Told Us: Assembling the Networked Ethos of Contemporary Maternity Advice* (Cambridge, MA: The MIT Press, 2022), 4–6.

2. Ruth Schwartz Cowan, *More Work for Mother: The Ironies of Household Technology from the Open Hearth to the Microwave* (New York: Basic Books, 1983), 16–17.

3. Ibid., 10.

4. Jessica McCrory Calarco, Emily Meanwell, Elizabeth Anderson, and Amelia Knopf, "'Let's Not Pretend It's Fun': How Disruptions to Families' School and Childcare Arrangements Impact Mothers' Well-Being" (SocArXiv Papers, Draft 1 November 2020), 1.

5. Ibid., 4–5.

## 8. MOTHERBOARD

1. By the early twentieth century, maternal impressionism was already widely discredited. The psychologist Havelock Ellis characterizes these beliefs as "dubious phenomena" in his 1928 book *The Psychology of Sex,* but then goes on to cite hair-raising examples, such as a mother who witnessed a cat killing her pet rabbit, gnawing off its paws, who gives birth to a child with deformed feet. Havelock Ellis, *Studies in the Psychology of Sex,* Volume 5 (Philadelphia: F. A. Davis Company, 1928), 217–18.

2. For studies on "fetal programming" see Hannah Cookson et al., "Mothers' Anxiety During Pregnancy Is Associated with Asthma in Their Children," *Journal of Allergy and Clinical Immunology* 123, no. 4 (2009): 847–53; and Curt A. Sandman et al., "Prescient Human Fetuses Thrive," *Psychological Science* 23, no. 1 (2012): 93–100. Notably, Sandman et al. found that a stable maternal emotional state before and after pregnancy,

even a negative one like depression, does not lead to the same negative outcomes as a radically altered state.

3. By the 1980s, improved tests allowed for self-monitoring of blood sugar. Information here and below from Irl B. Hirsch, "Introduction: History of Glucose Monitoring," *Role of Continuous Glucose Monitoring in Diabetes Treatment* (American Diabetes Association, 2018), <https://www.ncbi.nlm.nih.gov/books/NBK538968/>.

4. Anne L. Peters, "The Evidence Base for Continuous Glucose Monitoring," *Role of Continuous Glucose Monitoring in Diabetes Treatment* (American Diabetes Association, 2018), <https://www.ncbi.nlm.nih.gov/books/NBK538970/>.

5. The first commercially available insulin pumps were developed by Dean Kamen in 1976 and, though much smaller than Kadish's pump, were large and substantial enough to be coined the "blue brick." Jothydev Kesavadev et al., "Evolution of Insulin Delivery Devices: From Syringes, Pens, and Pumps to DIY Artificial Pancreas," *Diabetes Therapy* 11, no. 6 [2020]: 1251–69.

6. The pen needle was first introduced in 1985.

7. Nina Totenberg, "Sotomayor Opens Up About Diabetes for Youth Group," NPR, 21 June 2011.

8. Feudtner, *Bittersweet,* p. 9.

9. Looping began when diabetics discovered a security flaw in the Medtronic pumps, which were using a radio frequency. Erik Douds, "Learn About Looping: The Do-It-Yourself Artificial Pancreas," Beyond Type 1. They were able to use that frequency to communicate directly with the devices. The response to the looper community by biotech companies has been mixed—some have fixed the security vulnerabilities and made it harder to "loop," some have opened themselves up to more engagement from the DIY community, and others have worked to create more proprietary software that allows looping. Dana Lewis, who started the OpenAPS looping community, describes the experience of the closed loop system as follows: "I'd say 95 percent of my diabetes tasks have been removed on a daily basis . . . I do maybe three or four diabetes-related things a day. The cognitive burden reduction is so big." Katie Doyle, "The Future of OpenAPS with Dana Lewis," Beyond Type 1.

10. The hashtag was first coined in 2013 at the DiabetesMine D-Data Exchange event at Stanford University, <https://www.diabetes.co.uk/blog/2016/07/the-wearenotwaiting-movement-is-helping-people-with-diabetes-improve-their-health-now-not-later/>.

11. Mark C. Taylor, *Intervolution: Smart Bodies, Smart Things* (New York: Columbia University Press, 2021), 137.

12. Ibid., 174. Elsewhere, Taylor notes that diabetes itself represents a failure to distinguish between the self and the other—it is an immunological event in which the body attacks itself as if it is attacking a foreign invader.

13. Donna Haraway, "A Cyborg Manifesto: Science, Technology, and Socialist-Feminism in the Late Twentieth Century," *Manifestly Haraway* (Minneapolis: University of Minnesota Press, 2016), 6.

14. Ibid., 7.

15. Ibid., 68.

16. In a sweeping passage, Firestone describes her vision for a radical feminist future: "The reproduction of one sex for the benefit of both would be replaced by (at least the option of) artificial reproduction: children would be born to both sexes equally, or independently of either, however one chooses to look at it; the dependence of the child on the mother (and vice versa) would give way to a greatly shortened dependence on a small group of others in general . . . The tyranny of the biological family would be broken." Shulamith Firestone, *The Dialectic of Sex: The Case for Feminist Revolution* (William Morrow and Company, 1970), 12.

17. Julie Phillips, *The Baby on the Fire Escape: Creativity, Motherhood, and the Mind-Baby Problem* (New York: W. W. Norton, 2022), 139.

18. Shannon Mattern, "Maintenance and Care," *Places Journal*, 2018. <https://placesjournal.org/article/maintenance-and-care/?cn-reloaded=1>.

19. Some of the most extreme examples of this trope imagine artificial wombs that separate fetuses from human parents and put the developing child to use by the state. Such examples include the fetus farms of *The Matrix* or the social engineering of the World State in Aldous Huxley's *Brave New World*.

20. Hiʻilei Julia Kawehipuaakahaopulani Hobart and Tamara Kneese, "Radical Care: Survival Strategies for Uncertain Times," *Social Text* 38, no. 1 (2020): 13.

21. H. G. Wells, "Talk on Communications" (1932), in *H.G. Wells: The Spoken Word*, The British Library, 1996.

## 9. IN YOUR ELECTRONIC ARMS

1. "What a Cochlear Implant Sounds Like," <https://www.youtube.com/watch?v=1dhTWVMcpC4>.

2. In *The Computer's Voice: From Star Trek to Siri*, Liz W. Faber shows the influence of science fiction on the feminized voices of voice assistant technologies. Their examination of the 1974 comedy *Dark Star* with

its voice-interactive spaceship nicknamed "Mother" is especially apt. Liz Faber, *The Computer's Voice: From Star Trek to Siri* (Minneapolis: University of Minnesota Press, 2020), 59–67.

3. Ray Bradbury, *I Sing the Body Electric! And Other Stories* (New York: William Morrow, 1998), 121.

4. Mills writes, "Quality testing was a key aspect of quality control, an industrial production routine that commenced in the telephone industry at the outset of the twentieth century. The testing of mass-produced telephones with spoken words emerged concurrently with the mass testing of American ears." "Testing Hearing with Speech," *Testing Hearing: The Making of Modern Aurality,* ed. Viktoria Tkaczyk (New York, Oxford University Press, 2020), 27.

5. The building was designed by architects Francis Keally and Leonard Davis and was flanked by two 160-foot pylons and an enormous mural by Eugene Savage depicting different means of communication. Frank Monaghan, *Official Guide Book of the New York World's Fair* (New York: Exposition Publications, 1939), 75.

6. Dave Tompkins, *How to Wreck a Nice Beach* (New York: Stop Smiling Books, 2011), 37.

7. "The Vocoder," *Nature* 145, no. 3665 (1940): 157.

8. Monaghan, *New York World's Fair,* 81.

9. For more on what was known as the SIGSALY machine, which used both a vocoder and an elaborate system of phonograph recordings as single-use keys for encryption and decryption, listen to the *99% Invisible* podcast episode "Vox Ex Machina": <https://99percentinvisible.org/episode/vox-ex-machina/>.

10. Tompkins, *How to Wreck a Nice Beach,* 20. In order to decode the call, each participant in the phone call received a record printed with noise by the Muzak corporation. The noise recording was played over the line as a single-use decryption key. During the war, 1,500 records were printed for this purpose (Tompkins, 70).

11. Ibid., 20.

12. Michael Dorman, conversation, August 12, 2022.

13. Laura Mauldin observes that because 90 percent of deaf children have hearing parents, the non-deaf are the largest market for cochlear implants. Laura Mauldin, *Made to Hear: Cochlear Implants and Raising Deaf Children* (Minneapolis: University of Minnesota Press, 2016), 9.

14. Kenji Kansaku, "Neuroprosthetics in Systems Neuroscience and Medicine," *Scientific Reports* 11, no. 5404 (2021).

15. Mauldin, *Made to Hear,* 16.

16. Ibid., 21.
17. Geffen Records sued Young for $3.3 million in damages for not using his own voice. Young filed a countersuit and the case was settled out of court. Tompkins, *How to Wreck a Nice Beach,* 244.
18. Quoted in ibid.
19. Ibid.
20. William James, "The Stream of Consciousness" (1892), *Classics in the History of Psychology*, ed. Christopher D. Green, <https://shorturl.at/rsFV2>.
21. Laurie Anderson, "How We Made Laurie Anderson's O Superman," Interview with Dave Simpson, *The Guardian,* 19 April 2016. <https://www.theguardian.com/culture/2016/apr/19/how-we-made-laurie-anderson-o-superman>.
22. Ibid.
23. See also Hannah Zeavin, "How Parenting Tech Opens the Door to State Surveillance," *Wired,* 26 April 2023. <https://www.wired.com/story/how-parenting-tech-opens-the-door-to-state-surveillance/>.

## 10. SPINNING WEBS

1. George Eliot, *Middlemarch* (Harper & Brothers, 1873), 51.
2. Ovid, *Metamorphoses,* trans. David Raeburn (New York: Penguin Books, 2004), 210.
3. Ibid., 213.
4. Ibid., 216–17.
5. Alicia Ault, "Ask Smithsonian: How Do Spiders Make Their Webs?" *Smithsonian Magazine,* <https://www.smithsonianmag.com/smithsonian-institution/ask-smithsonian-how-do-spiders-make-webs-180957426/#:~:text=Spider%20silk%20is%20made%20of,spinnerets%20on%20the%20spider's%20abdomen>.
6. Yael Lubin, "Arachnid Matriphagy: These Spider Mothers Literally Die for Their Young," *Entomology Today,* 27 March 2015. <https://entomologytoday.org/2015/03/27/arachnid-matriphagy-these-spider-mothers-literally-die-for-their-young/>. Matt Simon, "Absurd Creature of the Week: The Spider Mother That Barfs Up Her Guts to Feed Her Kids," *Wired,* 8 May 2015. <https://www.wired.com/2015/05/absurd-creature-of-the-week-barfing-spider/>.

# IMAGE CREDITS